The

Farmette

COOKBOOK

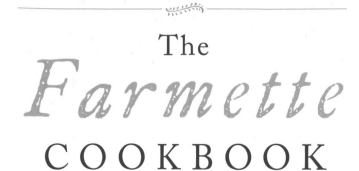

The
Farmette
COOKBOOK

RECIPES *and* ADVENTURES
from MY LIFE *on* AN IRISH FARM

Imen McDonnell

Roost Books

BOULDER
2016

Roost Books
An imprint of Shambhala Publications, Inc.
4720 Walnut Street
Boulder, Colorado 80301
roostbooks.com

9 8 7 6 5 4 3 2 1

First Edition
Printed in the United States of America

Distributed in the United States by
Penguin Random House LLC and in Canada by
Random House of Canada Ltd

BOOK DESIGN BY SHUBHANI SARKAR
sarkardesignstudio.com

Library of Congress Cataloging-in-Publication Data

McDonnell, Imen.
The Farmette cookbook: recipes and adventures from
my life on an Irish farm/Imen McDonnell.—First edition.
 pages   cm
Includes index.
ISBN 978-1-61180-204-7 (hardcover: alk. paper)
1. Cooking, Irish. 2. Country life—Ireland. I. Title.
TX717.5.M334 2016
641.59417—dc23
2015026646

For Richard, Geoffrey, and my Father

This book is also dedicated to my late mother-in-law,
Peggy McDonnell.

Peggy was extraordinary for many reasons. I spent so much time as a student of her gentle teaching in the kitchen and listening to stories of farming, past and present, over an afternoon cup of tea and slice of cake. She always treated me as if I was her own daughter, a gesture for which I will forever be grateful. Peggy taught me much about Irish cookery, but mostly she reminded me to always be kind and generous with your heart. Peggy passed away just as I began writing this book, and we had planned on putting the book together as a team. Writing this book has been bittersweet.

It is with Peggy's guardian spirit and all of the great memories we have that these words and recipes grace these pages.

CONTENTS

INTRODUCTION

We must be willing to let go of the life we have planned,
so as to have the life that is waiting for us.
—JOSEPH CAMPBELL

Girl Meets Farmer

It's hard to believe now, but I wasn't exactly the kind of girl who dreamed of country living. In fact, I had never even been on a real working farm in my life—except for a visit to Zander's maple sugar farm in Wisconsin during the fifth grade, which doesn't count because the only scent there was sweet syrup, not ripe, steaming slurry. As a young woman building an exciting career while living and working in Minneapolis, New York, and Los Angeles, quiet rural living had never occurred to me. I was accustomed to slipping into a pair of Weitzmans; I never considered pulling on a pair of rubber Wellington boots.

Then everything changed. Mad love swept me up and carried me across the Atlantic where I landed on a centuries-old family farm in the Irish countryside with the dashing man I would later call my husband. Listening to my heart, I left behind a career, a city, a nation, family, and friends

to share my life with a man (and eventually a son), a farm, and a new country with its timeless and sometimes peculiar traditions. Everything that made up my former identity was replaced with a dramatic new set of circumstances and a whole *lot* of muck to trek through.

Arriving in Ireland

When I first moved to Ireland, we took up residence in the village of Adare, County Limerick, an enchanting little town with a population of about twenty-five hundred, fifteen minutes from Limerick, which seemed like an ideal place to ease the transition between my cosmopolitan needs and the bucolic Irish countryside.

When I strolled from one end of my new hometown to the other, I encountered two thirteenth-century churches, a petite corner grocery store, a fish-'n'-chipper, a few pubs, a couple of quaint restaurants, a sweet café, the tidal River Maigue, the obligatory castle ruin, an itty-bitty post office that closed from 2:00 to 3:00 P.M. each day, a handful of thatched roof cottages, and a massive manor estate once inhabited by lords and ladies. Adare looked and felt like a scene out of medieval times. This was alluring when I first visited the village with Richard, but once it became my home, the romance seemed to fade a bit. I began to wonder, Where was my place here in this new country? What was my role?

Moving to the Farm

It was decided that we would move to the family farm once we were married, but in the fog of love, I hadn't fully understood what full-time farm living meant. In planning my move to Ireland, I secretly imagined that it would be only a matter of time until Richard and I would return to the States and build our life together there. But, I learned quickly that an Irish farmer will never leave his land, and this became especially apparent later on, when the heir to the milking parlor—our son, Geoffrey—was born.

In due course, we built our own eco-friendly house adjacent to the family farmyard, very near Richard's mother, father, and brother. Naturally, I insisted on incorporating as many modern, American-style kitchen features that I could, many of which would be unusual in an Irish farm home (such as a cheeky espresso bar, an indoor barbecue grill, and a large stainless steel refrigera-

tor, commonly referred to by appliance retailers in Ireland as an "American" fridge).

Still, it truly didn't hit me until about a year later. I'll never forget one particularly gray December afternoon—I was tidying our guest room when a cluster of cows contentedly grazing on our front lawn caught my eye, and it suddenly sank in: *We've built our home on a cow pasture, and we are on this farm to stay.*

Getting Used to Rural Living

At a time when so many young people are trying to trade their city lives for the quiet country life, I must confess, it took me a long time to get used to rural living. I was accustomed to spending my days organizing busy production shoots, commuting to a bustling office, grabbing a bagel and coffee on the way, grazing on catered meals for lunch, and eating, drinking, and socializing in fashionable restaurants for dinner. Ironically, I never once thought about how to prepare or source ingredients for the meals that I was enjoying so much.

There are no food delivery services or nearby restaurants in the middle of the Irish countryside. You won't find a corner bakery, a pizzeria, Chinatown noodles, Vietnamese *pho,* pour-over coffee, takeaway tacos, or a quick falafel fix. So, if this variety is woven into the fabric of your everyday life, you will grieve the loss intensely. When I first moved to the farm, our nearest "local" supermarket was forty-five minutes away. I would have to drive a couple of hours to Dublin to find an

organic, whole-foods grocer or exotic foods market comparable to what I would have had quick and easy access to in urban America.

It became quite clear that I had to teach myself how to cook and grow whole, healthy, interesting foods on our farm. My new family's pastures were rich with dairy cows, clutches of chickens, heaps of hedgerows, and superb soil to start a bountiful kitchen garden. As plausible as that notion was, the actual learning and doing seemed daunting and laborious.

However, I saw how this could be my contribution to the family farm, carving out my own unique niche, and this notion brought me joy. All the basic elements to get started were literally right in our front yard. Plus, I was determined to make sure Geoffrey would grow up with a healthy appetite and

a deep understanding of where his food comes from.

I took an organic growing class in County Clare, and we tilled a quarter-acre plot on the southeast side of our house. With Geoffrey by my side, I planted our garden with a rainbow of heirloom seeds and varieties of vegetables and fruits that are not easily found in Ireland, such as rainbow chard and globe artichokes. My kitchen was becoming my sanctuary. We were building a beautiful life together, and the future was beginning to look bright.

Starting My Blog (and Learning to Cook)

In the autumn of 2009, I began writing my blog, originally called *I Married an Irish Farmer* and later becoming simply *Farmette*. I needed an outlet for my creativity, to produce something and perhaps connect with other farming women. Blogging helped me adjust to all the crazy changes life had thrown my way. Comments by readers provided adult company when the farm kidnapped my husband for thirteen hours a day while I was alone at home with a toddler.

With all the time I was spending in the kitchen, I started quizzing my mother-in-law on her traditional Irish cooking skills and recipes. I discovered other doyennes of Irish country cooking and lingered over the cookbooks of Ireland, past and present. I photographed and recorded my culinary experiments and shared them on my blog. With the scent of a turf fire wafting through the house, I sat down each day and shared the details of my Irish country cooking journey with my family and a quickly growing audience.

My blog not only built my online community; I soon found that if you prepared homemade clotted cream and baked a mean scone, you might make a friend or two in the neighborhood.

I closely studied the ritual of Sunday lunch, pudding, and tea. I took to "wild crafting," our version of foraging for wild edibles. Each week, Geoffrey and I started visiting our charming local fishmonger to see what we could create with his daily catch from the sea. An abundance of raw milk from the farm and my father-in-law's honey provided inspiration for many of our meals and homespun indulgences.

Life on the Farm

The farm at Dunmoylan has been in the McDonnell family since the early nineteenth century. Dunmoylan, which refers to the townland on which the farm is situated, is Irish Gaelic for "land of the fort." Farming at Dunmoylan had humble beginnings, starting off with only a handful of milking cows, a horse and cart to deliver dairy to the creamery, and a hearth fire to prepare food in a thatched stone dwelling that would have been attached to the cowshed. Richard and his brother, David, are the seventh generation of McDonnells to be the honorable custodians of this land.

Today, Dunmoylan is a modern grass-fed dairy and free-range poultry farm with a focus on sustainability and renewable energy. Three homes are part of the farm at large, and we have adopted the traditional intergenerational approach to living. The "home" farmhouse is inhabited by my father-in-law, Michael. Our little homestead, adjacent to the farmyard, is named Dunmoylan Grove. David's home across the road was the original presbytery, built in 1872 for the local parish priests. In the farmyard, Richard milks Holstein Friesian dairy cows, morning and night, all year round. Richard also raises free-range poultry, which was proudly established on the farm in the 1960s by my late mother-in-law, Peggy.

There is a small orchard on the home farmyard. Originally planted in the 1940s for supplying an Irish cidery, it has since been cut back to a scale that provides just enough apples, pears, plums, gooseberries, and currants for our families each summer and autumn.

·My father-in-law is also a beekeeper. He keeps three hives in a wooded area near the River Shannon, and they keep us in honey all year.

Dunmoylan Grove is my "farmette." This is where we grow all of our vegetables and some fruit and raise small amounts of pastured livestock for meat. It's where I make wholesome magic with the milk from the home farm and press orchard apples and pears into juice.

While the farm and its working practices have been updated over time, my husband's family remains traditional with regard to family as well as community. Raw milk in the tea, big roast lunches, quaint country dinners, the observation of all holy days, traditional Irish music and dancing in the farm kitchen on St. Stephen's Day, the blessing of the farm on May Eve, a fresh shamrock on a lapel for St. Patrick's Day, a penny for luck on a sale of land or cattle, and unwavering support of small local businesses. Here in the Irish countryside, there is such a strong appreciation for old-fashioned values that it sometimes feels like we have stepped back in time.

A Note on Irish Food

Many classic Irish recipes have just a few simple ingredients: dairy, eggs, preserves, dried fruit, and flours. In fact, there are centuries-old cakes and pudding recipes that still rely solely on small variations of the same components, such as the Irish wedding cake, birthday cake, and Christmas cake. When I prepare some of the older recipes, I always make sure to pause and admire the thought and care that went into creating each dish through generations.

Over the years, I have been fortunate to meet and break bread with a bevy of magnificent Irish food producers, writers, chefs, and enthusiasts who have shown me that although we should respect all Irish food, there is more to Ireland than Guinness and beef pie. From Irish craft beers and ciders to smoked trout and salmon, farmhouse cheeses and cured meats, many Irish ingredients are available in stateside supermarkets and specialty food stores such as those listed in the Resources section of this book.

The Farmette Cookbook is a compilation of tried-and-true recipes that emphasize local, fresh ingredients and use my newly honed, traditional Irish kitchen skills. These are skills that have healed homesickness, forged new friendships, and provided an education that has taught me to respect the land and the animals that thrive on it. This book is also a tale of celebrating Irish traditions while finding common ground with new family and friends. It's about cultivating a love for the land and the quiet of the countryside and all the unpredictable cultural and practical differences I've encountered along the way.

So slip on some Wellies, tie on your best apron, and come with me on a fantastic Irish country food journey.

STOCKING THE LARDER

The larder was the place where food and cooking ingredients were stored before refrigeration came to Ireland. Nowadays, many people still refer to their pantry or fridge as the larder. It is essentially a place full of provisions for preparing meals. I use all of these terms interchangeably, and although we don't have a proper old-fashioned larder, I consider our kitchen cabinets and shelves the same thing.

This section is a reference tool for the recipes you will find in this book, since quite a few work with indigenous ingredients. A few of these foods may be unfamiliar, but many of them can be sourced online, and I've offered ways to concoct spice mixes that may not be easy to find.

The backbone of all Irish cooking is honest, wholesome ingredients, and traditional recipes are boosted by the quality of such ingredients. It is best to use fresh and local ingredients, organic when possible, of the highest quality for all of these recipes.

I have also added notes about equipment used in this book: how the items function, terminology, and kitchen methods that are used in Ireland and may not be familiar in other parts of the world.

Spices, Seasonings, Herbs, Oils

Mixed herbs. A mixture of savory herbs commonly used in Ireland and the United Kingdom, generally consisting of basil, marjoram, oregano, and thyme. You can prepare it yourself by combining the dried spices in equal proportions.

Mixed spice. A blend of sweet spices, similar to the pumpkin pie spice used in the United States. Cinnamon, nutmeg, and allspice are the dominant ingredients in mixed spice. The mix is often used in baking or to complement fruits or other sweet foods. It usually includes cinnamon (or cassia), nutmeg, allspice, ginger, coriander, caraway, and cayenne pepper.

Crab boil seasoning. My personal favorite spice mix for crab or seafood boils. It consists of mustard seeds, fresh dill, lemon zest, coriander seeds, cayenne peppercorns, bay leaves, dill seed, and allspice in equal proportions. To make your own, place all the ingredients in a sachet made of muslin and tie it with a string; place it in water to infuse.

Chipotles in adobo. Roasted and dried red jalapeño peppers in a sauce of chilies, tomatoes, garlic, vinegar, salt, and spices. Smoky and hot, they are available commercially in Latin food stores.

Baking Ingredients

Golden syrup. Available in the foreign food section of many supermarkets. There is no exact substitute in the United States, but light corn syrup is close. Also known as golden treacle.

Demerara sugar. A type of cane sugar with a fairly large grain and a pale amber color. It has a pleasant toffee flavor and can be used in place of light brown sugar.

Irish Atlantic sea salt. Sea salt cultivated from the Atlantic in the West of Ireland.

Muscovado sugar. An unrefined cane sugar from which the molasses is not removed. It is usually labeled "light" (with less molasses) or "dark."

Glacé cherries. Stoned maraschino cherries candied in sugar syrup. Very sweet with a hint of bitterness, they are used in many Irish fruitcake and bread recipes.

Mixed peel. Candied fruit peel, which is the term used in this book.

Currants. Tiny, dried, dark red, seedless grapes. This fruit was originally cultivated in the south of Greece.

Sultanas. Dried white seedless grapes. They tend to be plumper, sweeter, and juicier than other raisins. Referred to as golden raisins in this book.

Treacle. Dark molasses, which is the term used in this book.

Coarse wholemeal flour. A coarsely ground, soft, whole-wheat flour. King Arthur offers an excellent Irish-style wholemeal flour for baking brown and soda breads. Referred to as coarse-ground whole-wheat flour in this book.

Pudding rice. Short-grained white rice used for making rice pudding. Arborio rice works well too.

Fish

Trout caviar. Vibrant orange roe from trout.

Smoked haddock. Used in Irish seafood chowders and fish pies. Smoked haddock is often coated with a yellow dye that historically indicated it was smoked.

Kippers. A whole herring that has been split in butterfly fashion from tail to head along the dorsal ridge, gutted, salted or pickled, and cold smoked over smoldering wood chips (typically oak).

Wild Ingredients

Stinging nettle. A wild, herbaceous, perennial flowering plant that is native to Europe, Asia, northern Africa, and North America and is used in cooking and healing. The plant has stinging hairs that release histamines and create a rash when they come in contact with the skin.

Elderberry. Berries from the elder tree; green in the summer and purplish-red in the autumn.

Elderflower. The white blossom of the elder tree.

Sloes. Tiny, wild, bitter fruits of the blackthorn tree that are used to make sloe gin and other preserves.

Brambleberries. General term used for berries that commonly grow wild in hedgerows, such as blackberries, boysenberries, and raspberries.

Wild garlic, wood leek, wild leek, and spring leek. A broad-leafed allium also known as ramson or ramp.

Fraughan. A wild blueberry-like fruit; also known as bilberry.

Crab apples. Small, wild, tart apples.

Dillisk. A red seaweed high in vitamin B_{12} that is found along the coast of Ireland. Also known by its more common name, dulse.

Dairy

Rennet. An enzyme used in cheesemaking to set milk. Animal-based and vegetarian rennet are both available.

Dairy salt. Fine-grained salt that has no additives; used to flavor butter and in cheesemaking. Also called pickling salt, it is available at natural food stores.

Alcohol

Cider. Generally refers to hard cider, or pressed apples that have been brewed into a fermented, alcoholic beverage.

Porter. Dark style of beer originated in eighteenth-century London. Stout is derived from porter. The darker the porter, the more "stout."

Poitín. Grain alcohol or Irish moonshine; distilled in a pot still and has 40 to 90 percent alcohol. Formerly illegal, it is now available from the craft distillery Glendalough.

Apple jack. Apple brandy; Calvados.

Meat/Poultry

Eggs. All recipes in this book are best prepared with free-range and/or organic eggs.

Rasher. Thick-cut bacon with or without rind. Streaky rashers are usually cut thin and more fatty.

Black and white pudding. Blood sausage.

Oxtail. The tail of a cow. This inexpensive, flavorful specialty cut is available from butchers.

Minced beef, pork, or chicken. Ground beef, pork, or chicken.

Skirt steak. The cut from the plate of the cow.

Not the same as flank steak, it is best marinated or braised for tenderness and flavor.

Beef dripping. Rendered beef fat.

Goose fat. Rendered goose fat.

Ham hock. The cut of pork from the joint located between the ham and the foot (trotter). A frugal cut, it is flavorful when cooked long and slow.

Tools and Equipment

Cheeky espresso bar aside, I don't have a fancy, expensive, overly stocked kitchen, and you don't need one either. Some tools are helpful for modern cooks, but keep in mind that simplicity has been key for many Irish home cooks for centuries. Here are some of the tools and equipment that are used in various recipes in this book.

Kitchen and cooking stores carry many prepackaged types of *muslin*, including jam muslin, butter muslin, and cheesecloth. I recommend visiting a fabric store and ordering a large piece of unbleached muslin at a fraction of the price.

In Ireland, cake pans and pie plates are known as *tins*, as are cans of beans or tomatoes.

A *pudding basin* is an ovenproof custard dish or large ramekin.

A *grill* in Ireland serves the same purpose as an electric or flame broiler in an American oven.

A *hob* is the stovetop or cooktop; historically, the place behind the hearth where dishes were kept warm.

A *candy and jam thermometer* with a temperature range of 100°F to 375°F (40°C to 190°C)

is good for many recipes. Look for a model that labels certain temperatures such as liquid level, sterilize, jam, soft ball, hard ball, soft crack, hard crack, and caramel.

A stainless steel *meat thermometer* has a dial that displays a temperature range of 140°F to 194°F (60°C to 90°C).

A *fruit press* is a device used to separate fruit solids—stems, skins, seeds, pulp, leaves, and detritus—from fruit juice.

A deep stainless steel *preserving pan* is invaluable for making preserves. Find one that holds at least two gallons and has a pouring spout and a silicone handle.

A *milk separator* uses centrifugal force to spin and separate cream from milk.

An *ice cream maker* churns and freezes small quantities of ice cream for personal use. It's an absolute necessity in a dairy farm kitchen!

It's essential to have good-quality, sharp *knives* in your arsenal at all times. I can't live without these four key tools: a *chef's knife*, a *serrated knife*, a *boning knife*, and a *paring knife*. I also have a *cleaver*, which comes in handy when breaking down cuts of meat and seafood.

A *steamer basket* is a stainless steel or bamboo basket to hold vegetables or other foods over boiling water to steam cook.

I use a *balloon whisk* for cream and batters, but a small *flat whisk* is perfect for eggs and salad dressings. I mostly use *wooden spoons* when cooking, and they are required for working with meringue. I like to use *rubber and silicone spatulas and scrapers* as they are both sturdy and flexible. A *stainless steel fish slice* is the most versatile turner around.

A gradated *measuring cup* with metric and imperial measurements listed on the inside and outside for dry and liquid ingredients is the only measuring cup I use in the kitchen.

A *kitchen scale* is invaluable for weighing ingredients (instead of measuring them by volume). I have a vintage-style scale with a large dial and stainless steel bowl that measures weight in kilograms, grams, pounds, and ounces.

A *spiralizer* is a nifty little tool to have on hand for making ribbons of vegetable spaghetti or just to make things look pretty.

Butter bats and stamps are essential for molding and shaping homemade butter.

A *cheese basket* lends a tidy shape to homemade farmer cheese.

Despite never using one before coming to Ireland, I cannot live without my *electric tea kettle*. It is fast and convenient. Just about the only time I don't preheat water is when boiling potatoes. I use the kettle to heat water for everything else—coffee, tea, boiled eggs, pasta water, you name it.

I use a simple homemade *smoking tin and grate,* a large roasting pan fitted with a cooling rack and cover for stovetop and oven smoking.

For indoor stovetop or oven smoking, you need only sawdust, not woodchips. Try alder, hickory, oak, or cherrywood chip dust.

SOME NOTES ABOUT PREPARING THE RECIPES in this book.

Oven temperature: All ovens vary. The temperature can be affected by how old it is, how full, and how many times you open it. Always check for signs of doneness in aroma, color, or springiness or by inserting a skewer if baking a cake.

Mise en place: I recommend measuring out all of your ingredients before starting the recipe; this way you are much less likely to miss an ingredient or use the wrong ingredient. It makes preparing food so much easier!

The *Farmette*
COOKBOOK

CHAPTER I
Traditional Dairy Skills

HERE IN IRELAND, IT HAS BEEN SAID THAT FARMERS CAN TASTE THE FIELD FROM WHICH DAIRY COWS WERE GRAZING IN EACH CROCK OF BUTTER—GOÛT DE TERROIR, IF YOU WILL. THE DAIRY COWS OF IRELAND FORAGE ON GRASS OUTDOORS FOR UP TO TEN MONTHS OF THE YEAR. WHEN FRIENDS AND FAMILY VISIT, I ALMOST ALWAYS HEAR REMARKS OF SURPRISE ABOUT THIS. TOURISTS FIND IT FASCINATING TO SEE SO MANY ANIMALS IN THE FIELDS. NOW WHEN I TRAVEL BACK TO THE STATES, I FIND IT UNUSUAL TO SEE SO FEW COWS ON THE LAND.

Milk is the backbone of our family farm. This farm has been milking cows since the 1800s, when horses or donkeys carted the milk to and from the creamery every day on their own. My husband's grandmother could milk twelve cows by hand in ninety minutes flat before coming in to make breakfast for six children, herself, and her husband each morning. My father-in-law began milking cows at age seven, and if need be, he can still do it now in his seventies.

Time-honored dairy skills—some of which were once historical practices in Irish farm kitchens to make use of each day's milk and many of which I have adopted into my modern Irish kitchen—are anchored in our daily farm life.

Milk is a providential ingredient. It can go from liquid to a dense, creamy by-product. When warm, it can help you fall asleep. It is filled with calcium to help children grow strong bones, and even when it has gone sour, it is still good for you.

There is always a jug of raw milk in our fridge, and our son won't touch his morning porridge unless it has farm-fresh milk and honey mixed in. He says milk from the store "just doesn't taste like milk."

The great thing about milk is that even if you don't live on a dairy farm, you can find it locally. Cows are everywhere!

Farm-fresh milk has seasonal variations, a fact I learned only once I moved to the farm. I can now tell the difference between winter and spring milk. Spring milk has a purer, grassier flavor, which makes sense because the girls are back out to pasture full-time. During the depths of winter, the cows are fed hay and silage, and the milk always seems creamier and, I think, has less flavor.

The lower in fat a milk is, the more processed it is and the more sugar that has been added. Raw grass-fed milk is the least processed, so it is healthiest for you, but since there are health concerns for children, seniors, pregnant women, and people with immune deficiencies, not everyone can drink it. If you fall into any of those categories, prepare the recipes in this chapter only with pasteurized organic milk and cream.

Dairy milk is high in calcium as well as protein and vitamins A and D. Certain research suggests that consuming milk from grass-fed cows in its most pure, raw, organic state may potentially promote heart health, control diabetes, help vitamin absorption, and even aid in weight loss. I like to think of those facts as extra-special benefits that came with my new lifestyle.

All of the following recipes are best produced from raw milk and cream. Make friends with a farmer for your fresh milk if you haven't already. Most farmers will share only with a neighbor or friend. Many farms in the United States also offer milk-sharing programs. If you can't access fresh raw milk, then buy the highest-quality organic milk or cream you can afford. Look for milk products that are not ultrapasteurized.

There are several varieties of dairy milk to suit individual diet and lifestyle choices.

RAW MILK

Raw milk is full-fat milk straight from the cow's teat. It has not been pasteurized or homogenized. Many people claim that there are health benefits to drinking raw milk; it has beneficial bacteria cultures that make it more digestable, and many lactose-intolerant individuals have not experienced the same symptoms when using raw milk. I can vouch for this. Pre-farm life, I popped Lactaid tablets before and after eating or drinking dairy products. With raw milk, I don't have the symptoms of lactose intolerance I did then. Raw milk is hard to come by unless you have a relationship with a farmer (although you don't have to be married to one!), but finding it is worth the effort.

Raw milk should last in the refrigerator for ten days to two weeks. It is important to use sterilized glass containers for raw milk to ensure optimum safety and freshness.

PASTEURIZED MILK

Pasteurization is the process of heating milk to a specific temperature for a predefined length of time and then immediately cooling it after it is removed from the heat. This process slows spoilage caused by microbial growth in the milk, but it also kills the good bacteria that is present.

Pasteurized milk has a longer shelf life than raw milk. All milk found at the supermarket level in the United States, Ireland, and the United Kingdom has been pasteurized.

HOMOGENIZED MILK

Remember how milk used to come with the cream on top? That milk had not been homogenized. Homogenization is a mechanical process that breaks fat globules into smaller droplets so they stay suspended in the milk rather than separating out and floating to the top of the jug.

Homogenization was invented around the turn of the twentieth century and quickly became the industry standard—people preferred the convenience of milk that didn't have to be shaken vigorously to distribute the fat every time they wanted to use it. These days, we tend to see food processing as reducing the nutritive value of foods. In the States, you can buy nonhomogenized milk at Whole Foods Market and other natural food stores.

FORTIFIED MILK

Fortified milk is simply milk with added vitamins, such as vitamin A or D. Most milk options

4

at the supermarket are pasteurized, homogenized, and fortified.

ORGANIC MILK

Organic milk comes from cows that graze on organic fields and/or eat organic meal. The cost to the farmer is higher, and therefore, the price of the milk is usually substantially higher. It has been found, however, that organic milk has more nutritional value, containing higher concentrations of some beneficial omega-3 fatty acids and antioxidants.

BUTTERMILK

Buttermilk is the thin white liquid that separates from the fat when making butter. In Ireland, it is a much-loved baking ingredient. Fresh buttermilk has a thin, watery texture with a slight taste of butter. It is also an effective thirst quencher.

CULTURED BUTTERMILK

Cultured buttermilk is buttermilk that has been fermented either naturally or through inoculation. It is a sour, thick substance that can be used in baking. Because it has beneficial bacteria, many people find it easy to digest, but most would say it is hard to drink because of the sour flavor and thick texture. On the farm, if we want cultured buttermilk, we let buttermilk sit out on the counter to ferment naturally.

DAIRY CREAM: WHIPPING, DOUBLE, POURING, AND CLOTTED

Cream is the layer of milk fat that rises to the top of raw milk and is then skimmed off or separated to be used for whipping cream or to make butter, sour cream, or crème fraîche. When fresh, this cream is sweet in flavor. Cream has various percentages of milk fat. Double or heavy cream is about 50 percent fat, whereas clotted cream is up to 60 percent fat.

COUNTRY BUTTER

ONE OF MY VERY FIRST DAIRY ADVENTURES was learning how to make country butter. I was motivated to make my own since we live on a dairy farm, but I also wanted to have unsalted butter on hand, which at the time I could not source at nearby markets.

I experimented with churning techniques. First, I used a jam jar and shook it vigorously by hand, then a variety of vintage glass and wooden churns, and on to an electric hand mixer. I finally tried my trusty stand mixer, which is what I have come to rely on for quick and easy butter making. If you don't have a stand mixer, the next most convenient tool is an electric hand mixer; both methods take about the same amount of time.

Since you start with whole milk, you must first separate the cream from the milk. This can be achieved in two ways:

- *Naturally.* Here, you let a jug of milk sit in the fridge for twelve to forty-eight hours, depending on what type of cow the milk comes from. We keep British Friesian cows, whose milk has a lower butterfat content; Jersey cows have the creamiest milk. The cream will rise to the top and can be skimmed off for butter making.
- *With a separator.* My milk separator looks like a cross between a lamp and a spaceship, but it is very efficient. Using centrifugal force, it spins and separates the milk in a matter of minutes. A separator is handy if you plan to use cream (or make butter) on a regular basis, but it is a substantial investment, so keep that in mind when you look for one. If you prefer, you can simply use store-bought organic cream.

The sweet, creamy flavor and texture of country butter is unbeatable and well worth the effort.

Makes ½ lb (227 g) butter

About 2 gallons (7.5 liters) raw milk *or* 4 cups (2 pints; 1000 ml) organic dairy cream

Dairy or sea salt (optional)

SPECIAL TOOLS: Butter bats or wooden spatulas to shape butter

1. Skim the cream off the top of the milk. Pour the cream (fresh or store-bought) into the bowl of a stand mixer fitted with the whisk attachment. Beat on medium speed for 6 to 9 minutes, until the butterfat separates from the buttermilk (be careful of splashes!) and looks like scrambled eggs. Pour the contents of the mixing bowl into a sieve lined with muslin to strain out the buttermilk. Reserve the buttermilk for making pancakes, scones, or Best Brown Bread (see page 41).

2. Lift the muslin out of the sieve by the corners, gather together, and squeeze the buttermilk out, pushing down through the muslin until you've removed as much buttermilk as possible. Unwrap the muslin and place the baseball-size ball of butter in a large bowl of ice-cold water, washing and squeezing more buttermilk out in the water. If there is excess buttermilk in the butter, it will go rancid very quickly.

3. Place the butter on a flat surface and begin shaping it using your hands, traditional butter bats, or wooden spatulas. Keep the utensils in a bowl of ice-cold water before using, or the butter will begin to melt as you are shaping it. Mold the butter into a log or square.

4. If you wish, press a teaspoon of dairy salt or sea salt into the butter while you are shaping it.

5. Unsalted butter will keep for one week in the refrigerator; salted butter will stay good for up to two weeks.

Scullery
NOTES | You can add herbs, honey, fruit zest, liquor, or maple syrup to make delicious compound butters. Add a tablespoon of fresh dill and a pinch of minced garlic for a tasty topping for seafood, blend in a tablespoon of whiskey to melt over a steak, or mix in a teaspoon of cinnamon and sugar or a tablespoon of honey to use on pancakes or waffles.

CULTURED BUTTERMILK

FRESH BUTTERMILK IS THE LIQUID that separates from the butterfat when you are making butter. It is fresh and tangy but lightweight, and it looks like skim milk. Fresh buttermilk has fantastic leavening qualities and is great for baking, making cakes and breads incredibly moist. It is also quite refreshing to drink straight up!

When a recipe calls for buttermilk, however, it likely means cultured buttermilk. Buttermilk from the supermarket is often filled with additives, so making it from scratch will give much better results. Plus, like many fermented foods, once you make your first batch of cultured buttermilk you can use a portion of it as a starter for your next batch. This buttermilk tastes tangy but not sour.

Makes about 1 cup (250 ml)

4½ teaspoons white vinegar
or fresh lemon juice

About 1 cup (250 ml) whole milk

1. Place the vinegar or lemon juice in a glass measuring cup, and add enough milk to make 1 cup total liquid. Stir to combine and let stand for 10 to 15 minutes, until the mixture begins to curdle and becomes buttermilk. Stir it up slightly to combine, and store in the refrigerator.

Scullery NOTES | Use the buttermilk as called for in a recipe, or cover and refrigerate until you need it; it keeps for a week. For use as a starter, leave a tablespoon of cultured buttermilk in the bottom of a container and top up with fresh milk; you'll always have a bit of fresh cultured buttermilk in the fridge.

BUTTERED EGGS

SOME LIKE TO CALL BUTTERED EGGS "IRISH GOLD." I can see why—they taste like ambrosia. Buttering eggs was once a way of preserving them during the Lenten season. Farm wives and children would collect warm hen's eggs and rub butter on the shells to protect them from air, which ensured the eggs would keep until Easter. When they were finally eaten, the velvety butter flavor and, somehow, the texture melded with the egg and created an unbelievably rich flavor.

I keep buttered eggs on hand for when we entertain guests; soft-boiled buttered egg makes a simple breakfast special. Serve with buttered toast "soldiers," pieces of toasted bread cut into thin slices for dipping into the gooey soft egg yolk.

One dozen buttered eggs

1 cup (220 g) butter, semisoft

1 dozen hen's eggs
(preferably fresh from the coop)

1. Wash your hands thoroughly. Massage 2 tablespoons of butter onto each egg until it is thoroughly covered. There should be about a ⅛-inch layer of butter coating each egg.
2. Place the eggs in a basket and store in a cool place—in the United States, the refrigerator, in Ireland, a cool cupboard. Use buttered eggs as you would regular eggs: soft- or hard-boiled, in baking, fried, and so on.

Scullery
NOTES

These eggs keep for four weeks.

BASIC FARMER CHEESE

I LEARNED HOW TO CREATE THIS SIMPLE CHEESE from a cheesemaker at a food festival in an ecovillage in County Tipperary. She taught me the secret of making basic farmer cheese with just raw milk and white vinegar.

The moment I returned to the farm that evening, I followed her simple instructions, which resulted in a smashing success of soft, tangy, squeaky, curdlike clouds. I've experimented with variations on the same theme, using lemon or lime juice as a coagulator or substituting cream for milk to make a creamy mascarpone or ricotta (see pages 18 and 15, respectively). Raw milk is superb for cheesemaking, but if you can't find raw milk, organic milk from the grocery store works fine. Serve drizzled with olive oil and a side of capers or crumbled over a fresh garden salad and herb vinaigrette.

Makes 2 cups (550 g)

1 gallon (3.75 liters) milk
(not ultrapasteurized)

½ cup (125 ml) white vinegar

2 teaspoons fine sea salt

1. Line a colander with a double layer of cheesecloth or a single layer of butter muslin.
2. Pour the milk into a large, heavy-bottom saucepan, and bring to a boil over medium heat. Stir frequently to keep the milk from scorching. When it comes to a boil, immediately reduce the heat to low, and stir in the vinegar. The milk should immediately separate into curds and whey. If it does not separate, add a bit more vinegar, 1 tablespoon at a time, until you see the milk solids coagulate into curds swimming in thin, greenish-blue whey.
3. Pour the curds and whey into the lined colander. Rinse gently with cool water, and sprinkle the curds with salt. Tie up the cheesecloth, and press it a bit with your hands to remove any excess whey. Let the cheesecloth hang for 1 to 2 hours; open it, remove the cheese, and chop coarsely. Transfer and store in an airtight container.

Scullery
NOTES | This cheese will last for up to a week in the refrigerator.

FARMHOUSE *QUESO FRESCO*

THIS SIMPLE VARIATION on Basic Farmer Cheese makes the best salty, crumbly yet creamy *queso fresco*; it's perfect for tacos, nachos, and all things Mexican, including my Hot-Smoked Burren Salmon Tacos (see page 113) and Wild Garlic and Soft Irish Cheese Tamales (see page 133).

1. Follow the instructions for Basic Farmer Cheese, but replace the vinegar with ½ cup fresh lime juice. When you remove the cheesecloth, turn the cheese out onto a plate, and crumble.

Scullery NOTES | The longer the cheese is suspended, the drier and more crumbly it will become. You can also strain the cheese through a cheese basket, available at gourmet food shops.

IRISH FARMHOUSE RICOTTA

THIS IS NOT YOUR TRADITIONAL Italian ricotta cheese. *Ricotta* is Italian for "twice cooked" or "to cook again" and is usually made with the whey you get from making another cheese, such as mozzarella or a hard cheese. For proper ricotta, whey is heated, with or without additional vinegar, and the new cheese is strained and seasoned. Whole milk is never used.

This recipe is a variation on my Basic Farmer Cheese (see page 12), with added cream for a smoother, creamier consistency that works well for filling pasta shells or topping pancakes.

Makes about 1 generous cup (225 g)

3 cups whole milk (750 ml)

1 cup heavy cream (250 ml)

½ teaspoon coarse sea salt

3 tablespoons lemon juice, freshly squeezed

1. Pour the milk, cream, and salt into a 3-quart stainless steel saucepan, and heat the milk to 190°F (88°C), stirring occasionally to keep it from scorching on the bottom. Remove from the heat and add the lemon juice, slowly stirring once or twice. Let the pot sit for 5 minutes. The milk will separate and form curds and whey.
2. Line a sieve with cheesecloth and place it over a large bowl. Pour the curds and whey into the sieve, and let strain for at least 1 hour.
3. Eat right away or transfer to an airtight container and refrigerate until ready to use.

Scullery | Fresh ricotta will keep in the fridge for one week. Use really fresh milk for the best flavor
NOTES | and longevity.

CRÈME FRAÎCHE

I MADE CRÈME FRAÎCHE for the first time after tasting a delicate scoop of crème fraîche ice cream at a restaurant in County Donegal. My sole intention was to develop the same ultracreamy, dense ice cream for a dinner party. I first tried preparing the ice cream with store-bought crème fraîche, but since I wanted a thoroughly wholesome base, I decided to make it from scratch.

Homemade crème fraîche is a great way to use up leftover cream and buttermilk from the fridge. But most important, it tastes so much better than the expensive store-bought product.

Makes 1½ cups (375 ml)

1 to 2 tablespoons Cultured Buttermilk (see page 9)

2 cups (500 ml) heavy cream

1. Combine the buttermilk and cream in a saucepan over low heat and heat until lukewarm. Pour the mixture into a clean glass jar and cover partially with a clean tea towel. Let stand at room temperature for 8 to 24 hours, or until thickened. Stir and refrigerate at least 24 hours before using. Cover the jar with a lid to store.

Scullery **NOTES** | The crème fraîche will keep for about two weeks in the refrigerator. Crème fraîche is great in ice cream (in place of cream) and as a milder substitute for sour cream.

SOUR CREAM

I FIRST MADE SOUR CREAM by accident. I left a jar of cream and buttermilk on the counter over-night, and it thickened. I began researching whether we could use it for baking or cooking and discovered that I had homemade sour cream on my hands. A taste test confirmed this, and we enjoyed baked potatoes with a zesty sour cream and chive topping for supper that very evening.

Makes about 2 cups (480 g)

2 cups (500 ml) heavy cream

½ cup (125 ml) buttermilk

1. Pour the heavy cream and buttermilk into a large glass canning jar and fit it with a lid. Shake the mixture well for 1 minute. Cover the jar with plastic wrap or the lid; let stand at room temperature for 24 hours or until thickened.
2. It will keep for up to one week in the fridge.

Scullery
NOTES | If the cream does not thicken to your liking in 24 hours, put it in the fridge and it will thicken more. The only difference between sour cream and crème fraîche is that there is more buttermilk in sour cream, which gives it the trademark sour taste.

FARMHOUSE MASCARPONE

MASCARPONE COMES FROM the Italian word *mascarpa*, or cream cheese. If you can inhale half a pan of tiramisu in one sitting like I can, making the recipe using your own fresh mascarpone will put you over the edge (in a good way).

Thick, creamy, and sweet with a tiny bit of tang, this is another easy dairy delight. All you need is a little bit of lemon, heavy cream, and a thermometer.

Makes about 1½ cups (400 g)

2 cups (500 ml) heavy cream, pasteurized (but not ultrapasteurized)

1 tablespoon lemon juice, freshly squeezed

1. In a large saucepan, heat heavy cream over medium-high heat until it reaches 190°F (88°C) on a candy thermometer, stirring occasionally so it does not scorch on the bottom. Stir in the lemon juice and keep at the same temperature for 5 minutes, stirring constantly. The cream should thicken enough to coat the back of a spoon. Remove from the heat and allow to cool to room temperature, about 30 to 45 minutes.
2. Place a sieve lined with 3 layers of cheesecloth over an empty bowl. Pour in the cream, cover with plastic wrap, and place in the refrigerator. Allow the cream to strain for 8 to 12 hours, or preferably overnight.
3. When it is finished straining, transfer the cheese to an airtight container and store in the refrigerator.

Scullery
NOTES

Use fresh mascarpone cheese within a week.

CREAM CHEESE

NOTHING BEATS A NEW YORK BAGEL with a shmear of cream cheese. I can't tell you how many times I have longed for a little bagel shop to open just around the corner from the farm. It's never going to happen, but at least I can make spectacular cream cheese on my own.

The whole process takes two days, but you will be rewarded handsomely.

Makes about 13 oz (375 g)

---

2 cups (500 ml) whole milk

2 cups (500 ml) heavy whipping cream

2 tablespoons buttermilk

1 drop liquid vegetable rennet

¼ teaspoon fine sea salt

---

1. Warm the milk and the cream in a large, nonreactive pot until the temperature reaches about 70°F (21°C) on a candy thermometer. Don't let the mixture boil. Remove from heat. Stir in the buttermilk, then add the rennet.
2. Cover the pot and keep at room temperature overnight. The mixture will be set the next day.
3. Sprinkle the salt over the surface of the congealed mass, and whisk into small curds. Line a large colander with a piece of cheesecloth and place over a bowl large enough to hold the whey. Gently pour the contents of the pot into the colander and let it drain for about 30 minutes.
4. Gather the corners of the cheesecloth and tie them together to form a bag. Place the colander, with the cheese bag in it, back on the bowl. Put the whole thing in the refrigerator, and let the curds continue to drain overnight. The curds will meld together in the fridge and the cream cheese will be ready to use the next day.

Scullery NOTES | This cream cheese is particularly good in fresh cheesecake recipes. You can use the leftover whey for protein smoothies.

CLOTTED CREAM

CLOTTED CREAM IS COMMONLY ASSOCIATED with farms in the Cornwall and Devon regions of England; Cornish clotted cream has even garnered Protected Designation of Origin (PDO) status from the European Commission, but, after dipping into a tub of it made by a fellow Irish farmer, I decided I would try boldly to create this delicacy in my own kitchen. There is nothing like this thick, buttery textured cream; it is like a dreamy sweet ice cream that never melts.

Makes 1 cup (242 g)

4 cups (1000 ml) double or heavy cream (unpasteurized is best)

1. Preheat the oven to 200°F (100°C).
2. Pour the cream into a shallow, heavy-bottom pan. (I use a stainless steel roasting pan.) Place the pan in the oven and leave it for 8 to 10 hours, or overnight. A thick, golden crust will form on top when it is done. Remove from the oven and let sit in a cool place for 10 to 12 hours.
3. Remove the crusted "clotted" top with a slotted spoon, put it into a jar(s), and refrigerate for at least 2 to 3 hours before serving.

Scullery **NOTES** The clotted cream will keep in the refrigerator for three to four days. You can use the reserved cream underneath for other purposes if you wish, such as baking Creamiest Cream Scones (see page 55) and slathering it on any scones with jam.

SWEET CREAM ICE CREAM

ICE CREAM IS THE SIXTH FOOD GROUP on this farm. I love to experiment with different flavors, some more obscure than others: I've made everything from fresh hay–infused ice cream to sweet marjoram ice cream. One of my favorites is brown bread and whiskey. Just add your favorite flavorings to the ice cream maker at the beginning of the freezing cycle.

Makes 1 pint (475 ml)

SPECIAL TOOLS: An ice cream maker

6 large egg yolks

¾ cup (150 g) sugar

1¾ cups (420 ml) heavy cream

1¼ cups (360 ml) whole milk

Pinch of salt

1. Set a medium bowl in a large bowl of ice water.
2. In another medium bowl, whisk the egg yolks with ½ cup of the sugar until pale, about 3 minutes.
3. In a medium saucepan, combine the cream, milk, salt, and remaining ¼ cup of sugar, and bring to a simmer, whisking until the sugar is completely dissolved. Remove from the heat and allow to cool.
4. Pour the cream mixture into the beaten egg yolks in a thin stream while whisking to blend. Transfer the mixture back to the saucepan and cook over moderately low heat, stirring constantly with a wooden spoon, until the custard is thick enough to lightly coat the back of the spoon, about 4 minutes. Do not let it boil.
5. Pour the custard through a fine-mesh strainer into the bowl in the ice water. Let it cool completely, stirring frequently. Refrigerate the custard until very cold, at least 2 hours and overnight if possible.
6. Pour the custard into an ice cream maker with flavorings, if using, and freeze according to the manufacturer's instructions. Transfer the frozen custard to a plastic container, cover, and freeze until firm, at least 3 hours.

Scullery
NOTES

For brown bread and whiskey add ½ cup (45 g) caramelized brown bread crumbs and 1 tablespoon Irish Whiskey before churning in the ice cream maker. For fruit ice cream add ½ cup (45 g) chopped fruit.

IRISH COFFEE ICE CREAM

THIS RECIPE WAS INSPIRED BY the excitement of finding an American craft coffee roaster in Ireland. I was prepared to make coffee ice cream, a personal favorite for years, when my husband asked if I was making Irish coffee ice cream. I hadn't thought of putting whiskey in it, but I gave it a go, and we had ourselves one very tasty ice cream. (For more about my husband's affinity for Irish coffee, see page 312.)

Makes 1½ pints (713 ml)

SPECIAL TOOLS: An ice cream maker

1½ cups (375 ml) whole milk

¾ cup (150 g) granulated sugar

1½ cups (225 g) whole or ground coffee beans (Red Rooster in Ireland are great)

Pinch of salt

1½ cups (375 ml) heavy cream

¼ teaspoon vanilla extract

2 tablespoons Irish whiskey (optional)

4 tablespoons chocolate syrup (optional)

1. Heat the milk, sugar, coffee, salt, and cream in a medium saucepan over medium heat until the sugar is melted and it has just begun simmering but not boiling. Remove from the heat, and let sit at room temperature for 1 hour.

2. Strain the coffee mixture into a ceramic bowl. Mix in the vanilla (and whiskey, if using). Refrigerate overnight, then pour into your ice cream maker, slowly drizzling in the chocolate syrup (if using) as it churns. Freeze for 3 more hours before serving.

FARM-FRESH CONDENSED MILK
and EVAPORATED MILK

I MADE MY FIRST BATCHES of condensed and evaporated milk from scratch when I had a relentless hankering for Farmhouse *Tres Leches* Cake (see page 288) and no vehicle to drive to the market. Turns out, as with many homemade dairy recipes, these are time-consuming but simple processes that deliver incomparable flavor and texture.

SWEETENED CONDENSED MILK

CONDENSED MILK is cow's milk from which water has been removed and sugar has been added. It is great for desserts.

Makes about 1¾ cups (400 ml)

4½ cups (1 liter) whole milk

1 cup (200 g) granulated sugar
(or brown or raw sugar)

1 tablespoon butter, to thicken milk
(optional)

1. In a heavy-bottom pot, bring the milk and sugar to a boil over medium heat. Reduce the heat to low and simmer gently for about 2 hours, until the volume is reduced by half. The mixture should barely simmer and never bubble at any point. Stir every 15 minutes or so to keep the milk from burning on the bottom.

2. After 2 hours, stir in the butter (if using). Remove from the heat and let cool. The mixture will thicken further after it cools. Pour it into a jar and store in the refrigerator. Allow it to come to room temperature before using.

Scullery
NOTES | The no-butter version of this milk is perfect for making Vietnamese iced coffee. It will keep in the refrigerator for two weeks or more.

EVAPORATED MILK

EVAPORATED MILK is the same as condensed milk without added sugar.

Makes about 1¾ cups (410 ml)

2 quarts (scant 2 liters) whole milk

1. In a heavy-bottom pot, bring the milk to a boil over medium heat. Reduce the heat to low and simmer gently for about 2 hours, until the volume is reduced by 60 percent. The milk should barely simmer and never bubble at any point. Stir every 15 minutes or so to keep the milk from burning on the bottom.
2. Remove the pot from the heat and let it cool. The milk will thicken further after it cools. Pour it into a jar and store in the refrigerator. Allow it to come to room temperature before using.

Scullery **NOTES** Evaporated milk will keep in the refrigerator for two weeks or more.

FARMHOUSE YOGURT

AT HOME IN THE STATES, I was so spoiled with the many brands, flavors, and styles of yogurt that I never would have dreamed of making it from scratch. But when you have an Irish dairy farm literally at your doorstep and the nearest supermarket is nearly an hour away, it makes no sense *not* to milk it, so to speak. This recipe uses store-bought yogurt as a starter; its label must indicate that it contains "live bacteria cultures" for it to work.

Makes about 2 quarts (2 liters)

8 cups (2 liters) whole milk

½ cup (125 ml) plain yogurt

Seeds from 2 vanilla beans

1. In a saucepan over low heat, slowly warm the milk to 170°F (77°C) on a candy thermometer. Do not allow it to boil at any time. Turn off the heat, and bring the temperature down to 110°F (43°C). Stir 1 cup of the warm milk into the yogurt. Pour the mixture into the saucepan of milk and gently stir together. Stir in the vanilla seeds.

2. Now it is time to incubate the yogurt. You will need to keep it at a temperature of about 110°F (43°C) for 4 to 10 hours. Preheat the oven to 120°F (50°C), then turn it off. Put the lid on the saucepan, wrap it in two tea towels, and place it in the warm oven. The length of time it sits will depend on how thick and tangy you want your yogurt. The longer it sits at this warm temperature, the firmer and tangier it will get. Check the yogurt at the 4-hour mark to test the taste and texture; if you are not satisfied with the result, keep checking every 30 minutes until you are happy.

3. When the desired time is up, place the saucepan of yogurt in the fridge to chill completely. Once it is cold, stir. There may be a film on top, which you can stir into the yogurt or simply remove. Pour the yogurt into airtight containers and store in the fridge. Best eaten within ten days.

Scullery **NOTES** | Remember to save some of each batch of fresh yogurt to use as the starter for your next batch.

MILK JAM

MILK JAM, *CONFITURE DE LAIT, DULCE DE LECHE*—no matter what you call it, it's the beautiful by-product of a simmering pot of milk and sugar (and a prime suspect in the mystery of the ill-fitting jeans). I could eat milk jam by the spoonful, which is why I only make it for special occasions. Special occasions like "Hey, Mom, it's Wednesday!"

The milk I use is from our cows, but you can use any whole milk (grass-fed and organic is best but not necessary).

Pour it over ice cream, pudding, cake, apple pie, or crumble; prepare it with goat's milk for *cajeta;* spread it on cookies to make a sandwich; gift it for the holidays; or simply put it in a jar and dip a spoon in when the mood strikes.

Makes 2 cups (650 g)

4 cups (1 liter) whole milk

1⅓ cups (260 g) superfine sugar

½ teaspoon sea salt

½ teaspoon baking soda

1 teaspoon vanilla extract

1. Pour the milk into a pot that is large enough to hold the liquid with at least 4 inches to spare on top. Stir in the sugar, salt, baking soda, and vanilla. Bring to a frothy simmer over medium-high heat without stirring.
2. Turn the heat down to low, until the milk is barely simmering, and skim off the foam. Continue to simmer, uncovered, for 2 to 2½ hours, stirring about every 10 minutes and skimming off the foam when necessary. (If the heat is too high, the milk will boil and form a skin that won't disappear no matter how much you whisk it.)
3. Check the consistency at about 2 hours. Cook it a little longer if you want a thicker jam to use as a spread. It will also thicken up more while it cools and when it's in the fridge.
4. Remove from the heat, allow to cool to room temperature, then serve or pour into a glass jar with a lid and refrigerate.

Scullery
NOTES   Milk jam stays fresh for two to three weeks in the refrigerator.

MOONSHINE SYLLABUB

SYLLABUB IS A DRINK OR DISH made of milk or cream; curdled by the addition of wine, cider, or other acid; and often sweetened and flavored. Reputedly, the most traditional way to make it is by milking a cow directly into a jug of cider.

Since we live in Ireland, I like to use a splash of poitín (moonshine) instead of wine or brandy. This dessert is simple and creamy and presents beautifully, especially at a summery outdoor gathering, garnished with edible herbs and flowers.

Serves 4

⁓

⅛ cup (30 ml) Irish poitín

½ cup (100 g) sugar

Zest and juice of ½ lemon

1 cup (240 ml) heavy cream

1. In a small bowl, combine the poitín, sugar, lemon zest, and juice; stir to dissolve. In a large, chilled bowl, start beating the cream with a hand whisk or an electric mixer. Gradually add the poitín mixture, whisking constantly, until soft peaks form.
2. Serve immediately, or cover and chill until ready to serve.

Scullery NOTES | Serve the syllabub with sweet biscuits on the side.

IRISH CREAM

SIMPLE AND EVEN MORE DELICIOUS than store-bought, Irish cream is easy to make from scratch. If you make it just once, I guarantee you will prepare it time and time again. It's always a hit at the end of a dinner party and incredible as a festive coffee creamer during the holidays.

Makes 3 cups (720 ml)

1 cup (250 ml) heavy cream

1 teaspoon instant coffee powder

½ teaspoon cocoa powder

¾ cup (175 ml) Irish whiskey

1 teaspoon vanilla extract

1¾ cups (400 ml) Sweetened Condensed Milk (see recipe, page 26)

1. In a medium mixing bowl, combine 1 tablespoon of the cream with the coffee and cocoa powders to make a smooth paste. Slowly add the remaining cream, whisking until smooth. Add the whiskey, vanilla, and condensed milk; stir to combine.
2. Pour the mixture into a 24-oz jar and keep refrigerated until ready to serve, up to two weeks.
3. To serve, pour into a tumbler filled with ice or a cordial glass.

"COME IN, MAKE YOURSELF COMFORTABLE IN the sitting room." The blood rushed to my cheeks as I said "thank you" and nervously sat down on a beautifully upholstered high-backed armchair in front of a tiny, ornate fireplace burning with hot coals. "Can I get you a drop of sherry or a drop of Baileys?" I quietly breathed a sigh of relief as I chose the Baileys, a very warm and welcomed icebreaker.

It was my first time at the farm. I'd already met Richard's mother, father, and briefly, his brother, but it was time to meet the matriarch of the family, Mary McDonnell (may she rest in peace), otherwise known simply as "Grandma." Grandma lived in the little flat attached to the main farmhouse. But where she slept was only a matter of semantics; she clearly still ruled the roost at Dunmoylan. And deservedly so. In her day she could milk twelve cows by hand in a little over an hour before cooking breakfast for her six children and husband. Badass.

After I moved to the farm, my chat sessions with Grandma became more frequent. Over drops of Irish cream served in delicate cordial glasses, we swapped stories; she was kind yet opinionated, and as curiously interested in me as I was in her. At a certain stage, Richard told me, "Well, you passed the muster with Grandma," which was no easy feat apparently. I felt welcomed and proud.

CHAPTER 2

In the Bread Box

IRISH BAKING IS WORLD-RENOWNED YET STILL SO SIMPLE AND HOMESPUN. PEOPLE OFTEN TELL ME THAT THEIR GREATEST IRISH TRAVEL STORIES INCLUDE SAVORING A SIMPLE CUT OF BROWN WHEATEN BREAD OR TRADITIONAL SODA BREAD WITH COUNTRY BUTTER. BREAD BAKING IN IRELAND GOES BACK TO THE TIME WHEN THATCHED DWELLINGS STILL RULED THE COUNTRYSIDE. EVEN WHEN MY HUSBAND'S PARENTS WERE GROWING UP IN THE EARLY TWENTIETH CENTURY, TRADITIONAL FLATBREADS WERE STILL COOKED OVER AN OPEN FIRE OR IN GRIDDLES ON THE HEARTH LOCATED IN THE CENTER OF THE HOME.

Irish brown wheaten bread, also known as brown soda bread, is perhaps the most recognizable since it is commonly served up alongside velvety vegetable soups at pubs and inns around the country. The bread boasts a unique nutty flavor and has a crumbly yet moist texture that people long for after they've returned to their cozy homes abroad.

The tradition of making white soda bread goes back at least two centuries, born in a time before refrigeration, which meant fresh buttermilk needed to be used up quickly before it spoiled. White soda bread proved to be the perfect vehicle for buttermilk; the classic recipe has just four ingredients and only takes minutes to prepare—no proof or resting time required. The flavor and texture of white soda bread is distinctive, with a subtle hint of baking soda and a substantial bite, it is a hearty accompaniment to any meal. In many country houses, white soda bread is still made daily, and I make a loaf once every fortnight or so, more often when we have visitors.

As a farmer's wife, I have found it valuable to always have some tea bread on hand as we frequently entertain unannounced callers, various contractors, or just the occasional visiting neighbor.

You must be prepared! Tea breads, sometimes referred to as tea cakes, are essentially a cross between a bread and a cake and are usually baked in loaf form. Unlike American-style banana or pumpkin breads, Irish tea breads tend to be less sweet and heavier on dried fruit. Nevertheless, tea bread or tea cake is meant to be nibbled with a hot cup of tea or coffee, always a welcome snack.

This chapter offers a few of my favorite special bread recipes and a handful of toothsome baked treats.

BEST BROWN BREAD

OVER THE YEARS, I have received countless requests for the "best Irish brown bread recipe." Eventually, I developed one in my own kitchen. I am proud to say that this recipe garnered a top prize in an Irish bread baking competition, and many local family members and friends have adopted this formula as their own.

Makes 1 loaf

¾ cup (100 g) all-purpose flour

1 teaspoon sea salt

1 teaspoon baking soda

2 cups (275 g) coarse-ground whole-wheat flour (such as Bob's Red Mills Stoneground Whole-Wheat Flour)

2 tablespoons butter, room temperature

1½ cups (375 ml) buttermilk

1 large egg

1 tablespoon honey

1. Preheat the oven to 400°F (200°C).
2. In a large bowl, sift together the all-purpose flour, salt, and baking soda. Mix in the whole-wheat flour. Rub or cut in the butter until the mixture resembles coarse bread crumbs.
3. In a separate bowl, whisk together the buttermilk, egg, and honey.
4. Make a well in the center of the dry ingredients and pour in the liquids. Mix together with a spoon. The dough will be wet and sticky. Pour into a greased loaf pan and cut a line down the middle.
5. Bake for 40 to 45 minutes. Cool for 10 minutes, pop the bread out of the pan, and cover with a tea towel. It tastes best on the same day, but it will last for two or three days in the bread box.

Scullery NOTES | If you prefer, you can form a round with the dough and place it on a floured baking sheet or pour it into a well-oiled cast-iron pan. Cut the traditional cross though the center, and bake for 40 to 45 minutes.

TRADITIONAL WHITE SODA BREAD

WE ALWAYS FOLLOW THE TRADITION of Irish folklore that says before baking soda bread, you must cut a deep cross all the way across the top to be sure to let the fairies out. Of course, the cut serves the purpose of letting the heat penetrate the loaf while baking, but we love the ritual.

Makes 1 *loaf*

3⅓ cups (433 g) all-purpose flour

1 teaspoon fine sea salt

1 teaspoon baking soda

1¾ cups (375 ml) buttermilk

1. Preheat the oven to 450°F (230°C).
2. In a large mixing bowl, sift together the flour, salt, and baking soda. Make a well in the center and slowly pour in the buttermilk. Mix the dough with your hands, adding more milk if necessary, until the texture is soft, but not wet and sticky.
3. Turn the dough out onto a floured work surface and shape into a 1-inch-thick round. Cut a cross on the top.
4. Place on a stone or flour-dusted baking sheet in the oven for 15 minutes. Reduce the temperature to 400°F (200°C) for 30 minutes, or until the bread is cooked through. Tap the bottom of the bread to check for doneness; if it makes a hollow sound, it is ready. Let it cool for 10 minutes and serve slathered with Country Butter (see page 7).

Scullery
NOTES

This bread is best on baking day, but it will keep for two days in a bread box or airtight container.

Irish Fairies

THE WORD *FAIRY* (OR *FAERIE,* IN IRELAND) IS derived from the Gaelic word *Fé erie,* meaning "the enchantment of the Fées," and *Fé* is derived from "the Fates." The term originally applied to supernatural women who directed the lives of men and attended births. Now it has come to mean any supernatural creature, except monsters and ghosts, that is tied to the earth. In Ireland, the fairies are called the Aes Sídhe (singular, Aes Sídh; pronounced "ays-sheeth-uh"). Sídhe is also the name for the earthen mounds and hills that dot the Irish landscape. The country's mythology, legends, and folklore claim that the fairies live under these mounds, so the term *sídhe* has come to mean *fairy* in general, but it more properly refers to the palaces, courts, halls, and residences of these beings. However, they are known by a wide variety of euphemisms, including the Fair Folk, the Good Neighbors, the Little Folk, the Little Darlings, and the People of Peace.

FARMHOUSE MILK BREAD

PAN, BARREL, COBB, BLOOMER, brown, batch, granary, rolled, basket, milk—all names of beautiful breads that you will find in any Irish market or bakery on any given day, and all names of breads that baffled me upon moving to Ireland.

Milk bread in particular piqued my curiosity. After rooting around for a few weeks, I discovered the farm's recipe for an old-fashioned milk bread and couldn't wait to give it a try. I adjusted some measurements, added more milk, and used bread flour instead of all-purpose, and out came the softest, whitest loaf this side of the snow-capped Alps.

Makes 1 loaf

3 cups (750 g) bread flour, plus extra
  for dusting

1 teaspoon fine sea salt

5 tablespoons butter, diced

1 tablespoon sugar

2½ teaspoons (one 7-g packet)
  fast-acting dry yeast

1¼ cups (300 ml) milk

1. Grease a 9-inch loaf pan; set aside.
2. Combine the flour and salt in a large mixing bowl. Rub in the butter with your fingers until the mixture resembles coarse bread crumbs. Stir in the sugar and dry yeast.
3. Heat the milk in a small saucepan over medium heat until lukewarm. Stir the warm milk mixture into the dry ingredients. Use your hands to mix the dough until it comes away cleanly from the sides of the bowl.
4. Sprinkle a clean work surface with flour, and turn out the dough. Knead for about 10 minutes, until velvety smooth and elastic. Alternatively, you can use a stand mixer fitted with the dough hook for 7 minutes. Roll the dough into an oblong shape that will fit snugly in your loaf pan.
5. Put the dough in the pan, and cover loosely with plastic wrap. Put the pan in a warm, draft-free place and let rise for 30 minutes, until the dough has risen to the top of the tin.
6. Preheat the oven to 450°F (230°C).
7. Discard the plastic wrap, and lightly dust the top of the loaf with flour. Bake for 30 to 40 minutes, until the top of the bread is golden brown.
8. Let the bread cool in the pan for 20 minutes—but no longer. Turn it out of the pan; wrap in a clean tea towel so the crust stays soft but the loaf doesn't get soggy on the bottom.

GARDEN CARAWAY RYE

FEW MEALS ARE MORE SATISFYING than a proper Reuben sandwich prepared with caraway rye. Around the holidays, I get the urge to bake a loaf and feather together a sandwich of homemade sauerkraut, Swiss cheese, Russian dressing, and Irish spiced beef. Irish spiced beef is the closest thing to American-style corned beef on this fair isle, a cut that has been cured with cloves and savory spices, boiled in cider or stout, then sliced thin.

One year, I planted caraway in our kitchen garden specifically for this bread. Fresh caraway leaves have essentially the same flavor as the seeds but make the bread far more aromatic and flavorful. If you are a caraway lover, this bread is for you.

Makes 1 loaf

2¾ cups (340 g) bread flour

1¾ cups (230 g) rye flour

1½ cups (375 ml) water

1 teaspoon active dry yeast

1 tablespoon caraway seeds

1 tablespoon fresh caraway herb, finely chopped (optional)

2 teaspoons kosher salt

1. Grease a 9-inch loaf pan with vegetable oil spray, oil, or butter; set aside.
2. In a large mixing bowl or stand mixer with paddle attachment, combine the flours, water, yeast, caraway seeds, caraway herb (if using), and salt. Then knead the dough by hand or attach the dough hook and knead for 10 minutes. You should be able to stretch the dough until it is translucent without tearing it.
3. Cover the bowl with a tea towel and let the dough rise until it is double in size, from 2 to 4 hours.
4. Knead the dough again to force out gas and redistribute the yeast. Pat it into a rectangle about 1 inch thick. Cover with a towel and let rest for 10 minutes.
5. Shape the dough, starting on a long side of the rectangle; fold the dough over on itself and pound it down to seal. Keep folding in alternate directions and pounding until you have a squat, tubular shape.
6. Place the dough in the prepared loaf pan. Cover with a towel and let rise for 1 hour.
7. Preheat the oven to 450°F (230°C).
8. When the second rise is done, slash the dough lengthwise down the center. Bake for 30 minutes. Reduce the temperature to 375°F (190°C), and continue baking for another 15 to 30 minutes, until done.
9. Remove it from the oven, and let cool in pan for 10 minutes. Turn out and cover with a tea towel until ready to slice and serve.
10. This bread will keep in an airtight container or bread box for a week.

DIVINER'S TEA BRACK

ONE WET MARCH AFTERNOON, my husband announced that our local water diviner was going to come and help us locate a new well. Up until the moment he arrived, I honestly thought his visit was some kind of madcap prank. I simply couldn't believe that in the twenty-first century we would be enlisting the services of a person with a willow divining rod to find water on the farm.

But, as I have learned time and time again, many practices of the past are still very much alive in the Irish countryside. When I saw the man hiking in the fields behind our garden, I quickly made up a tea bread to share after he finished his work. We sat around the table sipping tea as I sliced piece after piece of this fruity brack, chatting for nearly an hour, and when the water diviner left, he thanked me for a tea cake as "fine as my mother's."

Brack is a cross between cake and bread and is often enjoyed with a cup of tea or coffee.

Makes 1 loaf

1 cup (200 g) mixed dried fruit

1 cup (240 ml) hot black tea
(Barry's Tea is perfect if you can get it)

1 cup (130 g) all-purpose flour

1½ teaspoons baking powder

1 teaspoon salt

½ cup (100 g) superfine sugar

1 large beaten egg

2 tablespoons orange marmalade

1. Preheat the oven to 375°F (190°C). Grease a 9-inch loaf pan.
2. Place the fruit in a small mixing bowl, pour the hot tea over the top, and allow to soak until the fruit swells, about 1 hour.
3. In a separate bowl, stir together the flour, baking powder, salt, sugar, egg, and marmalade. Pour in the fruit and any tea left in the bowl; stir thoroughly. Pour into the loaf pan, and bake for 1 hour.
4. Remove from the oven and allow to cool slightly before turning out of the tin. Serve the brack with butter and cups of tea.
5. Store any leftovers in the bread box, where it will keep for one week.

SODA FARLS

THE SODA FARL HAILS from Northern Ireland and is prepared on a griddle; it is made fresh in the morning, cooked until golden, and eaten immediately. Farls are delicious with butter and homemade jam or with savory foods such as smoked salmon, kippers, or thick dry-cured bacon. The soda bread quarters are slow cooked on a stovetop griddle or in a cast-iron pan for about fifteen to twenty minutes on each side. The farls will rise while cooking, and you may need to "harn" them (set them upright on the griddle, leaning against each other) to cook the edges.

Soda farls are perfect hot off the griddle, sliced down the middle, topped with butter, and slathered with jam or honey.

Makes 8 farls

3⅓ cups (450 g) all-purpose flour	½ teaspoon fine sea salt
1½ teaspoons baking soda	1¼ cups (300 ml) buttermilk

1. In a large bowl, sift together the flour, baking soda, and salt. Make a well in the middle, and add the buttermilk gradually, bringing the dough together with a mixing spoon. This recipe makes a soft dough, but the more buttermilk you incorporate, the better the bread tastes.

2. Turn the dough out onto a well-floured wooden surface, and knead it gently until you have a smooth, round shape, about 2 minutes.

3. Divide the dough in two, and knead both again to form balls. Roll each out to a fairly thick circle, about 10 inches (25 cm) in diameter, and cut into quarters.

4. Preheat a griddle or heavy skillet over medium heat. To check the temperature, dust with flour. Once the flour starts to color, brush it off, and turn the heat down to low. Your griddle is now ready.

5. Place the farls on the griddle until golden brown on one side, 2 to 3 minutes. Flip and cook for another 5 to 10 minutes. The farls will rise into triangular pillows. Test for doneness by pressing the middle—if they still hold the indent of your finger, you must flip them again and cook until firm.

6. Cool the cooked farls on racks, covered with a damp tea towel to keep them soft or uncovered if you prefer a drier crust. Slather in fresh butter and honey or marmalade to boost flavor.

Scullery NOTES | For a Northern Irish–style breakfast, soda farls are cut in half and then fried in bacon fat until they are crisp on both sides.

FARMER'S SUNDAY CAKE

FARMER'S SUNDAY CAKE STARTED OUT as a simple fruited soda bread, but when I doubled the fruit and added nuts, it became a bit more substantial. I serve a slice of this cake bread with a boiled egg and heaps of tea for light supper on Sunday evening, since the massive Sunday roast lunch with all the trimmings has finished only hours before.

Makes 2 loaves

¾ cup (170 g) butter, softened, plus more for greasing the pan

6¼ cups (800 g) all-purpose flour

1 teaspoon baking soda

1 teaspoon cream of tartar

1 cup (200 g) superfine sugar

1 cup (150 g) golden raisins

1 cup (150 g) dried currants

2 tablespoons glacé cherries

½ cup walnuts

2 tablespoons candied citrus peel, finely chopped

Grated zest of ½ lemon

2 eggs, beaten

2½ to 3 cups (600 to 720 ml) buttermilk

1. Preheat the oven to 450°F (230°C). Lightly grease two 9-inch loaf pans; set aside.
2. Sift together the flour, baking soda, cream of tartar, and sugar in a large bowl, and mix well. Rub in the butter with your fingers until the mixture resembles coarse bread crumbs. Add the raisins, currants, cherries, walnuts, candied citrus peel, and lemon zest. Mix well.
3. Make a well in the center of the flour mixture, and pour in the eggs and 2½ cups (600 ml) of the buttermilk. Stir into the flour mixture, working in a spiral motion from the middle toward the sides of the bowl, and adding a bit more buttermilk if necessary to make a moist but cohesive batter. Do not overmix.
4. Spoon the batter into the loaf pans and bake for 15 minutes. Reduce the temperature to 400°F (200°C) and bake for another 20 to 30 minutes.
5. Remove the loaves from the oven and let them cool in the pans for 10 minutes. Turn the loaves out and cover with tea towels until ready to serve.
6. This cake will keep for up to a week in an airtight container or bread box.

CREAMIEST CREAM SCONES

THERE IS NOTHING MORE DIGNIFIED and delicious than sipping afternoon tea and nibbling on fluffy scones covered in clotted cream and jam on a spring afternoon at the farm. After enjoying my first Queen's Tea at Adare Manor with my mother- and sister-in-law, I came home with dreams of cream scones.

The following weekend, I spent a day testing scone recipes in between feeding the spring calves. I began with a Victorian-era Mrs. Beeton recipe, a whole-grain scone, and finally created this recipe in which cream replaces the butter and milk, lending a lighter, airier texture. I like to add half a cup of fresh sliced strawberries, when they're in season, for a strawberries-'n'-cream version.

Makes 6 fluffy scones

1½ cups (200 g) all-purpose flour

1 tablespoon baking powder

1¾ teaspoons salt

¼ cup (50 g) superfine sugar

1 cup (240 ml) heavy cream

1. Preheat the oven to 425°F (220°C). Lightly flour a baking tray and place in the oven to preheat.
2. Sift the flour, baking powder, and salt together in a medium bowl. Add the sugar and ¾ cup of the cream; work the dough with a fork until you have even-size clumps. If the mix is too dry to hold together, add the remaining ¼ cup cream and mix thoroughly.
3. Place the dough on a floured worktop and knead 4 or 5 times. Dust with flour and roll flat with a rolling pin until 1½ to 2 inches thick. Cut out 2½- to 3-inch circles with a crimped scone cutter.
4. Place scones on the preheated tray, and bake for 6 to 8 minutes, until they have risen nicely and browned at the edges.
5. Serve with jam and whipped or clotted cream.

Scullery NOTES | Preheating the baking tray is essential for high-rising scones.

IRISH STOUT *and* TREACLE LOAF

BEFORE I MOVED TO IRELAND, the word *treacle* seemed to be about as modern as the word *brimstone*—and about as positive too; I'd only read about it in Victorian novels. This thick, midnight-black syrup with a tarlike consistency never crossed my kitchen path until I spotted it in an Irish supermarket and was enamored of the pretty red-and-gold Tate & Lyle packaging. I later discovered that treacle is the same as blackstrap or dark molasses commonly found in the United States. Eureka!

The treacle sat in my larder for a couple of months until I brought it out as an experiment in a brown bread recipe after getting word that it was a complementary addition. When you combine the treacle with stout, you get a deep, richly flavored, dense bread that's perfect for a special occasion or as a hostess gift.

Makes 1 loaf

2 cups (250 g) all-purpose flour

2 cups (250 g) whole-wheat flour

1¾ cups (150 g) rolled oats, plus more for sprinkling (optional)

1 tablespoon baking soda

½ tablespoon salt

2 cups (500 ml) buttermilk

2 tablespoons black treacle (or molasses)

¼ cup (60 ml) Irish stout

2 tablespoons honey

1. Preheat the oven to 400°F (200°C). Line a 9-inch loaf pan with parchment paper.
2. In a large mixing bowl, stir together the flours, oats, baking soda, and salt. Make a well in the middle, and pour in the buttermilk, treacle, stout, and honey. Using your fingers, lightly mix into a wet dough. Do not overmix or knead.
3. Spoon into the loaf pan, and slit the top of the dough with a knife. Sprinkle with rolled oats (if using). Bake for 45 to 50 minutes.
4. Remove the pan from the oven. Turn the bread out, transfer to a wire rack, and lay a slightly damp tea towel over the top; leave to cool completely. The tea towel will help keep the moisture in and the crust from becoming too hard.

Scullery **NOTES** | You might need to add a little more flour to bind everything together, depending on the consistency of your buttermilk. Treacle loaf is particularly splendid for grilled Gruyère and Granny Smith apple sandwiches!

NIAMH'S BLAAS

A FEW YEARS AGO I had the great fortune of meeting a fantastic blogger and cookbook author, Niamh Shields, who hails from Waterford, Ireland, but lives in London. Niamh had just finished her first book, *Comfort & Spice,* and the first recipe I baked from it was her Waterford blaas. The blaa is a soft, floury, yeast bread roll that dates back to the 1690s and has now been granted Protected Geographical Indication (PGI) status by the European Commission. PGI status is only assigned to unique, quality products that are distinguished by the use of simple ingredients, traditional skills, and local knowledge from a particular region. Blaa rolls have been a symbol of Waterford and a much-loved food for generations, and I can see why. The blaa is the perfect fluffy bun for sandwiches, burgers, and Irish breakfast sandwiches (called butties) alike.

Makes 8 large rolls

3½ teaspoons active dry yeast

2¼ teaspoons superfine sugar

1¼ cups (275 ml) lukewarm water

4 cups (500 g) bread flour, plus more
   for dusting

3 teaspoons sea salt

2¼ teaspoons unsalted butter

1. Dissolve the yeast and sugar in the water. Be sure the water is warm, not cold or hot. Let rest for 10 minutes. It should get nice and frothy, indicating that the yeast is alive and well.
2. Sift together the flour and salt to introduce air. Rub in the butter with your fingers until the mixture resembles coarse bread crumbs. Add the yeast mixture to the dry ingredients, and mix until combined. Knead for about 10 minutes, until the dough is smooth and elastic. (It will go from rough to shiny.)
3. Place the dough in a bowl, cover with plastic wrap, and let rest in a warm place for 45 minutes. Remove from the bowl and punch down, pushing the air out of the dough. Cover and let it rest for 15 more minutes, to give the gluten time to relax; this will make shaping easier.
4. Divide the dough into eight pieces. Roll each piece into a ball. Cover and let rest for 5 more minutes.
5. Dust a baking dish with flour, roll the balls in flour, then place the balls side by side. Let rise again in a warm place for 50 minutes.
6. Preheat the oven to 410°F (210°C). Roll the blaas in flour a final time, and bake for 15 to 20 minutes, until just barely golden. Store in a bread box for up to one week.

WELSH CAKES

WE STUMBLED UPON THESE CRUMPET-SIZE CAKES at a darling bakery in County Wexford, and I immediately inquired about how to make them. The clerk gave us a slapdash recipe, and I gave it a go a few days later. The mixed spice (see "Stocking the Larder," page xv) makes these cakes special; each currant-filled cake is a cross between a shortbread and a pancake, with a spicy-sweet flavor and a buttery, flaky texture.

Welsh cakes are perfect for a sunny Sunday morning, served with a fresh pot of tea before heading out to do a bit of weeding in the garden.

Makes about 16 cakes

1½ cups (225 g) all-purpose flour

⅜ cup (85 g) superfine sugar

½ teaspoon mixed spice (see page xv) or cinnamon

½ teaspoon baking powder

Pinch of salt

7 tablespoons (100 g) butter, cut into small pieces, plus extra for frying

⅓ cup (50 g) currants

1 egg, beaten

1 tablespoon milk

1. Combine the flour, sugar, mixed spice, baking powder, and salt in a bowl. Rub in the butter with your fingers until the mixture resembles coarse bread crumbs. Mix in the currants. Work the egg into the mixture until you have a soft dough, adding a splash of milk if it seems a little dry—it should be the same consistency as short (buttery) pastry.

2. On a lightly floured work surface, roll out the dough until it is ¼-inch thick. Cut out rounds using a 2-inch scone cutter, rerolling and cutting any trimmings. Grease a flat griddle or heavy frying pan, and place over medium heat. Cook the Welsh cakes in batches, for about 3 minutes on each side, until golden brown, crisp, and cooked through.

3. These cakes are delicious served warm with butter and jam, or simply sprinkled with superfine sugar. They will stay fresh in an airtight container for one week.

CHAPTER 3

Potatoes

IRELAND'S HISTORY WITH POTATOES IS PROFOUND. WHEN A BLIGHT CREATED A FAMINE THAT DEVASTATED THE COUNTRY IN THE 1800S, THE MODEST POTATO BECAME A REVERED AND CHERISHED VEGETABLE IN MOST IRISH HOUSEHOLDS.

I arrived in Ireland on the heels of the Atkins Diet era and hadn't eaten a spud in more than a year. I had been misinformed that potatoes were evil carbs, never to be ingested. I remember ridiculously swearing that I would not succumb to eating potatoes while living in Ireland. Well, let's just say that plan had to be abandoned within the first week.

Over the years, I have found the vast number of Irish potato creations and descriptive words that go along with them absolutely delightful. I even considered producing a documentary called "Práta," which is the Irish (Gaelic) translation of the word *potato*. The idea came to me as I sat at a wedding listening to my tablemates cheerfully carrying on about the texture of our freshly delivered, steamy-hot potatoes. Never had I heard potatoes discussed in such great detail or at such length. This "*práta*-talk" is truly a uniquely Irish gift.

Here's the inside scoop: terms such as *floury*, *soapy*, and *fluffy* are favorable potato textures, whereas *watery*, *hairy*, and *waxy* are no good at all. If you are planning a trip to Ireland, see if you can tell the difference as you taste your way across the country.

There are so many colorful ways to prepare potatoes, and often a few potato variations will be served at the farm dinner table. For formal meals, a *minimum* of boiled potato, mashed potato, and potato croquettes are served. Hash browns (called waffles), chips, and "roasties" are also on heavy rotation here.

I began growing both Irish heirloom potatoes and conventional classics a few years ago, and there is nothing more rewarding than going out to dig your own spuds for dinner.

I encourage everyone with a garden to grow potatoes. They are easy to plant (they can even be grown in containers!) and also yield beautiful flowers that can be cut and popped into a vase or used as a garnish.

CLASSIC COLCANNON

Did you ever eat Colcannon, made from lovely pickled cream?
With the greens and scallions mingled like a picture in a dream.
Did you ever make a hole on top to hold the melting flake
Of the creamy, flavoured butter that your mother used to make?

CHORUS:

Yes you did, so you did, so did he and so did I.
And the more I think about it sure the nearer I'm to cry.
Oh, wasn't it the happy days when troubles we had not,
And our mothers made Colcannon in the little skillet pot.

—TRADITIONAL IRISH FOLK SONG

COLCANNON AND CHAMP are both traditional Irish mashed potato dishes. Colcannon was traditionally made from mashed potatoes and kale (or cabbage), butter, salt, and pepper. It is often eaten with boiled ham or Irish bacon. You can also add scallions, leeks, or chives. "Old" potatoes or russet potatoes are best for this recipe—waxy varieties won't work.

Potatoes are a must in our farming family, and I love serving colcannon with a Sunday roast, which makes it all the more special. Since we have loads of kale and collards in the garden, I am always trying to work it into our weekly menus.

Serves 4

---

4 lb (1.8 kg) potatoes (or 7 to 8 large potatoes in jackets)

1 head green cabbage (or kale)

½ cup (120 g) butter, divided into three parts

1 cup (240 ml) whole milk (or cream)

Salt and freshly ground pepper, to taste

Fresh parsley (or chives), finely chopped, to garnish

---

1. Peel and put potatoes in an ovenproof or stainless steel pot filled with cold water and salt to boil.
2. While the potatoes are cooking, core the cabbage, thinly slice the leaves, and place in a large saucepan. Cover with boiling water from the kettle, and keep at a slow, rolling boil until the cabbage is just

wilted and has turned a darker green. This can take from 3 to 5 minutes, depending on the cabbage. Test it—slightly undercooked is better than overcooked.

3. Drain the cabbage well, squeeze out any excess moisture, and return to the saucepan. Add one-third of the butter and cover. Leave in a warm place (not on a burner) to let the butter melt into it while you continue to prepare the potatoes.

4. When the potatoes are soft, drain off the water and return the potatoes to the saucepan over low heat; leave the lid off so any excess moisture can evaporate. When they are perfectly dry, add the milk and another third of the butter. Allow the milk to warm but not boil—it is about right when the butter is fully melted and the pot starts to steam.

5. With a potato masher or fork, mash the potatoes thoroughly into the milk mixture. Do *not* pass through a ricer or beat in a mixer, as this will make the potatoes gluey.

6. Mix the cabbage thoroughly with the mashed potatoes. Place the last bit of butter on top and place it in a hot oven for 15 minutes.

7. Remove from the oven, season with a little salt and pepper, sprinkle with fresh parsley or chives, and serve.

Scullery
NOTES | Always boil potatoes in cold water to start for the best flavor and texture; potatoes will cook more evenly. Try your own special spin on colcannon by adding in finely chopped fresh herbs and even lemon zest, if you fancy.

CLASSIC CHAMP

CHAMP IS NATIVE TO NORTHERN IRELAND. It looks similar to colcannon and is made by blending scallions or green onions with creamy mashed potatoes. Champ is great on its own, served steaming hot with extra butter, or as a side dish for good-quality sausages.

Serves 4

3 lb (1.35 kg) potatoes, well scrubbed and left whole in their jackets

1 cup (240 ml) whole milk

1 large bunch spring onions, finely chopped

Salt and freshly ground black pepper, to taste

6 tablespoons butter

1. Boil the potatoes in salted water until soft. Drain and remove from the pan. Let stand until just cool enough to peel. Peel and mash thoroughly.
2. Boil the milk and stir into the potatoes, together with the spring onions. Season with salt and pepper, and stir well.
3. Pile the potatoes in a serving dish. Make a well in the center and add the butter. Serve immediately.

BOXTY

Boxty on the griddle
Boxty in the pan
If you can't make Boxty
You'll never get a man

—TRADITIONAL IRISH RHYME

BOXTY, OCCASIONALLY SPELLED "BOXDY," is basically a potato cake, eaten mostly in the north of Ireland, especially in counties Cavan, Fermanagh, Derry, and Tyrone. Boxty vies with champ and colcannon as Ireland's best-known potato dish. It may have originated in the late eighteenth and early nineteenth centuries, when potato harvests began to fail, as a way of using poor-quality potatoes that were deemed useless for boiling. The potato pulp was shaped into cakes and baked on heated flagstones or a griddle.

An indulgent dish, boxty is a delicacy on the farm. Serve it on a cool autumn evening; it's wonderful with a bit of homemade crème fraîche and stewed apples from the orchard.

Serves 4

6 medium potatoes

¼ cup (38 g) all-purpose flour

1 teaspoon sea salt

1 tablespoon butter (or sunflower oil)

Fresh herbs, chopped, for garnish

1. Peel the potatoes. Line a colander with cheesecloth and place over a large mixing bowl. Using a box grater, grate the potatoes into the colander. Gather the corners of the cheesecloth together and squeeze the liquid from the potatoes into the bowl. Put the dry grated potato in another bowl and discard the liquid.

2. Add the flour and salt to the grated potato and mix gently.

3. Melt the butter in a heavy iron pan, and pour in the potato mixture to make an even layer, about ¾ to 1 inch thick. Cook over medium heat until nicely brown on one side, about 15 minutes; flip the whole boxty cake and cook on the other side for another 15 minutes, or until brown. It's much better to cook the boxty slowly than too fast. It should be crisp and golden on the outside and cooked through on the inside.

4. Remove from the heat, cut into quarters, garnish with herbs, and serve with crème fraîche, applesauce, or just on its own.

HARISSA POTATO LATKES

CRUNCHY POTATO LATKES are traditional Jewish fare throughout the world. The word *latke* means "little oil" in Hebrew, and latkes are essentially grated potatoes prepared with oil. Similar to Irish boxty but with the addition of an egg, they are a crunchy, fried, addictive potato cake that I am happy to have in my repertoire.

On a summer trip stateside, I had the pleasure of tasting tiny latkes laced with harissa. Two weeks later, back in County Limerick, I was still thinking about them. I decided to whip up a batch on a whim for a simple Friday supper, and the family loved them, despite their being a bit spicy for the Irish palate. Nothing a dollop of farm-fresh yogurt couldn't help!

Makes 6 to 8 latkes

2 large baking potatoes (about 1 lb), peeled	1 teaspoon salt
1 small onion (4 oz), peeled	¼ teaspoon freshly ground pepper
¼ cup (38 g) all-purpose flour	Peanut oil, for frying
1 large egg, lightly beaten	Farmhouse Yogurt or Crème Fraîche (see recipes pages 29, 16), for serving
2 tablespoons harissa	

1. With a box grater, coarsely shred the potato and onion. Transfer to a colander or wrap in a cheesecloth sling, and squeeze out as much liquid as possible. Let stand for 2 minutes, then squeeze again.

2. In a large bowl, whisk together the flour, egg, harissa, salt, and pepper. Stir in the potato mixture until all pieces are evenly coated.

3. In a medium skillet, heat 2 tablespoons peanut oil over moderately high heat until simmering. Drop heaping spoonfuls of the potato mixture into the skillet, and flatten them with the back of the spoon. Cook the latkes until the edges are golden, about 90 seconds; flip and cook on the other side until golden, about 1 minute. Remove from the skillet and drain on paper towels. Repeat with the remaining potato mixture, adding more oil to the skillet, as needed.

Scullery **NOTES** | These latkes are best fresh out of the frying pan and plunged in yogurt or crème fraîche.

POTATO, RASHER, *and* ROSEMARY PIZZA

INSPIRED BY A PIZZA I SAMPLED at a food festival in Donegal, this recipe features some of my favorite local ingredients: Crowe's Farm streaky rashers and Ardsallagh Goat's Cheese along with truffle oil, minced garlic, and the fresh rosemary that grows in our front yard. This pizza does not have a tomato sauce, but the crust is just as delicious with passata (tomato purée) and the toppings of your choice, if you prefer.

Makes 6 small thin-crust pizzas

FOR THE CRUST

3½ cups (500 g) bread flour

2½ teaspoons (one 7-g packet) dry fast-acting yeast

2 teaspoons sea salt

¼ teaspoon sugar

1⅓ cups (300 ml) lukewarm spring water

1½ tablespoons extra virgin olive oil, plus more to brush

FOR THE TOPPINGS (PER PIZZA)

3 bacon strips, cooked

1 medium russet potato, thinly sliced and parboiled

1 teaspoon minced garlic

2 to 3 rosemary sprigs

1½ teaspoons truffle oil, to drizzle

1 teaspoon fennel seeds

1. In a large mixing bowl, combine the flour, yeast, salt, and sugar. Stir in the water, and then the olive oil. Mix until you have a soft dough.

2. Gather the dough into a ball and turn onto a lightly floured work surface. Knead by hand for about 10 minutes, or in a stand mixer fitted with the dough hook for 5 minutes, until the dough feels silky and springy. Place in another bowl and cover with a cloth or plastic wrap. Let rest in a warm place until the dough has doubled in size, about 1 to 2 hours.

3. Half an hour before baking the pizzas, preheat the oven to 500°F (250°C). Place a pizza stone or heavy baking sheet in the oven to preheat.

4. Divide the dough into eight equal parts. (While working with one section of dough, cover the remainder with plastic wrap or a tea towel so it doesn't dry out.) Working on a lightly floured board, roll out each ball of dough until very thin, and place each on a square of parchment paper. Prick the dough several times with a fork and brush lightly with olive oil.

5. Top each pizza with the bacon, potato, garlic, and rosemary. Using a light hand, drizzle a little truffle oil over the top and sprinkle the fennel seeds. Slide the pizzas on the parchment paper onto the pizza stone, and bake for 7 to 10 minutes. Using the parchment paper, quickly slide each pizza out of the oven onto a cutting board. Serve immediately with a tossed green salad and a glass of bold red wine.

POTATO BREAD

AS MUCH LOVE AS THE HUMBLE SPUD GETS in Ireland, potatoes have not fully entered the Irish bread realm. For me, potato bread conjures warm memories of nibbling on powder-topped toast with my cousins at my grandmother's house on Saturday mornings stateside. This easy potato bread recipe is the closest I've come to emulating the bread from my local childhood bakery. The recipe makes two loaves—one to eat immediately and one to freeze for later. The bread doesn't taste like potato; it just has an extraordinarily moist texture that makes it stand apart from other white yeast breads.

Makes 2 loaves

1 cup (325 g) mashed russet potatoes

2 eggs, beaten

½ cup (113 g) butter, soft, plus more
   for the bowl

½ cup (100 g) sugar

1 teaspoon salt

2¼ teaspoons (one 7-g packet)
   active dry yeast

½ cup (118 ml) warm water

5 cups (625 g) bread flour

1. Grease two 8-by-4-inch loaf pans with butter; set aside.
2. In large bowl, mix together the mashed potatoes, eggs, and butter. Stir in the sugar, salt, yeast, and warm water. Mix in enough flour to make a dough that you can knead by hand.
3. Turn the dough out onto a floured board, and knead until smooth and elastic, about 10 minutes. Coat another bowl with butter, and place the dough in it. Flip the dough to lightly grease both sides. Cover with a tea towel or plastic wrap and let rise for 1 to 2 hours, until double in bulk.
4. Punch down the dough. Turn it out onto a lightly floured board and briefly knead out the bubbles. Divide the dough in half and shape into two loaves.
5. Place in the prepared loaf pans. Cover and let rise a second time for 40 minutes, or until double in size.
6. Preheat the oven to 375°F (190°C). Bake the loaves for 40 minutes, or until the bread sounds hollow when you tap the top. Remove from the oven and turn out of the loaf pans; let cool on a wire rack.
7. Serve with lashings of country butter. The bread will keep in a bread box or an airtight container for a week.

Scullery
NOTES | Using a ricer for the mashed potatoes makes the bread softer.

SEA SALT *and* CIDER VINEGAR CRISPS

I FIRST PREPARED THESE POTATO CHIPS from scratch for a spring gathering I hosted at the farm when Geoffrey was five years old. I baked up tea cakes, little milk jam meringue tarts, sausage rolls, and a big bowl of salt and vinegar crisps for the occasion.

In keeping with the seasonal theme, we had two beautiful, snow white-and-brown calves in the back garden for the children to bottle-feed, and our two baby donkeys they could pet. Halfway through the party, one of the sweet calves trotted right into our kitchen. Luckily, another farming girlfriend was there and helped me ease the calf back out onto the grass, but it was no easy feat!

Salt and vinegar chips are a favorite on the farm, and while there are many supermarket options, this from-scratch version trumps all of them. You can also bake the crisps instead of frying for a lighter option.

Serves 4

2 large russet potatoes, unpeeled

⅔ cup (160 ml) cider vinegar, plus 1 tablespoon

Frying oil (such as vegetable or peanut),

enough to fill a fryer or to brush slices before baking

1 tablespoon sea salt

SPECIAL TOOLS: A mandoline

1. With a mandoline, thinly slice the unpeeled potatoes to about an ⅛-inch (2.5-mm) thickness. Place the potato slices in a bowl, and pour the ⅔ cup of cider vinegar over them; stir to coat all slices. Set aside.

2. Fill a fryer (or a deep saucepan) with the oil of your choice and heat to 350°F (175°C). Fry a few slices at a time until golden brown, being careful not to overcrowd the fryer. Time will vary, depending on the size and thickness of the slices, but the average is 3 to 5 minutes.

3. Remove the chips and place on paper towels to drain. Let cool for a few minutes, then toss in the remaining cider vinegar; sprinkle with sea salt.

4. Repeat with the remaining slices, ensuring that the oil is at 350°F (175°C) when frying. You may need to pause between batches to let the oil heat up again.

Scullery **NOTES**

For a healthier version, bake the chips: Preheat the oven to 400°F (200°C). Line two baking sheets with foil and lightly grease with cooking spray. Place the vinegar-soaked potato slices in a single layer on the two sheets. Brush each slice with vegetable or peanut oil. Bake for 10 to 15 minutes, or until golden brown and crisp. If some of the smaller pieces are baking faster after 10 minutes, remove those and keep baking the rest. Let cool for a few minutes, then toss with the sea salt and cider vinegar mixture.

CHAPTER 4

Orchard

EACH SEASON ON THE FARM BRINGS A NEW BOUNTY OF FRUIT. FOR SOMEONE WHO WAS ONCE A NEW ARRIVAL STRAIGHT FROM THE PROVERBIAL CONCRETE JUNGLE, BEING ABLE TO EAT AND COOK WITH FRESH ORCHARD PRODUCE IS AN EVERLASTING THRILL.

From about 1948 to 1958, Dunmoylan had a substantial apple orchard, which, with the growth of the dairy component, has been pared down significantly over the years. Still, behind the farmhouse and cowshed are a variety of apple, pear, and plum trees from that era. In the last twenty years, my father-in-law has planted several more fruit trees on the farm. In 2014, I planted the first cherry, apricot, and apple trees here in my garden.

If you have the space to grow a few fruit trees, you will be rewarded handsomely for years, even generations. In fact, you may have so much fruit on hand that you need to be extra-creative with ways to prepare or store your bounty. We relish not only the fruit we harvest but also the blossoms of sweet fruits. One of my new favorite drinks to sip on a hot summer day is apple blossom cordial with a splash of sparkling soda. You can make fritters out of virtually any sweet fruit blossoms, and children will go mad for them.

Over time and with a lot of experimentation, these orchard recipes have become part and parcel of our Irish country life.

APPLE JACK FRITTERS

THESE FRITTERS ARE A SPECIAL TREAT during harvest time on the farm. After an autumn day of picking apples and pears from our small orchard, I inevitably find myself in the kitchen whipping up dozens of these treats for a gang of hungry farmers. We sit around the table and guttle fritters and cups of milky tea until it's time to bring the cows in.

Serves 4

3 Granny Smith apples (or any semisweet variety), cored, peeled, and cut into ¼- to ½-inch slices

Juice of 1 lemon

1 teaspoon lemon zest

2 tablespoons vanilla or superfine sugar

1 teaspoon vanilla extract

1 teaspoon cinnamon

2 tablespoons Calvados or apple jack (or Longueville House apple brandy if you can find it)

1 cup (130 g) all-purpose flour

1 cup (235 ml) apple cider

2 tablespoons olive oil

4 cups (950 ml) vegetable oil, for frying

Powdered sugar, to serve

Whipped cream, to serve (optional)

1. Put the apple slices in a bowl with the lemon juice and zest, vanilla sugar, cinnamon, and Calvados to macerate for at least 1 hour.
2. Put the flour in a separate bowl and whisk in the cider, followed by the olive oil. Whisk until completely smooth. Let sit for 1 hour.
3. Heat the vegetable oil in a large saucepan over high heat to 350°F (175°C). Dip the apple slices in the batter, then drop them into the oil, frying in small batches. When they are golden, remove with a slotted spoon, and place on paper towels to drain.
4. When you are finished, pile the apples on a serving platter and sprinkle liberally with powdered sugar. Serve hot with or without whipped cream, as you prefer.

Scullery NOTES | This batter is best when made in advance and allowed to sit for at least 1 hour. Omit the brandy and cider for a children's version.

GRANDMA'S GOOSEBERRY TART

THE FIRST TIME I PICKED GOOSEBERRIES with my mother-in-law, Peggy, we collected a massive basketful. We divided the berries into two lots of five pounds each; I took one, and she took the other. Peggy made jam, and I decided to bake a deep-dish American-style pie.

The next afternoon, I took my first gooseberry tart to tea. Afterward my father-in-law, Michael, kindly asked me if I would try making the next tart like his mother would have done, doubled up on gooseberries with a very short (buttery) crust. I went back to my kitchen with his instructions, and an hour later the most beautifully fruity pie popped out of the oven. That evening, Michael granted it the honor of being "just about as good as Grandma's gooseberry tart."

Makes one 9-inch pie

1 batch Basic Short Pie Crust
(see page 165)

2 cups (300 g) gooseberries, topped
and tailed

½ cup Kiddie Elderflower Honeysuckle
Cocktails (see page 335)

½ cup (100 g) superfine sugar

1. Preheat the oven to 350°F (175°C).
2. On a lightly floured surface, roll the cold pastry into two 9-inch (3-mm-thick) circles. Put one aside and press the other into a 9-inch pie plate. Prick the bottom of the crust with a fork, and place a sheet of parchment paper over the top. Fill with dry beans, rice, or baking weights. Bake for 15 minutes, or until cooked but still pale. Remove from the oven and take out the baking parchment and beans. This technique is called blind baking.
3. Combine the gooseberries, cocktail, and sugar in a saucepan over medium heat. Cook until the gooseberries are just softening. Check the flavor and add more cocktail, if desired.
4. Spoon the gooseberry compote into the partially baked crust, and cover with the other pastry circle and press together. Make three cuts in the top crust, and return the tart to the oven for another 40 minutes, or until pastry is golden.
5. Serve the tart dusted with granulated sugar and a scoop of Sweet Cream Ice Cream (see page 23).

GEOFFREY'S PLUMMY JAM DOUGHNUTS

ONE SUMMER, GEOFFREY AND I DECIDED to open our very own farm stand. We made jam doughnuts in the morning and sold them with fresh milk at the farm gate each sunny day. We filled the doughnuts with plum jam, and they were a great success, although our best customer was a man named Daddy.

For many years, the only doughnuts in Ireland were jam-filled, a fact that led to many doughnut binges whenever I went stateside for a visit: old-fashioned cake, yeast, and raised doughnuts glazed with everything from cherry almond bark to bacon grease.

Over time, I've come to revere the classic jam doughnut. If you don't have homemade plum preserves, you can use any preserves you have in your pantry.

Makes a baker's dozen (13 doughnuts)

2¼ teaspoons fast-acting dry yeast

¼ cup (60 ml) warm water

1 cup (250 ml) whole milk, warmed slightly

¼ cup (60 g) superfine sugar

1 tablespoon (20 g) butter, melted

2 eggs, lightly beaten

3¾ cups (165 g) all-purpose flour

½ cup (75 g) plum jam (or any flavor)

4 cups vegetable oil, for deep frying

Confectioner's sugar, for dusting

SPECIAL TOOLS: A pastry bag fitted with a ½-inch tip

1. In a small mixing bowl, combine the yeast, water, milk, and sugar. Cover and let sit in a warm place for about 10 minutes, or until mixture is frothy. Stir the butter and eggs into the yeast mixture.

2. In a separate bowl, sift the flour, then stir in the yeast mixture and mix until it forms a soft dough. Cover with a light tea towel and place in a warm place for about 45 minutes, or until the dough has doubled in size.

3. Turn the dough onto a lightly floured surface and knead for about 5 minutes, or until smooth. Roll out to about a 1-inch (2-cm) thickness. Cut into 2½-inch (5-cm) rounds and place on a baking tray lined with plastic wrap.

4. Cover loosely with oiled plastic wrap, and place the tray in a warm place for 10 to 20 minutes, or until almost doubled in size.

5. Pour the oil into a deep saucepan and bring it up to 350°F (175°C) over high heat. Deep-fry the doughnuts in batches until well browned, turning once. Remove from the pan and place on kitchen paper to drain; while still hot, toss in confectioner's sugar.

6. While you let the doughnuts cool slightly, fill the pastry bag with jam. Insert the tip into the end of each doughnut, and pipe approximately 1 to 2 teaspoons of jam inside. Serve.

Scullery
NOTES | Marmalade makes a particularly lovely filling as well.

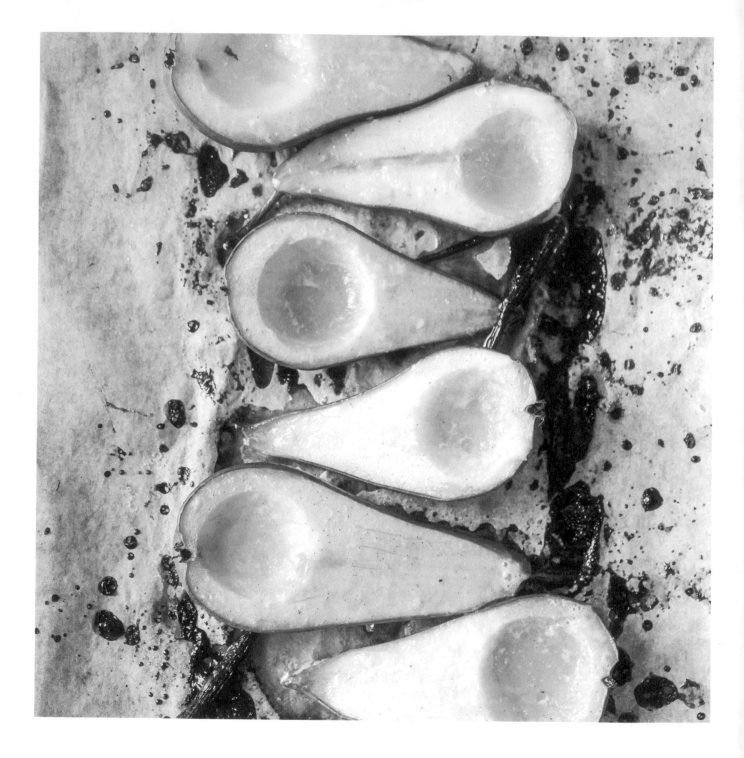

Roasted pears can be prepared in advance for convenience.

ROASTED PEAR CHEESECAKE

IF YOU FIND YOURSELF with a glut of pears at the end of the fall harvest, try roasting and serving them with custard or mixed into a bowl of porridge. Roasting brings out the pure pear essence and creates a caramelized sweetness and tender texture that is tremendously satisfying.

This cheesecake is both rustic and decadent. The pure roasted-pear flavor contrasted with the cream cheese is wildly addictive. You can roast your pears up to a day ahead for this recipe.

Makes one 9-inch cheesecake

6 tablespoons unsalted butter, melted

1½ cups (135 g) crushed gingersnaps

4 small ripe pears (any variety), peeled, cored, and cut in ¼-inch thick slices

¼ teaspoon ground ginger

16 oz (450 g) cream cheese, room temperature

1¼ cups (250 g) granulated sugar

2 large eggs, room temperature

3 teaspoons vanilla extract

1 cup (230 g) sour cream, room temperature

Whipped cream, to serve

1. Preheat the oven to 350°F (175°C).
2. In a medium bowl, combine the butter and crushed gingersnaps. Press the mixture into a 9-inch springform pan, working the crumbs over the bottom and then up the sides. Bake for 10 minutes, remove from the oven, and set aside to cool.
3. Turn the oven up to 400°F (200°C).
4. In a small bowl, toss the pears and ground ginger. Place in a roasting pan and roast for 20 minutes, until soft and caramelized. Remove from the oven and allow to cool for about 1 hour.
5. Line the crust with the pears, overlapping the slices slightly.
6. In a large bowl, beat the cream cheese for 2 minutes with an electric mixer on medium speed. Add 1 cup of the sugar and beat for 2 minutes. Add the eggs, 1 at a time, and mix until combined. Stir in 2 teaspoons of the vanilla. Pour the mixture over the pears in the crust.
7. Turn the oven down to 350°F (175°C). Bake until the top is barely set but still slightly wobbly, about 50 minutes. Remove from the oven and transfer to a wire rack; leave the oven on.
8. In a small bowl, combine the sour cream with the remaining sugar and vanilla. Pour over the cheesecake. Bake for 8 more minutes. Remove from the oven and replace on the wire rack; cool to room temperature.
9. Cover with plastic wrap and refrigerate for at least 4 hours before serving.
10. Slice and serve with a dollop of fresh whipped cream.

APPLE BLOSSOM CORDIAL

FOR THE FIRST TWO YEARS after moving to the farm, I spent hours photographing the wellspring of delicate apple blossoms in the orchard and along nearby country roads. It was only much later, after picking a blossom and sneaking a taste of a petal, that I realized the blossoms' fragrant, sweet flavor would make the perfect summer elixir. (You can also make fritters with the blossoms, but I prefer this refreshing spring nectar for the summer months.)

Makes two 16-oz (1-liter) bottles

11 cups (2.2 kg) sugar, either granulated or superfine

5½ cups (1.5 liters) water

2 unwaxed lemons

1 orange

1 lb freshly picked apple blossom petals, plus more to garnish

1. Sterilize two 16-oz bottles (see page 92).
2. Put the sugar and water into the largest saucepan you have. Heat gently over medium heat, without boiling, until the sugar is dissolved, stirring occasionally.
3. Pare the zest from the lemons using a vegetable peeler, discard the pith, and slice the lemons into rounds. Repeat with the orange.
4. Once the sugar has dissolved, turn the heat up and bring the pan of syrup to a boil, then turn off the heat.
5. Fill a large mixing bowl with cold water and plunge the apple blossoms into it. Gently swish the blossoms to loosen any dirt or insects. Lift the flowers out, shake gently, and put in the sugar syrup along with the lemon and orange slices and zest; stir well.
6. Cover the pan and leave to infuse on the kitchen counter for 24 hours.
7. Line a colander with cheesecloth and sit it over a large bowl or pan. Ladle in the syrup, letting it drip through slowly. Discard the bits left in the towel. Use a funnel and ladle to fill the sterilized bottles.
8. The cordial is ready to drink right away. Serve with chilled club soda on ice, and garnish with fresh apple blossoms.

Scullery **NOTES** | You can also freeze this cordial in plastic containers or ice cube trays and defrost as needed. It will keep for up to six weeks in the fridge.

THIRSTY FARMER PRESSED
SOFT PERRY *and* APPLE CIDER

MAKING CIDER ON IRISH FARMS was the norm until the early 1900s. Our farm once had an enormous orchard that supplied the local Irish cidery when it first opened in the 1940s. Following a hankering for American-style apple cider one autumn afternoon, I ordered a small apple press and began the tradition of pressing apples each fall. Since we love hard cider, I tried to make both apple and pear versions with varying degrees of success. In the end, we chose to stick with the soft apple and pear juices, or "soft ciders," as we like to call them.

Good apple varieties for cider include Golden Delicious (sweet), McIntosh (tart), and Cox Pippin (bitter). Pears such as Huffcap (bitter) and Bosc or Bartlett (sweet) work very well for soft pear cider.

Makes 3 to 6 gallons (11–23 liters)

SPECIAL TOOLS: A small fruit press

1 bushel (20 kg) apples or pears
(have a variety of sweet, tart, and bitter)

---

1. Wash your hands thoroughly, then rinse the apples or pears with warm water. Sanitize the bottles (any size will work, but I use 1½-pint [750-ml] bottles), then thoroughly wash your hands again. (For sterilizing instructions, see page 92.)
2. Grind the whole apples or pears to a fine pulp in a food processor (this pulp is then called pomace). Grinding initiates cellular breakdown and releases the juices in the fruit. The finer the pomace, the more juice will be extracted and (usually) the darker and cloudier the cider will be.
3. Load the pomace into the mesh fabric bag, and press it in the apple press according to the manufacturer's instructions.
4. If you wish, you can pasteurize the resulting cider by heating it in batches to 160°F (70°C) in a large stainless steel pot, then letting it cool and refrigerating it for up to 24 hours to allow any sediment to settle to the bottom. Strain through cheesecloth into sterilized bottles.
5. Apple and pear cider will keep in the refrigerator for about a week and in the freezer for six months.

ORCHARD PRESERVES *and* CONSERVES

THE ART OF PRESERVING was once an absolute necessity for survival during the long winter months, no matter where you lived in the world. Nowadays we have freezers, and the reasons for preserving have more to do with convenience than necessity. Here on the farm, we try to eat with the seasons as much as possible, and since I tend to (enthusiastically) oversow in the kitchen garden, I spend a great deal of time harvesting and processing a surplus of produce that must be made into jams, jellies, chutneys, vinegars, oils, mustards, and pickles to put up and have on hand for the year.

PRESERVING BASICS

1. To get started preserving, you'll need to gather tongs, a wide-mouth funnel, and a variety of measuring cups. A large, wide, nonreactive pot like an enameled Dutch oven is a good vessel for cooking preserves. A deep stockpot makes a good canning pot. Just pop a round rack into the bottom of the pot to allow the water to circulate fully around the jars.

2. Choose your recipe based on what ingredients you have in abundance. Always work with the freshest produce you can find (or harvest).

3. To sterilize the jars, remove the lids and rings from the jars you plan to use. Place the jars on top of the rack in your stockpot. Fill the pot with enough water to cover the jars, place a lid on the pot, and bring it to a boil. Put your lids in a small saucepan and bring them to the barest simmer on the back of the stove. While the sterilizing pot comes to a boil, you can prepare your preserves.

4. When your recipe is complete, use long-handled tongs to remove the jars from the canning pot (pouring the water back into the pot as you remove the jars), and lay them out on a clean towel on your kitchen worktop.

5. Carefully fill your jars with preserves. Depending on the recipe, you'll need to leave between ¼ and ½ inch of headspace (the room between the surface of the product and the top of the jar). Wipe the rims of the jar with a clean, damp paper towel or the edge of a kitchen towel.

6. Apply the lids and screw the rings on the jars to hold the lids down during processing.

7. Carefully lower the filled jars into the canning pot; you may need to remove some of the water to prevent it from overflowing. Bring the pot back to a boil, and start a timer. The length of processing time varies from recipe to recipe. When the timer goes off, remove the jars from the water bath. Place them back on the towel-lined countertop and let them cool.

8. The jar lids should begin to ping soon after they've been removed from the pot. The pinging is the sound of the seals being formed, and the center of the lids will become concave as the vacuum seal takes hold.

9. After the jars have cooled to room temperature, remove the rings and check the seals. You do this by grasping the jar by the edge of the lid and gently lifting it an inch or two off the countertop. The lid should hold fast. Once you've determined that the seals are sound, replace the rings and store your jars in a cool, dark place for up to a year. Jars that don't seal can become refrigerator preserves and should be used within a week.

GOOSEBERRY JAM

GOOSEBERRY JAM is such a treat to make as well as eat; the green berries turn pink during the preserving process. Gooseberries are naturally high in pectin, so no added pectin is needed for this recipe.

Makes ten 8½-oz (240-g) jars

2 lb (1 kg) gooseberries, topped and tailed

Juice of ½ lemon

1½ cups (350 ml) water

5 cups (1 kg) granulated sugar

1. Sterilize ten 8½-oz jars (see page 92). Put 2 or 3 small plates in the freezer (these will be used to test the setting later on).
2. Put the gooseberries, lemon juice, and water in a large, wide pan. Bring to a boil over medium heat, then turn the heat down and simmer for 15 minutes, until the fruit is soft and pulpy. Add the sugar and stir over low heat for another 10 minutes, until the sugar is completely dissolved. You don't want it to boil at this point, as the sugar could crystallize. Once you can't feel or see any grains of sugar, bring the mixture back to a boil; boil hard for 10 minutes, skimming the surface as needed and stirring occasionally. The jam will start to turn a pinky-red hue as it cooks.
3. Spoon a little jam onto a chilled saucer, leave to cool, then run your finger through it. If it's done, the jam will "wrinkle." If this doesn't happen, boil for another 5 minutes, then keep testing and boiling until it does.
4. Do a final skim on the finished jam, then pour it into the sterilized jars and seal (see page 92). Store in a cool, dark place; the jam will be good for up to six months. Keep in the fridge once it's opened.

BLACK CURRANT JAM

BLACK CURRANT JAM is a staple in most Irish country kitchens. This tasty, dark-hued jam is easy to make because it always sets up nicely.

Makes ten 8½-oz (240-g) jars

2 lb (1 kg) black currants, topped and tailed

Juice of ½ lemon

1½ cups (350 ml) water

5 cups (1 kg) granulated sugar

Crab Apple Juniper Jelly

Chive Blossom Vinegar

Farmhouse Piccalilli

Tomato Chili Jam

Black Currant Jam

Sweet Marjoram Oil

Blackberry Mint Jam

Apple Mint Jelly

Gooseberry Jam

1. Sterilize ten 8½-oz jars (see page 92). Put 2 or 3 small plates in the freezer (these will be used to test the setting later on).

2. Put the black currants, lemon juice, and water in a large, wide pan. Bring to a boil over medium heat, then turn the heat down and simmer for 15 minutes, until the fruit is soft and pulpy. Add the sugar and stir over low heat for another 10 minutes, until the sugar is completely dissolved. You don't want it to boil at this point, as the sugar could crystallize. Once you can't feel or see any grains of sugar, bring the mixture back to a boil; boil hard for 10 minutes, skimming the surface as needed and stirring occasionally.

3. Spoon a little jam onto a chilled saucer, leave to cool, then run your finger through it. If it's done, it will "wrinkle." If this doesn't happen, boil for another 5 minutes, then keep testing and boiling until it does.

4. Do a final skim on the finished jam, then pour it into the sterilized jars and seal (see page 92). Store in a cool, dark place; the jam will be good for up to six months. Keep in the fridge once it's opened.

BLACKBERRY MINT JAM

AT THE END OF EACH SUMMER, we harvest a bounty of wild ripe blackberries from the hedges on the farm. I'm reminded of the late Irish poet Seamus Heaney and his beautiful poem "Blackberry Picking," in which he evokes the sensuality, hope, and naivete of picking blackberries in the countryside during his childhood.

Blackberry jam is great on its own, but the mint adds a refreshing quality that takes the sweetness down a notch.

Makes ten 8½-oz jars

2 lb (1 kg) blackberries, topped and tailed	Juice of ½ lemon
½ cup mint leaves, finely chopped	3¾ cups (1 kg) granulated sugar
1½ cups (350 ml) water	

1. Sterilize ten 8½-oz jars (see page 92). Put 2 or 3 small plates in the freezer (these will be used to test the setting later on).

2. Put the blackberries, mint leaves, water, and lemon juice in a large, wide pan. Bring to a boil over medium heat, then turn the heat down and simmer for 15 minutes, until the fruit is soft and pulpy. Add the sugar and stir over low heat for another 10 minutes, until the sugar is completely dissolved. You

don't want it to boil at this point, as the sugar could crystallize. Once you can't feel or see any grains of sugar, bring the mixture back to a boil; boil hard for 10 minutes, skimming the surface as needed and stirring occasionally.

3. Spoon a little jam onto a chilled saucer, leave to cool, then run your finger through it. If it's done, it will "wrinkle." If this doesn't happen, boil for another 5 minutes, then keep testing and boiling until it does.

4. Do a final skim on the finished jam, then pour it into the sterilized jars and seal (see page 92). Store in a cool, dark place; the jam will be good for up to six months. Keep in the fridge once it's opened.

TOMATO CHILI JAM

HOT AND RICHLY TOMATO FLAVORED with a hint of sweetness, this gooey sauce is easy to make and has the power to transform simple scrambled eggs into a lavish breakfast. We are never without a jar of tomato chili jam in the pantry.

Makes about six 6-oz (170-g) jars

1 lb (500 g) tomatoes

1 tablespoon minced garlic

4 large red chilies

One 2-inch piece gingerroot,
   peeled and roughly sliced

1½ cups (300 g) golden superfine sugar

2 tablespoons Thai fish sauce

Scant ½ cup (100 ml) red wine vinegar

1. Sterilize six 6-oz jars (see page 92).

2. Purée the tomatoes in a food processor with the garlic, chilies, and ginger. Pour into a heavy-bottom saucepan.

3. Add the sugar, fish sauce, and red wine vinegar; bring to a boil, stirring slowly. Reduce the heat and simmer for 30 to 40 minutes, stirring occasionally. The mixture will turn slightly darker and be sticky.

4. Pour into warm, dry sterilized jars and seal while the mixture is still warm. The longer you keep this jam, the hotter it gets. Mine stores for years, and once opened it will last for six months in the fridge.

CRAB APPLE JUNIPER JELLY

THIS JELLY CAN EASILY BECOME cloudy during the cooking process, but don't be disheartened—it is still edible, and the taste and texture are pure nirvana. In other words, don't go crazy trying to make sure it is completely clear. Go for the rustic look like I do!

Makes ten 8½-oz jars (six 500-ml) jars

8 lb (4 kg) crab apples

3¾ cups (1 kg) superfine sugar

Juice of 1 lemon

10 juniper berries

1 cinnamon stick

1. Sterilize ten 8½-oz (six 500-ml) jars (see page 92).
2. Wash the apples, removing any bruised fruit. Put them whole into a saucepan, and fill with just enough water to cover the apples. Bring to a boil over medium heat, then turn the heat down and simmer until the fruit is soft, about 30 minutes.
3. Pour the pulp into a jelly bag or several layers of cheesecloth, and let drip into a pan overnight. Do not squeeze the bag, or it will make the juice very cloudy.
4. The next day, put a dessertspoon in the refrigerator to chill (this will be used to test the setting later on). Measure the juice out into a saucepan, and add sugar in the ratio of 10 parts juice to 7 parts sugar. Add the lemon juice, the juniper berries, and the cinnamon stick; bring to a boil, stirring to dissolve the sugar.
5. Keep at a rolling boil for 40 minutes, skimming off the froth as needed. To test the set, dip the chilled dessertspoon into the jelly. It is done when it solidifies on the back of the spoon.
6. Pour into warm, sterilized jars and seal tightly while the mixture is still slightly warm. Store in a cool, dark place for up to six months. Once opened, it will stay fresh in the refrigerator for one month.

FARMHOUSE PICCALILLI

PICKLES IN IRELAND are not necessarily the same sort of dill or sweet-and-sour cucumber and gherkin pickles we are used to in the United States. Think malty, cider vinegary, zesty, sweet, savory, spicy, chunky, and cloyingly tangy. Often there are no cucumbers involved at all. A pickle can be a gorgeous sandwich spread, a ploughman's lunch, or, better yet, piccalilli (relish) on a charred sausage. These pickle recipes came to Ireland via the United Kingdom, but Great Britain borrowed them from India. Whatever way you look at it, piccalilli is true (fermented) perfection in a jar.

2½ lb vegetables (choose 5 to 6 from among the following: cauliflower, turnips, asparagus, radishes, green beans, cucumbers, zucchini, green or yellow tomatoes, carrots, small pickling onions or shallots, peppers), washed and peeled

½ cup (100 g) fine sea salt

½ cup (60 g) cornstarch

2 tablespoons ground turmeric

2 tablespoons English mustard powder

2 tablespoons ground ginger

1 tablespoon caraway seeds

2 teaspoons cumin seeds

2 teaspoons coriander seeds

5 cups (1.2 liters) white or cider vinegar

2½ cups (300 g) granulated sugar

½ cup (100 g) honey

1. Sterilize six 12-oz (340-g) jars (see page 92).
2. Cut the vegetables into small, bite-size pieces. Place in a large colander over a bowl, and sprinkle with the salt. Mix well, cover with a tea towel, and leave in a cool place for 24 hours. Rinse the vegetables with ice-cold water and drain thoroughly.
3. Blend the cornstarch, turmeric, mustard powder, ginger, caraway seeds, cumin seeds, and coriander seeds with just enough of the vinegar to make a smooth paste. Put the rest of the vinegar in a saucepan with the sugar and honey, and bring to a boil. Remove from the heat and pour 1 cup of the hot vinegar over the spice paste; stir well and return to the pan. Bring the mixture gradually back to a boil. Boil for 3 to 4 minutes to allow the spices to release their flavors into the sauce.
4. Remove from the heat and carefully fold the well-drained vegetables into the hot, spicy sauce. Pack the piccalilli into warm, sterilized jars and seal immediately with vinegar-proof lids. Store in a cool, dark place for about six weeks before opening. Use within a year.

CHIVE BLOSSOM VINEGAR

POSSIBLY THE PRETTIEST VINEGAR there ever was and a fantastic use for those chive blossoms in your kitchen garden, chive blossom vinegar makes salad dressings sing. I even sprinkle it on my fish and chips. Try it on the Sea Salt and Cider Vinegar Crisps (see page 76).

Makes one 8-oz (226-g) bottle

————— ⚶ —————

2½ cups (80 g) chive blossoms, snipped right beneath the head	1½ cups (350 ml) champagne, white wine, or white vinegar

1. Sterilize one 8-oz bottle (see page 92).
2. Plunge the chive blossoms into a bowl of cold water, and swish them gently to flush out any dirt or insects. Put the flowers into a colander and shake off the excess water.
3. Stuff the blooms into a pint jar, and pour in just enough champagne, wine, or vinegar to submerge the flowers, using a metal spoon to push down any errant blooms that want to float over the top.
4. Place a square of parchment paper over the opening of the jar, and screw on the top. Put the container in a dark, cool spot; steep for at least one to two weeks or up to a month.
5. Open and taste a spoonful. When you're happy with the strength of the brew, strain it through a fine sieve into an 8-oz sterilized bottle (see page 92), and toss the spent blossoms. Store in a cool, dark place for up to 6 months.

SWEET MARJORAM OIL

BECAUSE WE HAVE a veritable forest of sweet marjoram growing in our garden, I make this infused oil as a base for salad dressings and marinades. It has a sweet, spicy flavor similar to that of oregano.

Makes about one 16-oz (452-g) bottle

————— ⚶ —————

4 cups (120 g) packed sweet marjoram leaves	2 cups (473 ml) extra virgin olive oil

1. Sterilize one 16-oz bottle (see page 92).
2. Purée the marjoram leaves and olive oil in a blender until smooth. Pour into a saucepan, and gently simmer over medium heat for 1 to 2 minutes. Pour through a fine-mesh strainer into a bowl to remove most of the marjoram. Cover with a tea towel and allow to sit for a few hours.
3. Pour the oil into the sterilized jar and seal (see page 92). Store in a cupboard for up to 6 months.

GARDEN APPLE MINT JELLY

OUR SUNDAY LAMB ROAST would not be complete without a side of apple mint jelly. The apple cores are included in this recipe as that is where most of the natural pectin comes from.

Makes approximately four 8-oz (226-g) jars

4 lb (2 kg) tart apples (like Granny Smith), unpeeled, chopped into big pieces, including the cores

1½ cups (120 g) lightly packed fresh mint leaves, freshly chopped

2 cups (470 ml) water

2 cups (470 ml) white vinegar

3½ cups (800 g) sugar

1. Sterilize four 8-oz jars (see page 92). Put 2 or 3 small plates in the freezer (these will be used to test the setting later on).

2. Combine the apple pieces, mint, and water in a large pan. Bring to a boil, then reduce the heat and cook for 20 minutes, until the apples are soft. Add the vinegar, and return to a boil. Lower the heat, cover, and simmer for 5 more minutes.

3. Use a potato masher to mash the apple pieces to the consistency of thin applesauce. Spoon the apple pulp into a couple layers of cheesecloth (or a large, fine-mesh sieve) suspended over a large bowl. Let strain for several hours. Do not squeeze. You should have 4 to 5 cups of resulting juice.

4. Measure the juice, then pour into a large pot. Add the sugar (⅞ cup for each cup of juice). Heat gently over low heat, stirring to make sure the sugar dissolves and doesn't stick to the bottom of the pan and burn.

5. Bring to a boil over high heat. Cook for 10 to 15 minutes, using a metal spoon to skim the surface as necessary. Continue to boil until it reaches 220°F (104°C) on a candy thermometer. Additional cooking time of anywhere from 10 minutes to 1 hour or longer may be needed, depending on the amount of water, sugar, and apple pectin in the mix.

6. To test, spoon a little jelly onto a chilled saucer, leave to cool, then run your finger through it. If it's done, it will "wrinkle." If this doesn't happen, boil for another 5 minutes, then keep testing and boiling until it does.

7. Pour the jelly into the sterilized jars to within ¼ inch of the top and seal. Store in the refrigerator for up to six months.

CHAPTER 5

From the Sea

ONE THING IS CERTAIN: IRELAND'S PURE SHORES PROVIDE AN ENDLESS BOUNTY OF FINE FISH AND SEAFOOD TO ITS LUCKY INHABITANTS. IRELAND IS RENOWNED FOR THE QUALITY OF ITS BEEF AND LAMB, BUT THERE IS NOTHING BETTER THAN SMOKED WILD ATLANTIC SALMON, PLUMP NATIVE OYSTERS, KERRY CRABS, AND DUBLIN BAY PRAWNS. EVEN THE LITTLE WHITE BAGS OF PERIWINKLES SOLD AT THE SEASHORE ARE SUPERB.

I cherish our fishmonger, McMahon's. John and Angela McMahon have run their shop in the nearby village for decades, and Geoffrey and I try to visit at least once a week.

Ireland has a rich fishing history, from sea fishing to inland river fly-fishing and lake fishing. We have hosted friends for fly-fishing on the Blackwater River in Cork and deep-sea fishing around the Aran Islands with equal pleasure and results.

Lakes, rivers, and coastal stretches are filled with an extraordinary mix of cold- and warm-water fish. There are still waters that have seldom, if ever, seen a rod and line, so treasures are still out there to find.

Here, crab and lobster cost a fraction of their market price in the United States. This means we host plenty of traditional Southern-style crab boils on the farm in summer. I buy fresh lobster to use for lobster rolls, which I prepare with a snow white, superairy Irish blaa, a bread roll that hails from County Waterford (see page 59). Eating fish on Friday is a common practice during Lent, but it doesn't end there. It would be possible to become a pure pescetarian with all the gifts from the sea we are fortunate enough to have in Ireland.

FISH PLAYS AN IMPORTANT ROLE IN IRISH folklore too. One of our favorite fish-related Irish children's fables is the tale of Fionn mac Cumhaill and the Salmon of Knowledge.

According to the story, an ordinary salmon ate nine hazelnuts that fell into the Well of Wisdom and gained all the world's knowledge. The first person to eat its flesh would, in turn, gain this knowledge.

The poet Finn Eces spent seven years fishing for this salmon. One day, Eces caught the fish and gave it to Fionn, his servant and the son of Cumhaill, with instructions not to eat it. Fionn cooked the salmon, turning it over and over, but when he touched the fish with his thumb to see if it was cooked, he burnt his finger on a drop of hot fish fat.

Fionn placed his burned finger into his mouth to ease the pain. Little did Fionn know that all of the salmon's wisdom had been concentrated into that one drop of fat. When he brought the cooked meal to Finn Eces, his master saw that the boy's eyes shone with a previously unseen wisdom. For the rest of his life, Fionn could draw upon this knowledge merely by biting his thumb. The deep knowledge and wisdom gained from the Salmon of Knowledge allowed Fionn to become the leader of the Fianna, the famed heroes of Irish myth.

COUNTY KERRY CRAB BOIL

THE CRAB AND LOBSTER WE GET from our local fishmonger come from nearby Kerry or Clare, two stunningly rugged, coastal Atlantic counties that border ours. The brown Kerry crab, with its succulent claw meat, and Clare's luscious lobster tails are both world-class ingredients in my book.

A classic summer crab boil is especially fun as a small dinner party al fresco, if weather permits. The crab boil is more a method than a recipe; the fun of it is in the preparation and laid-back ritual that makes it especially delicious. We invite a few friends or neighbors over for Sunday lunch and serve up the boil under the horse chestnut trees, with ice-cold craft cider and elderflower or apple blossom cordial on the side.

I have given the ingredient amounts per person, so you can tailor the boil to suit the number of guests.

Serves 1

New potatoes (2 to 3 per person)

Crab boil seasoning (I recommend Zatarain's or the DIY version; see Scullery Notes)

Sea salt, to taste

Smoked spicy sausage (1 to 2 per person)

Live brown Kerry crabs (3 to 4 small or 1 to 2 large crabs per person)

Sweet corn (1 ear per person, cut in half)

Melted butter, for dipping

1. Put the potatoes in an oversized pot; they should cover the bottom. Add enough water to cover them by about 2 inches. Add the crab boil seasonings and a few generous pinches of sea salt.
2. Char or sear the sausages to seal in flavor.
3. Place the crabs, corn, and sausages in the pot, and cover. Put the pot over high heat. When the water reaches a rolling boil, reduce the heat to medium high. Cook for another 12 to 18 minutes, until the crabs are cooked through.
4. Hold the lid of the pot ajar and dump the water into a sink, keeping the food in the pot.
5. Pour the contents of the pot onto the center of a table covered with newspaper or brown paper. Make sure you have plenty of serving supplies: melted butter; little forks; claw crackers or hammers to get at the crabmeat; loads of napkins; and bottles of chilled pinot blanc, rosé wine, sangria, or cold cider.
6. Everyone digs in and feasts!

Scullery
NOTES | For a DIY crab boil seasoning to serve 6, fill a large muslin sachet with 1 tablespoon of each of the following spices and herbs: mustard seeds, coriander seeds, chili peppers, bay leaves, dill seeds, allspice, fresh lemon rind, and fresh dill fronds.

CLASSIC DUBLIN LAWYER

THE ORIGINS OF DUBLIN LAWYER, a rich dish of lobster, cream, and whiskey, are allegedly unknown, but I'm told that this dish has been served around Dublin for at least a hundred and fifty years. I can testify that it has been been served in our house for the last eight.

After tasting this succulent dish at a seafood festival in the eponymous capital city, I vowed to prepare it at home. Now, Dublin Lawyer has become a much requested meal for special occasions—and sometimes just because.

I prefer to serve it with the meat still in the tails, allowing each person to dip the meat into the sauce as they wish.

Serves 2

SPECIAL TOOLS: A kitchen torch

Two 2-lb lobsters, fresh

1 cup (235 ml) Irish whiskey

12 tablespoons butter

1 cup (235 ml) heavy cream

Salt and pepper, to taste

Lemon slices, for garnish

Chopped parsley, dill, or chervil, for garnish

1. See instructions for cooking lobster in the Lobster Blaas recipe (page 118). Steam or boil the lobsters for about 8 to 9 minutes. Remove from the pot. Split the lobsters in half. Clean out the top halves of the body, but leave the tail meat intact.
2. Heat the whiskey in a small saucepan over low heat. In a large skillet, melt the butter over medium heat until foamy. Add the heated whiskey, and flambé with a kitchen torch. Allow the flame to die down completely before adding the cream. Heat through. Season with salt and pepper.
3. Divide the butter mixture evenly between two dipping bowls, or pour into the cleaned top halves of the lobsters. Serve the lobster with lemon slices and sprinkled with chopped parsley, dill, or chervil.

Scullery
NOTES If a thicker sauce is desired, allow the sauce to simmer for another 2 minutes.

IRISH DULSE MISO SOUP

AS MUCH AS I EMBRACE THE FARM LIFESTYLE, there are days that I double-damn the notion that I can't walk out my door and down the street with my family for a steaming hot bowl of Asian soup, a freshly wood-fired pizza, the perfect doughnut that *someone else* made, or a grande soy "holiday spiced" latte. But then I stumble upon a memoir, discover a blog, or meet someone who shares a similar lifestyle, and if I am lucky, this conjures up cravings that result in a new recipe to whittle down my whinging.

One book that forged this connection was *Japanese Farm Food* by Nancy Singleton Hachisu, and the dish was seaweed soup. Ireland has long been revered for its dulse and carrageen moss, so after spending a weekend enthralled with a book about a kindred soul who moved to Japan for the food and ended up falling in love with a farmer, I was craving a big, steaming hot bowl of miso soup.

I rooted through my cupboards and found miso and a small container of dried Irish dulse. I boiled the water and made up a makeshift bowl of miso soup. I ladled it up, closed my eyes, took one slurpy mouthful, and was transported to my favorite Japanese restaurant back in New York City.

Serves 4

FOR THE DASHI

4 cups (940 ml) water

16 to 20 square inches (103–129 sq cm) kombu

½ cup (60 g) loosely packed katsuobushi (dried bonito flakes)

FOR THE SOUP

3 tablespoons white or brown miso

3 to 4 cups (705–940 ml) homemade dashi (or quick dashi, available in Asian specialty markets)

2 teaspoons dried, ready-to-use dulse seaweed (or Irish dillisk)

1 green onion

---

1. **MAKE THE DASHI:** Place the water and kombu in a pot, and let the kombu soak for about 15 minutes. Place the pot over medium heat. Just before the water starts to boil (watch for bubbles starting to break around the edge of the pot), remove the pot from the heat, and sprinkle the katsuobushi over the surface.

2. After 3 or 4 minutes (the katsuobushi will have sunk to the bottom of the pot by this point), strain the stock through a strainer lined with muslin.

3. **MAKE THE SOUP:** Put 1 tablespoon of miso in a ladle (or strainer) and stir it into the dashi until it is thoroughly mixed. Continue this process until all of the miso is used. For each 1 cup of dashi, you will need about 1 tablespoon of miso.

4. Soak the dried dulse in water for 10 minutes to rehydrate; drain well. Finely slice the green onion. Divide the dulse and green onion between 4 bowls.

5. Return the miso soup to a slight simmer until heated through. Pour into the bowls and serve.

Scullery
NOTES

Be careful not to boil the soup, or the miso will lose its flavor. The dashi will keep for up to four days in the refrigerator. Be sure to store the dashi stock in a tightly covered container.

HOT-SMOKED BURREN SALMON TACOS

EVERY TUESDAY NIGHT, the farm kitchen is transformed into a *taqueria*. Whether we use our own chicken, whatever is fresh and fun at the fishmonger, or a fresh cut from the local butcher, a little Mexicana on the schedule saves us a three-hour drive to the nearest margarita and mole.

Our favorite standby is Hot-Smoked Burren Salmon Tacos. Combining smoky chipotle with garden-fresh kale and cabbage verde, these fish tacos pack a rich and flavorful yet balanced punch, not to mention plenty of omega-3s and antioxidants.

Serves 4

½ cup (125 g) mayonnaise

½ cup (125 g) sour cream

1 tablespoon adobo sauce from tin of chipotle peppers in adobo sauce (or 1 tablespoon chili powder)

1 tablespoon ground cumin

2 tablespoons lemon juice

Salt and pepper, to taste

1 cup (250 g) shredded white cabbage

2 cups (500 g) kale (stems removed), finely chopped

1 small green chili pepper, finely chopped

A big handful of fresh cilantro, chopped, plus extra for garnish

1 garlic clove

Juice of 1 lime

1 lb (450 g) hot-smoked salmon (or your favorite hot-smoked fish)

8 flour tortillas, warmed

2 limes, cut in wedges, for garnish

1. MAKE THE CREMA: Mix the mayonnaise and sour cream together in a large bowl. Add the adobo sauce, cumin, and lemon juice; season with salt and pepper to taste.
2. MAKE THE VERDE: In a food processor, pulse the cabbage, kale, chili pepper, cilantro, garlic, lime juice, and salt to taste until coarsely chopped.
3. ASSEMBLE THE TACOS: Flake the hot-smoked salmon into each tortilla, and top with a spoonful each of crema and verde.
4. Serve with lime wedges and cilantro. Feast.

Scullery NOTES | You can also flake the salmon into the crema, mix, then fill the tortilla and top it with verde. Burren Smokehouse Salmon is available in the United States in Dean & DeLuca stores, gourmet food markets, and online. (See the Resources section.)

I FIRST MADE THESE SPECIAL SALMON TACOS after an extraordinary day spent fishing with Birgitta Curtin of Burren Smokehouse in County Clare. She was heading out to fish on the River Lee in Cork for the first of the wild Atlantic spring salmon in Ireland, and I asked if I could go along and document her adventure.

Irish Atlantic salmon spend the first years of their lives in rivers before migrating to the sea to grow. To complete their life cycle, they return to their river of origin to spawn. The fish Birgitta was after would have traveled as far as Greenland and back to Ireland to lay their eggs. The wild salmon season begins in May and ends in August, with strict regulations in place to prevent overfishing.

I arrived at a marina on the River Lee on a cool, rainy morning in mid-May. Birgitta was suited up in chest-high waders and ready to go, but the fish weren't exactly going along with the plan. After a couple of hours, we decided to pull up anchor and drive to the River Nore in County Kilkenny. We met the award-winning snap-net fishing duo Mark and Tricia Murphy, who took us out on their traditional Irish cot-style fishing boats for the afternoon. It was absolutely calm and serene as we floated up and down the river, pulling a snap-net between the two handcrafted, flat-bottomed boats.

The McDonnells are all fans of smoked salmon, so when I came home with a few packages of Burren Smokehouse's tender, delicate, hot-smoked salmon, I absolutely had to experiment with using it as a taco ingredient. It was Tuesday, after all.

OYSTERS *and* STOUT

THE NATIVE IRISH OYSTER *Ostrea edulis* can be found throughout the coastal regions of Ireland and has been considered traditional fare dating back to the thirteenth century. The best way to enjoy the full flavor of Irish oysters is to eat them raw, served in the half shell to hold their succulent juices. Topped with fresh lemon juice or a drop of Tabasco sauce and with a cold pint of Guinness on the side, oysters make for a wonderful summer supper. This is less of a recipe and more of an excuse to gather friends around and have your own little oyster fest!

Serves 6 (3 oysters each)

18 raw, fresh oysters, shucked

Sea salt and ground black pepper

Lemon juice

Tabasco sauce

6 pints Irish stout

1. Open the oysters and arrange on a platter filled with crushed ice, making sure to keep any seawater in the shells. Season as you wish with sea salt, black pepper, lemon juice, and Tabasco, then tip into your mouth. Follow each oyster with a hearty glug of stout, if you can manage it!

OYSTER CULTURE IS PROBABLY ONE OF THE most environmentally friendly types of farming, as it never requires feed or medication. It has also an extremely low and often negative carbon footprint; oysters feed themselves on elements that are naturally found in the seas where they grow. The oyster farmer's task is simply to accompany the natural growth of the mollusks by managing stocking densities and thereby naturally influencing shell shape and growth rates. Irish oysters are coveted and exported to meet a huge demand in France as well as the United Kingdom; Belgium; Germany; and more distant markets such as the Ukraine, China, and Japan.

One of the best ways to experience eating Irish oysters is to attend the Galway International Oyster Festival that takes place each September and has evolved from very modest beginnings. In September 1954, only thirty-four guests attended the very first Oyster Festival Banquet; now thousands of people from around the world gather annually to eat oysters and drink Guinness. We try to go every year, and our visit is always filled with loads of delicious fun and frolic.

LOBSTER BLAAS

A LOBSTER BLAA IS A HYBRID of the all-American lobster roll, prepared using an authentically Irish bun called a blaa (page 59), a very soft, white bread roll dusted with flour.

I came up with my version of lobster blaas just after I returned from a visit to Martha's Vineyard, Massachusetts, where the seafood roll is a supreme specialty. I had boiled a mess of lobsters for supper on a midsummer's night, and after supper, I picked the shells clean and put the meat in the fridge. I had a dozen fresh-baked blaas on hand, and I just couldn't resist snitching one to make a lobster roll. The bun had the perfect texture, and I was transported back to the wharf restaurant on the Vineyard.

Serves 6

1 large onion, cut in half

2 tablespoons coarse sea salt

4 large garlic cloves, smashed and peeled

3 bay leaves

1 teaspoon black peppercorns, cracked

Four 1½-lb lobsters

8 tablespoons salted butter

1 teaspoon garlic powder

6 top-sliced hot dog–style blaa buns (see page 59)

2 tablespoons mayonnaise

Fine sea salt

1. Pour 2 inches of water into a large clam or lobster pot. Put in the onion halves, cut sides down, and add the salt, garlic, bay leaves, and black peppercorns. Bring to a boil over high heat.

2. Put in the lobsters, head up, with the first two sitting on the onion halves and the other two loosely stacked; make sure all the lobsters are evenly spaced. Cover and cook over medium-high heat until bright red all over, about 6 minutes.

3. Transfer the lobsters to a large rimmed baking sheet, and let cool. Working over the sheet to collect all the juices and fat, twist the tails and the claws from the bodies. Pull off the tail ends or flippers from the tail shells and push the tail meat out of the shells with your thumb.

4. Cut down the top of the tails and discard the dark vein. Twist the knuckles from the claws. Cover the claws with a kitchen towel and, with a mallet or the back of a large knife, gently crack the claws on both sides to loosen the shells from the meat. Break the shells off the claws, and pull out the meat, preferably in one piece. Break up the knuckles and push out the meat.

5. Cut the tails down the center, and keep all of the lobster meat in big chunks. You should have about 5 cups of meat. Put the meat and the collected juices in a large skillet, and set aside.

6. Heat a griddle. Meanwhile, in a small saucepan, melt the butter with the garlic powder and stir. Open the hot dog buns, and brush only the insides with some of the garlic butter. Toast the buns on the hot griddle on medium-high heat until golden brown and crisp, about 2 minutes per side. Reduce the heat to medium if the griddle gets too hot.

7. Gently reheat the lobster meat over low heat until barely hot. Remove the skillet from the heat, stir in the mayonnaise, and season with fine sea salt. Pack the lobster meat into the toasted buns and drizzle each with a little more garlic butter. You should have a nice pink-orange sauce developing around the meat as a result of the mayo and lobster juice cooking just a bit.

8. The cooked lobster meat and juices can be refrigerated overnight. Bring to room temperature, then reheat gently if you are assembling the rolls the following day.

Scullery **NOTES** | Save the lobster bodies and shells for bisque or stock. You can store them in the freezer for up to one month.

COMFORTING FISH PIE

THE WEATHER IS A SIGNIFICANT INGREDIENT in the recipe of Irish life; it is always in the background, influencing everything on some level—like a family member with a strong will and personality. There are times when it is so wet and fierce that the screaming wind will keep you up at night no matter how exhausted you are from a day of moving cattle.

I discovered early on that the Irish embrace the weather with humor. They chat about it tirelessly, always acknowledging and even damning the rain and gray, but if it's sunny for more than three days, fear sets in and the grave grumbling of too much heat commences. You will hear weather talk no matter where you go, and it is more than just chatter—it is embedded into the charming fabric of Irish life.

When I first moved here, I felt a chill in my bones for at least a year. Even when it wasn't raining, everything felt damp. No matter how warmly I dressed, I felt cold. My favorite thing to do was wrap up in a warm blanket in the evenings in front of a roaring turf fire with Richard. We ate fish pie fresh from the oven and sipped mugs of hot tea. To this day, that soothing dish topped with mashed potato still makes me feel warm—inside and out.

The classic Irish fish pie is usually a blend of fresh and smoked seafood and fish in a velvety cream sauce topped with fluffy, floury mashed potatoes. You can often find handy prepared seafood mix/fish pie portions at fishmongers and supermarket fish counters.

Serves 4

---

2 lb (1 kg) floury potatoes, such as Golden Wonder, Maris Piper, or King Edwards	¾ lb (350 g) white fish fillets and/or salmon fillets
¼ cup (50 g) butter	¾ lb (350 g) smoked white fish
Splash of milk	½ lb (200 g) small peeled prawns
Salt and pepper, to taste	¼ cup (50 g) butter
2 cups (500 ml) fish stock	½ cup (50 g) all-purpose flour
½ cup (100 ml) white wine	¾ cup + 1 tablespoon (200 ml) heavy cream
Small bunch of parsley, separated into leaves and stalks	½ cup (25 g) grated carrot

---

1. Preheat the oven to 375°F (190°C).
2. Peel the potatoes and dice into even small chunks. Place in a large pan, cover with cold water, add a

generous pinch of salt, and bring to a boil. Simmer for about 20 minutes, or until tender. Drain the potatoes, and let them sit in the colander for a few minutes. Return them to the pot and mash until smooth; beat in the butter and milk. Season well with salt and pepper; set aside.

3. Put the fish stock, wine, and parsley stalks into a large pan; bring to a simmer. Add the prawns and all the fish, and simmer for 5 minutes. Lift the prawns and fish out with a slotted spoon, remove any skin, and cut into large chunks. Discard the parsley stalks.

4. Melt the butter in a medium pan over low heat, then whisk in the flour. Cook, stirring constantly, for a couple of minutes, being careful not to let it brown. Gradually stir in the fish stock. Bring to a boil, then simmer for about 20 minutes.

5. Take the sauce off the heat, stir in the cream, parsley leaves, and carrots; season to taste. Add the fish and prawns, and toss to coat.

6. Place the seafood and sauce in a baking dish, and top with the mashed potatoes. Bake for 35 minutes, until the top is golden.

7. Spoon generous portions onto each plate, and serve with braised greens and glasses of sauvignon blanc.

FIRE-ROASTED CLARE CRAB COCKTAIL

I HAD BEEN SELECTED to be a "food ambassador" for the Wild Atlantic Way, the world-famous scenic route spanning seven stunning counties on Ireland's west coast, and was lucky enough to be sent around to several excellent restaurants in County Clare to taste and choose the best dish that each chef had specially prepared for a regional event. When our group arrived at Aidan McGraths's Wild Honey Inn—a gem on the edge of the Burren in Lisdoonvarna, Clare—we were treated to a most unforgettable crab cocktail. It was at once zesty, creamy, spicy, and filled with the freshest, most robust crab flavor.

I later tried to re-create the dish and never quite achieved it, but through all of my testing, I came up with a special crab cocktail of my own that is undeniably tasty in a spicy-smoky sort of way.

Makes 8 cocktails

14½ oz (400 g) organic, fire-roasted diced tomatoes, undrained

½ cup (118 ml) tomato juice

1 clove garlic, minced

1¼-inch sliced red onion, chopped

1 tablespoon apple cider vinegar

1 tablespoon olive oil

½ teaspoon salt

3 drops red pepper sauce

1 tablespoon horseradish

1 small cucumber, peeled, diced or spiralized (turned into thin noodle shape with spiralizer tool) (to make about ¾ cup)

6½ oz (185 g) white crabmeat

2 teaspoons coarsely chopped fresh dill weed

¼ cup (60 g) spiralized or julienned carrot

1 tablespoon lemon zest

2 teaspoons chopped fresh herbs, such as chervil, celery leaves, or chard flowers

1. Place all of the ingredients except the cucumber, crabmeat, dill weed, carrot, lemon zest, and herbs in a food processor. Cover and pulse until the mixture is coarsely puréed. Stir in half of the cucumber.
2. Spoon about ⅓ cup of the tomato mixture into each of 8 martini or wine glasses. Spoon about 1 heaping tablespoon crabmeat onto the center of each cocktail. Sprinkle with the dill weed, carrot, remaining cucumber, lemon zest, and herbs, and serve.

Scullery
NOTES | Frozen crabmeat can be used instead of fresh, if you wish. Chill the tomato-cucumber mixture up to 1 hour before spooning into glasses; the flavors will have melded more fully.

IRISH TROUT CAVIAR BLINIS

TRADITIONAL BLINIS, or buckwheat pancakes, and Ireland's trout caviar are a match made in heaven. The large golden-orange beads of roe have a fresh, subtle flavor and pop on the tongue when you bite into them. Topped with a dollop of crème fraîche, these blinis are sure to impress any guest.

Makes 6 blinis

⅓ cup (40 g) buckwheat flour

1 teaspoon sugar

½ teaspoon salt

½ teaspoon baking soda

1 large egg, plus 1 large egg yolk

1 cup (227 g) Crème Fraîche (see page 16)

Grated peel of 1 lemon (about 1 tablespoon), plus juice, for serving

Vegetable oil, for frying

4 oz (120 g) trout caviar

Chives and wild herbs and flowers, for garnish

1. In a medium bowl, whisk together the flour, sugar, salt, and baking soda.
2. In a small bowl, combine the egg, egg yolk, ½ cup of the crème fraîche, and half of the lemon peel; stir into the dry ingredients (the batter will be slightly lumpy).
3. In another small bowl, combine the remaining ½ cup of the crème fraîche and the remaining lemon peel.
4. Heat a nonstick griddle over medium-high heat, oil lightly. Working in batches, drop a tablespoonful of batter in the oil for each blini. Cook until the bottoms are golden, about 2 minutes. Flip and cook through, about 1 minute more.
5. Top each blini with some lemon, crème fraîche, trout roe, and herbs.

IRISH SEAFOOD CHOWDER

ONE OF THE FOODS for which I receive the most requests from farm visitors is a steaming bowl of seafood chowder. True, this chowder can be found on nearly every gastropub menu in the country, but as with most comfort foods, the homemade version—served with cuts of warm, buttered brown bread—is more satisfying. A medium-size bowl makes a meal!

Serves 6

1 lb (500 g) mussels, in the shell

1 cup (240 ml) white wine

1 cup (200 g) peeled and diced russet potato

1 carrot

2 stalks celery

1 medium onion

4 tablespoons butter

Heaping ½ cup (50 g) all-purpose flour

2 cups (500 ml) cream

2 cups (500 ml) milk

1 cup (240 ml) prepared fish or vegetable stock

2 cups (400 g) smoked fish (such as haddock, cod, or salmon), cut into bite-size pieces

½ cup (100 g) scallops, shelled

Salt and pepper, to season

1. Wash and beard the mussels. Steam in a large pot with the white wine. When the mussels have all opened, they are cooked. Remove from the heat, drain the mussel juice, and remove the cooked mussels from their shells. Set aside.
2. Dice the potato, carrot, celery, and onion into small, equal pieces. Melt 1 tablespoon of the butter in a large pot, and cook the diced vegetables over low heat until translucent, about 10 minutes.
3. In a separate saucepan, stir together the remaining butter and flour over low heat to form a roux.
4. Bring the cream, milk, and stock to boiling in another saucepan. Whisk in the butter and flour mixture, and bring back to a simmer, stirring continuously.
5. When the potato, carrot, celery, and onion mixture is cooked, add the diced fish and scallops, followed by the thickened cream and stock mixture and the cooked mussels.
6. Bring the soup back to a simmer, adjust the seasoning if necessary, and serve in bowls with white soda bread or Best Brown Bread (see page 41).

Scullery
NOTES Reserve some mussels in the shell for a beautiful garnish.

CHAPTER 6

A Walk on the Wild Side

ONCE UPON A TIME, IN MY PREFARM LIFE, THE TERM *FORAGING* APPLIED ONLY TO SAMPLE SALES OR AN EARLY OPENING AT SAKS OFF 5TH ON A SATURDAY MORNING. THINGS ARE MUCH DIFFERENT IN THE IRISH COUNTRYSIDE.

Nevertheless, it is only fitting that I discovered early on that foraging also encompassed making your own sweet spirits. My first foray involved plucking plump, violet-colored sloe berries from the blackthorn tree and soaking them in cheap gin for a few months.

Since moving to the farm, I've become a bit of a foraging fanatic. I never dreamed of finding such delicious treats growing wild in our back garden and around the farm, but over the years, wild-food forays have become a weekly part of life. When the weather permits, Geoffrey and I pack up our explorer basket—complete with binoculars, gloves, pruning shears, a tiny spade, and our cameras—and head off to hunt for and gather all things edible.

We often find ourselves lost in the dense hedgerows and ancient woods of the farm in our search for spring wild garlic (ramson), autumn field mushrooms, summer fraughans, capers, nettles, elderflower, winter sloes, hazelnuts, wood sorrel, watercress, and whatever else pokes up and presents itself to say hello.

This chapter shares several of our crafty foraging adventures in the Irish countryside along with some tasty recipes for wild fruit, flowers, greens, and nuts. I have detailed how to identify and when to pick several varieties of wild edibles that grow not only here, but around the world. Part of the fun is learning the stories behind these foraged finds. Consider shadowing a seasoned forager before beginning your pursuit of wild edibles in your neck of the woods!

WILD GARLIC *and* SOFT IRISH CHEESE TAMALES

LONG BEFORE I WAS FAMILIAR with "ramps" and "ramsons" (or other wild alliums like wild leek, spring garlic, and wild onion), I was visiting the honeybee hives in the woods with my father-in-law. I wandered off to admire yet another storybook-worthy babbling brook when I stepped on a plant and the scent of woodsy garlic hit the air with a vengeance. I returned to where Michael keeps the bees and explained what I had discovered. He told me the plant was "wild spring garlic," and to him it was somewhat of a nuisance, especially when it used to grow near the hives—which made for garlic-scented honey during one particular season. I went home that afternoon; looked up this peculiar plant online; and found that it has many names, including ramps, ramsons, spring garlic, and spring leek, and it grows not only here in Ireland, but also in the States.

We've made many things with these gems, including wild garlic pesto and wild garlic–infused oil. I've even pickled the bulbs and used them for double dirty martinis on a Friday night. One day, over a transatlantic phone call, my friend Sonia suggested making soft cheese tamales with the wild garlic. My mouth watered just hearing those words.

Crafting the tamale is a bit fussy but not time-consuming. They are soft, piquant, sheep-cheesy, and woodsy. You can use any soft cheese, but we prefer Irish goat or sheep's milk varieties.

Makes about 20 medium-size tamales

20 corn husks

2½ lb (1 kg) masa harina

1½ cups (355 ml) chicken or vegetable stock, warmed

2 cups (450 g) lard

3 roasted poblano peppers, chopped coarsely

1 cup (125 g) wild garlic (or ramps), finely chopped

4 cups (550 g) Farmhouse *Queso Fresco* (see page 13)

1. Soak the corn husks overnight (or for at least 4 hours).
2. Stir the masa harina and warm stock together; let stand for 20 minutes.
3. With an electric mixer, beat the lard until fluffy; gradually mix in the masa and stock until the dough reaches a smooth, spreadable consistency. (It is ready when you drop a tiny bit into a glass of water and it floats to the top.) Set aside.
4. Pulse the poblano peppers and wild garlic together in food processor.
5. Pat dry the corn husks. Using the back of a spoon, spread a heaping tablespoon of masa dough on the wide end of a corn husk. Leave a bit of space from the widest edge, and leave about 2 inches of space at

the top edge to fold over. Place a spoonful of cheese and peppers in the middle of the masa. Wrap the sides of the tamale over one another, then fold down the top. Tie together with pieces of corn husk.

6. Once you've assembled all the tamales, bring a large pot of water to a boil.

7. Place the tamales in one layer in a steamer basket, folded end down (you may need to do two batches). Once the water is boiling, place the steamer basket in the pot, cover with a lid or towel, and steam for 1 to 1½ hours. Open one tamale to check for doneness; when the masa dough is cooked and the husks begin to separate, your tamales are ready to eat.

8. Serve warm with a fresh green salad and a margarita!

| *Scullery* NOTES | The tamales can be frozen. Reheat by steaming them for 15 to 20 minutes, or by wrapping them in foil and heating them in a 350°F (175°C) oven for 15 minutes. |

SWEET FARMER CHEESE DANISH
with Elderflower Glaze

THESE DANISHES ARE REGULARLY REQUESTED for weekend farm breakfasts, so when there is time, I make up a few batches to serve and freeze. Because this pastry dough is made with sour cream, it has a distinctively tender texture, more like a puff pastry than an authentic layered Danish pastry. The delicate elderflower garnish and essence in the glaze are sweet and aromatic yet do not overpower the star of the show: the fresh farmer cheese on the inside.

Makes 4 pastries

FOR THE PASTRY

1 cup (245 g) sour cream

½ cup (113 g) butter

½ cup (100 g) granulated sugar

1 teaspoon salt

4 teaspoons (two 7-g packets) fast-acting dry yeast

½ cup (118 ml) warm water

2 eggs, lightly beaten

4 cups (500 g) all-purpose flour

FOR THE FILLING

1 cup (225 g) Basic Farmer Cheese (see page 12)

¾ cup (150 g) granulated sugar

1 egg, lightly beaten

1 teaspoon vanilla extract

⅛ teaspoon salt

FOR THE GLAZE

2½ cups (312 g) confectioner's sugar, sifted

¼ cup (60 ml) Kiddie Elderflower Honeysuckle Cocktails (see page 335)

Fresh elderflowers, for garnish

1. **MAKE THE PASTRY:** Put the sour cream, butter, sugar, and salt in a small saucepan over low heat. Warm until the butter is melted and the sugar is dissolved. Remove from the heat and allow to cool to room temperature.

2. In a large mixing bowl, dissolve the yeast in the warm water for 10 minutes. Stir in the sour cream mixture along with the beaten eggs and flour. Mix to form a very soft dough. Cover the bowl with plastic wrap and put it in the fridge to rise overnight. (You can also do this on the same day. Just put the dough in the fridge for 2 to 4 hours and then proceed.)

3. **MAKE THE FILLING:** Using an electric mixer, beat together the farmer cheese, sugar, egg, vanilla, and salt in a large mixing bowl until well combined.

4. **ASSEMBLE THE PASTRIES:** Generously dust a clean work surface with flour. Tip out the dough and knead it 6 or 7 times, just until smooth and pliable. Divide the dough into 4 equal pieces and roll each piece into a 12-by-8-inch rectangle.

5. Spread one-quarter of the filling on each piece of dough. Starting at one of the long sides, roll up the dough jelly-roll style. Pinch the seams and ends together to seal in the filling. Place the pastries seam-side down on a buttered baking sheet, and cut five or six Xs in the top of each one with a sharp knife. Each Danish should be slightly flattened and should now measure 3½ to 4 inches wide by about 12 inches long.

6. Cover the baking sheet with a clean tea towel and set aside in a warm, draft-free place for about 1 hour, until the pastries have doubled in size.

7. Preheat the oven to 375°F (190°C).

8. Bake the pastries for 20 to 25 minutes, until golden. Remove from the oven and transfer to wire racks until they are at room temperature.

9. While the Danishes are cooling, make the glaze by sifting the confectioner's sugar into a large bowl. Whisk in the elderflower cordial a little at a time, until it has a nice drizzling consistency. Drizzle the glaze over the cooled Danishes, then sprinkle with elderflowers.

Scullery **NOTES** | You can make the dough and the filling a day in advance, then make up the pastries on the morning you wish to eat them.

FRAUGHAN COBBLER

with Pouring Cream

AS A CHILD, I loved my mother's blueberry cobbler. She hailed from Falmouth, Massachusetts, and blueberries were one of her favorite ingredients. The cobbler crust on her Cape Cod Cobbler was sconelike and not sugary, whereas the blueberry filling was a supersweet gooey glaze. A scoop of vanilla bean ice cream on top created the perfect little slice of heaven in a dish on a late summer's day.

When I discovered the wild fraughan (or bilberry) in Ireland, I boldly replaced the purple fruit in my favorite childhood recipe as an experiment, and it was a treat.

Serves 6

2½ cups (360 g) fresh or frozen fraughans (or blueberries)

1 teaspoon vanilla extract

Juice of ½ lemon

1¾ cups (400 g) granulated sugar

½ teaspoon all-purpose flour, plus 1¾ cups (75 g) more

1 tablespoon butter, melted

4 teaspoons baking powder

5 tablespoons butter, cold and cut in pieces

1 cup (235 ml) milk

1 pinch ground cinnamon

Pouring, whipped, or ice cream, to serve

---

1. Preheat the oven to 375°F (190°C).
2. Lightly grease an 8-inch square baking dish. Place the fraughans in the baking dish, and mix with the vanilla and lemon juice. Sprinkle with 1 cup of sugar and ½ teaspoon of flour, then stir in the melted butter. Set aside.
3. In a medium bowl, stir together 1¾ cups flour, the baking powder, and 6 tablespoons of sugar. Rub in the cold butter with your fingers, or cut in with a pastry blender, until the mixture resembles coarse bread crumbs. Make a well in the center, and quickly stir in the milk. Mix just until moistened. You should have a very thick batter (or very wet dough). You may need to add a splash more milk to make sure the dough is not too dry. Cover and let rest for 10 minutes.
4. Spoon the batter over the fraughans, leaving only a few small holes for the berries to peek through. Mix together the cinnamon and 2 teaspoons of sugar; sprinkle over the top.
5. Bake for 20 to 30 minutes, or until the top is golden brown. A knife inserted into the topping should come out clean. Remove from the oven and let cool until just warm before serving.
6. Spoon into dessert bowls and top with cream or ice cream.

| Leftover cobbler stores in the fridge for two to three days. You can substitute blueberries for the fraughans, if you prefer.

FRAUGHANS ARE CLOSELY RELATED TO BLUE-berries. In fact, in some European languages, the direct translation for *fraughan* is "blueberry." Fraughans do not grow in clusters; the fruit is smaller and somewhat darker in color than that of a blueberry, but when ripe, the flavor is fuller and more pronounced. If fraughans are not picked at their peak, they can be bitter, so be sure to do a taste test before harvesting.

In Ireland, fraughans are traditionally gathered on the last Sunday in July, known as Fraughan Sunday.

BRAISED FIELD MUSHROOMS

FIELD MUSHROOMS ARE ALWAYS A TREAT to find on our farm or in other parts of the country-side. There is an incredible Irish mushroom festival in County Leitrim that we attend each autumn; it takes place on an estate that boasts more than three hundred species of wild mushrooms and is always an adventure to attend.

If you don't have access to wild mushrooms, you can use any style from the market. Always use caution when selecting wild mushrooms: if you are not skilled at foraging for wild edibles, bring along an expert to steer you away from poisonous species.

Serves 4 to 6

2 tablespoons olive oil

2 medium brown-skinned onions, peeled and diced

2 carrots, finely diced

2 celery stalks, finely diced

2 garlic cloves, peeled and sliced

3 lb (1.5 kg) mixed wild mushrooms, half thickly sliced and half diced

1 small bunch thyme

One 14-oz (400-g) can chopped tomatoes

¼ cup (50 g) butter

2 to 3 tablespoons soy sauce

2 tablespoons Worcestershire sauce

3 cups (700 ml) water

Salt and pepper, to taste

1. Preheat the oven to 350°F (175°C).
2. Heat a casserole dish or deep frying pan over a medium-high heat. Add the onion, cover, and cook, stirring occasionally, until soft and slightly golden, about 10 minutes. Add the carrots, celery, and garlic; cook for another 5 minutes. Add the mushrooms in batches, stirring until they cook down, about 5 to 7 minutes. Add the thyme, tomatoes, butter, soy sauce, Worcestershire sauce, and water. Bring to a simmer, then place the dish in the oven.
3. Bake, uncovered, for 2 to 2½ hours, stirring every half hour. The mushrooms are ready when they are tender and the liquid has reduced to a saucy consistency.
4. Taste and season with a little extra soy sauce, salt, and pepper if needed.
5. Serve on a crusty baguette or sourdough bread.

Scullery NOTES | You can add diced bacon lardoons to this dish for a meatier version. As an alternative to the stovetop method, you can also use a slow cooker on medium for 4 to 5 hours. Braised dishes taste even better once they have been chilled and reheated, so you can make up several portions to serve later in the week.

NETTLE, SWEET PEA,
and TURF-SMOKED HAM SOUP

I'LL NEVER FORGET MY FIRST NETTLE STING. I was working in my kitchen garden on a spring afternoon and accidentally brushed up against a nettle. The sting was painful but didn't warrant my reaction—I swore at that blasted nettle. I damned it. Then, oddly, I began to cry. About the pain, my late father, the bloody Irish weather. Life had a bit of a sting to it at the time.

So nettles and I didn't always get along. But this has changed. I began bravely experimenting with nettles. We had a few good natters and made a deal: if I wear gloves and blanch them in hot water, they won't make me cry. In fact, I discovered that if you put them in hot water for long enough, you can even create a flavorful and nourishing cup of tea.

Then, I made this nettle soup. It is tempered with peas and turf-smoked ham, and it fulfills me in ways I never imagined a soup could. Just like this new life.

Nettle leaves cover the Irish countryside during the spring and summer. In the States, they can be found at farmers' markets and specialty stores. In the wild, they grow on short grass prairies throughout the country.

Be sure to wear thick gardening gloves when you pick nettles and when you blanch them so you don't get stung. Don't worry—once they are cooked, they no longer sting.

Serves 4 to 6

5 oz (150 g) young nettle leaves

¼ cup (50 g) butter

10 oz (275 g) potatoes, peeled and chopped

4 oz (100 g) onion, chopped

4 oz (100 g) garden peas

Salt and freshly ground black pepper, to taste

3½ cups (1 liter) chicken stock

1 cup (200 g) shredded turf-smoked Irish ham (or regular smoked ham), plus 2 tablespoons for garnish

½ cup (125 ml) cream or whole milk (optional)

Wild garlic oil, for garnish

Kale flowers, for garnish

1. Remove the sting from the nettles by placing them in a heatproof bowl or a pot. Boil 1 cup of water in a kettle, and pour it over the nettles. Let sit for 30 seconds, then drain. Roughly chop the leaves; set aside.
2. Melt the butter in a large, heavy-bottom pot. Add the potatoes, onions, and peas; toss until well coated. Sprinkle generously with salt and freshly ground black pepper. Cover and cook over low heat for 10 minutes, until the vegetables are soft and translucent.

3. Add the chicken stock and bring to a boil, then reduce to a simmer and cook until the vegetables are tender. Add the chopped nettle leaves and ham to the pot, and simmer for 2 to 3 more minutes. Be careful not to overcook the soup, or the vegetables will discolor and lose their flavor.

4. Remove from the heat, and purée the soup. Add the cream (if using)—check the consistency of the soup first, as you don't want it to be too thin; stir it in and reheat. Taste and adjust the seasoning if necessary.

5. Ladle into serving bowls, add the remaining shredded ham, drizzle with wild garlic oil, and sprinkle kale flowers to garnish.

Salting and Smoking at Home

THE MAGICAL COMBINATION OF SALT AND smoke is one of the oldest ways of imparting flavor and preserving precious protein. Many people think smoking at home is tricky, requiring special equipment and fancy skills, but it's not. Anyone can rig up a DIY smoker in his or her own kitchen with a bit of ingenuity.

First, you must start by salting the food you are preserving, which draws water from the flesh and makes the smoked flavor more pronounced. When possible, use flaky or coarse salt because it's less harsh and easier to rinse off. Scatter an even layer of salt on a large, nonmetallic plate or tray, then place the meat or fish on top, and scatter a further layer of salt on the top, being sure to cover the flesh completely. Leave for between 5 and 50 minutes, depending on the size—specifically, the thickness—of what you want to smoke.

In some cases, you won't need to salt first. For example, with a cured ham, you won't want to add any extra salt as it has already been brined. However, fish, such as small mackerel fillets, should be salted and left for 5 to 10 minutes. A large, 16-oz meaty fish fillet or a rib-eye steak needs around 40 to 50 minutes. After the salting period, give the meat or fish a quick, thorough rinse under cold water, pat dry with paper towels, and you're ready to smoke.

For basic home smoking, start with a large, lidded saucepan. Place a piece of aluminum foil in the bottom of the pan. Fit a metal cooling rack or metal steamer insert into the pan about 3 inches above the bottom.

Next, add enough sawdust, wood pellets, or small pieces of peat (Irish turf; see the Resources section) to form a 2-inch-thick layer on the bottom of the pan. Different substances give different flavors. I like Irish turf with ham, oak with red meat or trout; alder also matches well with fish. But experiment—beech, bay, cherry, apple, and hickory all have their own characters. You can even add some woodsy herbs such as bog myrtle or rosemary to the mix for added depth of flavor.

If you have a very sensitive smoke alarm (like we do), you need to open as many windows and doors as you can to give yourself as much ventilation as possible.

Cover the pan and put it on the stove over high heat. When the wood starts smoldering, turn the heat down to low and place the meat, poultry, or fish on the rack; cover; and cook until you get the result you like. Smaller cuts will take 15 to 20 minutes, while larger pieces can take 30 to 40 minutes. If the weather's fine, you can rig up your smoker outside on the barbecue or even over a campfire.

IRISH HEDGEROW SHANDY

I TASTED MY FIRST HEDGEROW COCKTAIL at one of the most exquisite country estates in Ireland: Ballyvolane House in Fermoy, County Cork. Justin and Jenny Green had been perfecting their Hedgerow Martini for their winter guests, and it was essentially a symphony of sloes and brambleberries (picked from those charming rows of border shrubs and trees throughout Ireland) mixed with gin or vodka, and for me, shaken, not stirred.

When I created my version of the cocktail for guests at our house, I added early ripened sloes to last season's fresh blackberries and loads of elderberries from our tree, spiked it with a bit of hard cider and some fresh pressed juice, and it became a sort of hedgerow shandy.

We have modified this cocktail using other foraged fruits and herbs, including nettles and fraughans. Tailor the recipe for your region and the seasons.

Makes 4 shandies

1 cup (150 g) blackberries

½ cup (75 g) elderberries

1 tablespoon superfine sugar

½ cup (75 g) ice

½ cup (120 ml) sloe gin
(to taste and comfort level)

½ cup (120 ml) Irish hard cider

½ cup (120 ml) grapefruit juice,
freshly squeezed

1. Purée the blackberries, elderberries, and sugar in a food processer. Push the mixture through a sieve to remove the seeds. Pour 1 tablespoon into the bottom of a jam jar; cover with the ice. Making one shandy at a time, pour in ⅛ cup sloe gin, ⅛ cup cider, and ⅛ cup grapefruit juice. Shake and pour into a glass of your choosing. Garnish with elderberries and blackberries.
2. Sip and smile.

Scullery **NOTES** | You could have fun with any in-season foraged fruits or herbs from your area for this cocktail, using these basic proportions as a guide.

LAVENDER SLOE GIN JELLIES

ABOUT FIVE YEARS AFTER I ARRIVED in Ireland, I had my first delicious taste of genuine sloe gin. I immediately wondered why it had taken me so long. Ironically, I soon discovered that there was no shortage of sloes in our farm's hedgerows, and I vowed to go sloe picking the following year and make my very own infusion.

Sloe gin has a complex flavor, perfectly sweet and fruity, yet slightly tart. It is not to be confused with the syrupy, commercially produced sloe-flavored gin on the market, which is far different. Having lavender plants in our front garden beds, I got to thinking about how a lavender-and-sloe-gin martini would taste. Tucking a few sprigs under the berries would give the sweet sloe gin a subtle and complementary lavender essence. The result was a combination for the ages and a new farm tradition.

These jellies can be served as a dainty dessert or even as a middle course during a formal meal. The suspended lavender sprig makes each jelly look as beautiful as it tastes.

Makes 1 quart (1 liter) sloe gin

SPECIAL TOOLS: 8 jelly molds or shot glasses

FOR THE LAVENDER SLOE GIN

1 lb (454 g) sloes, washed

2 to 3 sprigs fresh lavender (no flowers)

2 cups (400 g) granulated sugar

One 25-oz (75-cl) bottle medium-quality gin

FOR THE JELLIES

4 leaves vegetable gelatin

1½ cups (350 ml) lavender sloe gin

¾ cup (150 g) granulated sugar

⅔ cup (150 ml) water

1. **MAKE THE SLOE GIN:** Sterilize a 32-oz (1-liter) glass jar or wide-necked bottle (see page 92).
2. Wash the sloes well and discard any bruised or rotten fruit. Place the lavender sprigs at the bottom of the jar. Prick each fruit several times with a fork, then place the sloes on top of the lavender. Using a funnel, add the sugar, then top up with gin to the rim. Seal well and store in a cool, dark place.
3. Shake every day until the sugar is dissolved. Allow to infuse for at least three months; it's best if left to mature for a year. After three months, strain the grog, and enjoy on the rocks, with a splash of tonic, or as a martini.
4. **MAKE THE JELLIES:** Soak the gelatin in a bowl of cold water to soften, about 10 minutes. Meanwhile, measure out the gin, sugar, and water.
5. Pour the sugar and water into a saucepan and bring to a boil. Remove the soaked gelatin from the

cold water and dissolve it in the pot with the sugar and water. Once the gelatin has dissolved, remove it from the heat and let cool for a couple of minutes.

6. Pour the sloe gin into the syrup and give it a quick stir. Pour the mixture into the jelly molds and chill immediately. Allow it to set for at least 4 hours, but overnight is better.

7. Serve individual jellies with a spoon alongside.

Scullery
NOTES | The sloe gin keeps for up to a year. I like to store it in the freezer once it is ready, which seems to enhance the flavor a bit more. You can substitute vodka for gin as well.

SLOES GROW ON THE BRANCHES OF THE blackthorn tree. They look a bit like a blueberry but can be slightly more oblong in shape. Unlike their close relative, the damson or wild plum, you'd be best advised not to eat them raw as they are extremely bitter and can make your mouth quite dry.

They are ripe from October to early November. And as far as I can tell, sloes are really only useful to humans when steeped in alcohol. The process of making sloe gin has been going strong since the 1800s in our neck of the woods, and the odd bit of folklore has it that sloes should only be pricked with the thorn from the branch itself and never a metal fork, unless it is silver.

WILD HAZELNUT *and* VANILLA SLICE

TREMENDOUSLY POPULAR IN IRELAND and the United Kingdom, a slice is a three-layered puff pastry that actually originated in France where it is known as a mille-feuille, custard slice, cream slice, or napoleon. This pastry traditionally has two custard cream layers and one layer of jam or whipped cream. Sometimes the slice is topped with icing. Other ingredients like cocoa, confectioner's sugar, roasted almonds, and pulverized nuts can be used to decorate the pastry.

This sweet marries my love of fresh vanilla slice with rich, nutty wild hazelnut. We enjoy it in late autumn each year, after the wild hazelnuts have dried.

Makes 8 to 10 slices

18 oz ready-prepared puff pastry, thawed

FOR THE FILLING

1½ cups (375 ml) whole milk

1½ cups (375 ml) heavy cream

¼ cup (60 g) butter

2 teaspoons vanilla extract

⅔ cup (150 g) superfine sugar

⅓ cup (40 g) cornstarch

½ cup (125 ml) water

6 large egg yolks

FOR THE GLAZE

3 tablespoons whole milk

1¼ cups (156 g) powdered sugar

1 cup (110 g) chopped hazelnuts
   (wild foraged, if you can find them),
   for garnish

1. Preheat the oven to 350°F (175°C). Line two 8-by-12-inch baking trays with parchment paper.
2. Cut the pastry in half lengthwise, and roll each piece out to an ⅛-inch-thick rectangle. Trim each piece to fit the baking trays, and line the trays with the pastry. Top each tray of pastry with another baking tray as a weight and bake for 35 minutes, or until puffed and golden. Remove from the oven and let cool.
3. **MAKE THE FILLING:** Place the milk, cream, butter, vanilla, and sugar in a saucepan over medium-low heat; cook until hot but not boiling.
4. In a small bowl, mix the cornstarch and water to a smooth paste; whisk into the hot milk mixture. Gradually add the egg yolks, stirring constantly while simmering for 6 minutes, or until the mixture has thickened. Remove from the heat, and let cool to room temperature.

5. **ASSEMBLE THE SLICES:** Reline one of the baking trays with parchment paper. Place one of the pastry sheets on the tray, and spread the custard filling over it. Top with the remaining pastry, and refrigerate for 2 hours, or until set.
6. **MAKE THE GLAZE:** Mix together the milk and confectioner's sugar in a small bowl. Drizzle the glaze over the pastry and sprinkle liberally with the hazelnuts.
7. To serve, slice into rectangular pieces.

ON A SUNNY, LATE SUMMER AFTERNOON, I was helping Richard move some cattle from one field to the next. I am always distracted by searching for various wild edibles in the trees and hedges. Just when we had all the cows together in an orderly group, I caught a glimpse of what looked like clumps of small green pods hanging from a tree growing around the hedge of the paddock. I shielded my eyes with my hand, squinted through the glaring sun, and yelled for Richard to stop everything and come over to have a look. He had no idea what I was so excited about, but if he had known it wasn't an emergency with the cattle, he would not have come so quickly. Much to his chagrin, I showed him the green pods. He poked around the branches and finally grunted, "Oh, that old hazel tree. Forgot about that one. It's been here my whole life."

The flowery green pods were hazelnuts ripening on the tree. I don't think I was ever more giddy about a foraged find! I picked a few and brought them home, cracked them open and ate them, and made plans for returning for a proper harvest.

The next evening, I went back to the hazel tree with Geoffrey. The pods were all gone. I was gutted. How could they be there one day and gone the next? I asked Richard if we had really found them or had the unusual Irish heat played tricks with my mind.

Turns out the window for obtaining these gems is very, very small. You must pick them when you see them, green with bits of brown in the tips. They don't look ripe, but you can put them in a basket, and they will ripen and dry out in a few weeks. Which is exactly what I have done every year since that first discovery.

Hazel trees are small and hardy—more like shrubs, really—and thrive in hedgerows, woods, and scrubland. They can be found throughout the countryside, and not only are the nuts a valuable source of food, but the leaves were traditionally fed to livestock. The flexible branches were used in thatching, building fences and shelters, and making furniture and firewood.

BRAMBLEBERRY PIE

(for Beatrix Potter)

ANY BERRY THAT GROWS on thorny canes or trailing vines ("brambles") is considered a bramble-berry. Everywhere you turn in the countryside, hedges are teeming with brambles. And on all of our arms and legs you see evidence of "bramble wounds," or scars from picking these gems every summer.

Brambleberries for baking purposes can loosely refer to any fruit that grows on a prickly shrub, such as raspberries, blackberries, boysenberries, tayberries, loganberries, marionberries, gooseberries, and more. My romantic nature loves the word *brambleberry* simply because it conjures up having tea with Beatrix Potter. (In *A Tale of Beatrix Potter,* author Margaret Lane describes Potter's cottage dining room table, where one could find "bramble jelly and toasted teacakes," which sounds like a dream.)

This is a simple fruit pie, but if you pick your hedgerow berries at just the right time, the wild berries are pure, sweet ambrosia. When you serve the pie, imagine yourself under the roof of an old thatched cottage around a table with friends and maybe a few furry creatures as well.

Makes one 9-inch pie

One 9-inch double pie crust from Peggy's Apple Tart on a Plate (see page 193)

5 cups (785 g) brambleberries (including raspberries, blackberries, marionberries, black or red currants, or other bramble-berries)

¼ cup (30 g) flour

¼ cup (50 g) granulated sugar, plus 1 teaspoon extra

¼ cup (50 g) light brown sugar

1 tablespoon quick-cooking tapioca

1 tablespoon lemon juice

1 teaspoon salt

1 tablespoon butter

Whipped cream or ice cream, for serving (optional)

1. Put an oven rack on the lowest rung, and preheat the oven to 375°F (190°C).
2. Lightly dust your counter and rolling pin with flour, then unwrap one dough disk. With short strokes from the center outward, roll the dough into a 12-inch circle (about ⅛ inch thick), turning 90 degrees after every three or four passes of the rolling pin to keep it from sticking. Transfer the dough to a 9-inch pie pan, letting it fall into place. (If you push or stretch the dough, it will shrink back when baked.) Trim the overhang to ¼ inch. Cover with plastic wrap, and refrigerate at least 15 minutes and up to overnight. Meanwhile, roll the second disk into an 11-inch circle. Transfer to a baking sheet, cover with plastic wrap, and refrigerate at least 15 minutes and up to overnight.

3. While the crusts chill, put the berries in a large bowl. Sprinkle with the flour, ¼ cup granulated sugar, brown sugar, tapioca, lemon juice, and salt. Stir gently until the berries are well coated. Taste and add more granulated sugar, if you like.

4. Pour the berry mixture into the chilled bottom crust and dot with the butter. Unwrap the top crust, and lay it over the pie. Fold the bottom crust over the edge of the top crust, and crimp the edges together. Cut several vents or holes in the top crust, and sprinkle with the remaining teaspoon of sugar.

5. Put the pie on a rimmed baking sheet and bake until the crust is browned and the filling is bubbling, 60 to 75 minutes. (Cover the edges with foil if they become too dark before the middle of the top is nicely browned.)

6. Remove from the oven and let cool until the bottom of the pie pan reaches room temperature, at least 3 hours. Serve with whipped cream or ice cream, if you like.

CANDIED CRAB APPLES

IF YOU WERE TO WALK INTO OUR KITCHEN during crab apple season, you might mistake it for a confectionery. It has all the right trappings: steaming stainless steel pots of bubbling sugary concoctions on the stove, candied apples drying on waxed paper, tiny bottles of food coloring lining the countertop, finely chopped nuts of every sort in bowls ready for dipping. It looks and smells like candy heaven.

Building this kitchen confectionery first began when my father-in-law said he had spotted a crab apple tree bursting with fruit in a hedge while checking cattle. Geoffrey and I met Granddad at the gate of the pasture, ladder and empty rucksack in hand. We walked together toward the tree, which was heavy with fruit. It was on the edge of a shallow stream running through the paddock, so Michael had no choice but to plant the ladder in the water and climb on up. As he plucked the abundant fruit, Geoffrey and I tried to catch any falling apples. Each time an apple dropped into the water, the current whisked it away before we could retrieve it. We came away soaked but smiling and with an overflowing sack of dainty apples.

That batch became the first of a tasty yearly ritual.

Makes 10 to 15 apples

10 to 15 small ripe crab apples with stems intact, for dipping

3 cups (675 g) granulated sugar

½ cup (120 ml) golden syrup (or light corn syrup)

1 cup (250 ml) water

½ teaspoon red food coloring

1 cup (110 g) finely chopped hazelnuts or peanuts (optional)

1. Clean and dry the crab apples; set aside. Line a baking sheet with parchment paper.
2. Stir together the sugar, golden syrup, and water in a saucepan over medium heat until the sugar has dissolved. Turn up the heat and boil until the syrup reaches 310°F (150°C) on a candy thermometer.
3. Remove from the heat and stir in the food coloring. Allow to cool slightly, until bubbles disappear.
4. Dip one apple completely in the syrup, and swirl it to coat fully. Hold the apple above the saucepan to drain off excess, then dip in the chopped nuts (if using). Place on the baking sheet. Repeat the process with the remaining apples. If your syrup thickens or cools too much, warm it over low heat before proceeding.
5. Let the apples cool completely before serving.

Scullery **NOTES** | Do not allow the candy mixture to go above 310°F (150°C), or it will burn. Be very careful—this mixture is extremely hot. This is not a project for unsupervised children.

CHAPTER 7

Sweet and Savory Pies and Tarts

I LIKE PIE. EVERY SORT OF PIE. BUT I'M EMBARRASSED TO ADMIT THAT BEFORE MOVING TO THESE GREEN PASTURES, I CONSIDERED PIE TO BE AN EXCLUSIVELY AMERICAN TREAT. AFTER ALL, WHO CAN BEAT AN APPLE PIE ON THE FOURTH OF JULY? WELL, I SOON FOUND OUT THAT NO ONE REALLY BOTHERS ABOUT THE FOURTH HERE (NATURALLY). AND SAVORY, NOT SWEET, CREATIONS SEEM TO BE AT THE TOP OF THE IRISH PIE LIST.

Once I recovered from my astonishment, nothing was more pleasing to discover (and taste) than the many ways in which Ireland creates a sensational savory pie. Previously, the closest encounter I'd had with savory pie had been the processed, frozen potpies of my Midwestern childhood—not exactly a taste memory for the record books.

Some of my new favorites include a chicken and leek pie that can easily double up to feed an army, free-form galettes that utilize odds and ends from the crisper, and an easy shepherd's pie that goes a long way toward helping out a busy or down-on-his-luck neighbor. I can't leave out the creamy sweet or fruit pies that make for the perfect ending to a meal. Easy to prepare and handy to freeze, these delectable dinner pies are absolute winners for farm living.

In this chapter, I have included recipes for both sweet and savory pies that will fill your heart with joy and your belly with deep satisfaction.

PERFECT PIE CRUST

FOR ME, MAKING PASTRY was a persnickety technique. Perfecting this craft takes time and experience. And since I have somewhat impatient leanings when it comes to fussy baking techniques, the curve was steeper than I would have liked.

After a series of kitchen tests, complete with some massive flops, I finally got pastry down to a science of three recipes that we can all understand and use easily. Nearly all of the pie and tart recipes in this chapter use one of them.

BASIC SWEET PIE CRUST

THIS CRUST IS PERFECT for many fruit or custard cream pies and tarts.

Makes one 9-inch single crust

¾ cup (56 g) butter, softened

Scant ½ cup (112 g) superfine sugar

1 small egg

4 drops vanilla extract

1¼ cups (156 g) all-purpose flour

1. In a large mixing bowl, lightly beat the butter and sugar with a wooden spoon until light and creamy. Add the egg and vanilla, and mix until combined. Add the flour and mix to a paste, just until the dough comes away from the bowl cleanly. Be careful not to overmix, or the pastry will become elastic and doughy. Wrap in plastic wrap and refrigerate for 30 minutes or (even better) overnight.
2. Before using, gently knead the pastry, taking care that it remains cold and firm. On a lightly floured surface, roll out the pastry into a ⅛-inch-thick sheet, or as called for in your recipe.

Scullery **NOTES** | This recipe can be doubled to make a double-crust pie. The pastry freezes well, and you can store it in the fridge for up to a week and in the freezer for one month.

BASIC SHORT PIE CRUST

THIS IS MY GO-TO PASTRY for most savory pies and tarts.

Makes one 9-inch single crust

1½ cups (187 g) all-purpose flour

½ cup (56 g) butter, cut in pieces

Pinch of sea salt

¼ cup (60 ml) cold water

1. Place the flour, butter, and salt in a large mixing bowl. Rub the ingredients together with your fingers until the mixture resembles coarse bread crumbs. Do not overmix, or the butter will begin to melt from the heat of your fingers.
2. Add the water, and mix with a wooden spoon until a firm dough forms. Cover the bowl with plastic wrap, and refrigerate for 30 minutes or overnight.
3. Gently knead the pastry before using, taking care that it remains cold and firm. On a lightly floured surface, roll out the pastry into a ⅛-inch-thick sheet, or as called for in your recipe.

Scullery NOTES | This recipe can be doubled to make a double-crust pie. This pastry freezes well, and you can store it in the fridge for up to a week and in the freezer for one month.

PUFF PASTRY

THIS IS A LIGHT, FLAKY PASTRY that can be used for pie crusts, canapés, and sweet pastries.

Makes one 24-oz (700-g) pastry

2 cups (250 g) bread flour

1 teaspoon fine sea salt

1 cup (227 g) butter, room temperature but not soft

¾ cup (177 ml) cold water

1. Sift the flour and salt together in a large bowl. Roughly break the butter into small chunks, add them to the bowl, and rub them in until you see only small bits of butter. Make a well in the center and pour in about two-thirds of the cold water, mixing until you have a firm, rough dough. Add extra water if needed to bring the dough together. Cover the bowl with plastic wrap, and let it rest in the fridge for 20 minutes.

2. Turn the dough out onto a lightly floured board, knead gently, and shape into a smooth rectangle. Roll it in one direction only, until it has become three times as long as it is wide. Keep the edges straight and even. Do not overwork the dough; it should have a marbled appearance.

3. Fold the top edge down to the center, then the bottom edge up and over that to the top fold. Give the dough a quarter-turn (to the left or right), and roll out again in one direction until the width is three times the length. Fold as before, cover with plastic wrap, and chill for at least 20 minutes before rolling out to use.

Scullery
NOTES | Puff pastry freezes well; you can store it in the fridge for up to a week and in the freezer for one month.

RUSTIC TURF-SMOKED HAM
and LEEK GALETTE

YOU MAY HAVE GATHERED that I am smitten with the fragrance and feel of a turf fire. Turf is ancient peat found in the boglands of Ireland and consists of many layers of leaves, herbs, and roots. Used for centuries as a source of fuel for fire here, the warmth and smell of burning Irish turf is positively mystical.

After I'd tasted a joint of beef cured with turf, I was inspired. I had read about farmers from a century ago cooking ham over a hearth turf fire but had never sampled such a thing firsthand.

I decided to experiment with turf in my kitchen. When Richard brought home a big bag of dried turf from the bog near the farm for fuel, I smoked a small piece of ham simply by burning small chips of turf in a covered roasting tin. The result was a subtle, traditional cottage fire scent with uniquely local flavor. (For instructions on creating a home smoker, see page 147.)

The leeks and cheese bring out the smokiness of the ham in this rustic tart.

Serves 4

1 tablespoon olive oil

3 leeks, thinly sliced

1 recipe Basic Short Pie Crust
   (see page 165)

1½ cups (150 g) soft farmer cheese with
   garlic and herbs (or Boursin)

1½ cups (150 g) turf-smoked ham
   (or any smoked ham) cut into chunks

½ cup (100 g) grated Glebe Brethan cheese
   (or Gruyère cheese)

1. Preheat the oven to 350°F (175°C). Line a baking sheet with parchment paper; set aside.
2. Heat the oil in a frying pan. Fry the leeks until soft, about 5 minutes. Cool.
3. Roll out the pastry into a rough circle and place on the baking sheet. Spread the farmer cheese over the pastry to within ½ inch of the edge. Scatter the leeks, ham, and grated Glebe Brethan cheese over the farmer cheese. Fold just the edges of the pastry over the filling, leaving the top open.
4. Bake for 20 minutes, until the crust is golden. Cool slightly and serve.

FOR EONS, THE IRISH HAVE HEATED THEIR homes and cooked their food using peat or turf taken from bogs as fuel. Turf was cut by hand, using a two-sided spade called a *sleán*. Entire families often helped to cut the turf on the bog, which involved turning each sod of turf to ensure the sun and wind could help in the drying process. The turf was then placed upright, or "footed," for further drying. Footing the turf was a back-breaking job and involved placing five or six sods of turf on end and leaning against each other. Finally, the turf was brought home and stored in sheds or ricks. In the midlands and the west of Ireland, the tradition of using turf or peat as fuel continues in many homes to this day.

FISH-'N'-CHIP PIE

THIS RECIPE CAME ABOUT ENTIRELY BY ACCIDENT. I had been trying unsuccessfully for years to get Geoffrey to eat peas. He loves so many green vegetables, particularly the ones we grow such as brussels sprouts, broccoli, and kale, but I couldn't get him to swallow one measly pea. After trying minty, mushy, mangetout, marrow root, sugar snap, raw, steamed, shelled, and sautéed peas, I had almost given up. Even the darling "Give Peas a Chance" T-shirt from a stateside visit to Whole Foods couldn't charm him.

About a year later, it dawned on me. What if I popped some peas into a fish-and-chips tart? Going out for fish-and-chips is a bit of an indulgence here on the farm, so I figured I could get away with such a lark. Soon I found myself in the kitchen, donning an apron, layering peas and fish in a creamy sauce, and topping the filled pie crust with a handful of chunky chips before popping it into the oven.

Voilà, the peas were eaten. In fact, Geoffrey thought the pie was better than any fish-and-chips he'd had before, and we grown-ups thought it was pretty darn good too.

Makes four 6-inch pies

1 recipe Basic Short Pie Crust
  (see page 165)

1½ lb (675 g) potatoes, peeled

2 tablespoons oil

1 tablespoon lemon juice

Sea salt and black pepper, to taste

2 tablespoons (25 g) butter

1 onion, finely chopped

¼ cup (25 g) all-purpose flour

1¼ cups (300 ml) milk

1 teaspoon minced garlic

1 lb (450 g) cod fillets

1 cup (100 g) peas, fresh or frozen

1 tablespoon freshly chopped mint leaves

Sea salt and malt vinegar, to serve

1. Preheat the oven to 350°F (175°C). Grease four 6-inch springform tart pans. Roll out the pastry until it is ¼ inch thick. Line the bottom and sides of each tart pan with the pastry. Blind bake the crusts for 8 to 10 minutes, remove from the oven, and allow to cool. (For instructions for blind baking, see Grandma's Gooseberry Tart on page 82.)

2. Turn the oven up to 400°F (200°C).

3. Cut the potatoes into chunky steak fries. Place in a saucepan of boiling water, bring back to a boil, and cook for 3 minutes. Drain. Stir in the oil and lemon juice, and season with salt and pepper. Set aside.

4. Melt the butter in a medium-size saucepan over low heat. Add the onion and cook until softened.

Add the flour and cook for 1 minute. Gradually add the milk and garlic, stirring continuously until the sauce thickens and comes to a boil. Season with salt and pepper. Remove from the heat.

5. Skin the cod fillets and cut into small chunks. Stir into the sauce.

6. Boil the peas in a separate saucepan, drain, and pulse in a blender with the mint.

7. Spoon a layer of the pea mixture into each tart case, followed by a layer of the creamy fish filling. Spoon the chips over the fish mixture. Bake for about 25 to 30 minutes, until the potato topping is golden.

8. Remove from the oven, and serve with sea salt and malt vinegar.

IRISH LOBSTER MAC *and* CHEESE PIE

MAC AND CHEESE HAS BEEN A REGULAR DISH in my cooking repertoire ever since Geoffrey became acquainted with it on an early childhood trip to the States. He adores it homemade, with any number of cheeses, but will also devour a box of the organic store-bought version if he must.

In fact, it was Geoffrey who suggested mixing seafood into his mac and cheese. Family from America had been visiting, and we'd just returned from a day trip to Killarney National Forest. It was one of those trademark rainy Irish days, and by the time we returned to the farm, I was weary from driving, and we were all a bit chilled and craving the warmth of a fire and something comforting for supper.

I opened the fridge, and there was leftover lobster meat from the Classic Dublin Lawyer (see page 108) that I'd prepared the evening before. Geoffrey asked if we could have lobster macaroni and cheese, and I thought that sounded just right for the day.

I boiled some pasta and made the cheese sauce, flaked in the lobster meat, popped on some quick puff pastry lids, and baked the dishes in the oven. Now, I'm not sure I would buy and boil a lobster just for this purpose, but these little soup bowl–style pies brought supreme comfort and delight to everyone on that night.

Makes 6 small pies

8 oz (227 g) elbow macaroni

¼ cup (56 g) butter

¼ cup (30 g) flour

½ teaspoon salt

Dash of black pepper

2 cups (480 ml) milk

2 cups (226 g) shredded cheddar cheese (we like smoked cheddar)

2 cups (500 g) cooked lobster meat, shredded

1 egg

¼ cup (60 ml) milk

1 recipe Puff Pastry (see page 165)

Quinoa, for sprinkling

1. Preheat the oven to 400°F (200°C).
2. Cook the macaroni according to the directions on the package.
3. In a separate medium saucepan, melt the butter over medium heat. Stir in the flour, salt, and pepper, then slowly add milk. Cook and stir until bubbling. Add the cheese and stir until melted. Stir in the lobster meat.
4. Drain the macaroni, add it to the cheese sauce, and stir well to coat. Divide between 6 individual round baking dishes or ovenproof ceramic bowls.

5. Beat together the egg and milk to make an egg wash. Cut the puff pastry into 6 circles, slightly larger than the top of each baking dish. Brush the outer edge of each circle with the egg wash. Place each crust egg-wash-side *down* on the filled dishes; lightly press the pastry onto the edge of the dish. Brush the crusts with additional egg wash and sprinkle with quinoa. Cut a slit in the top of each crust so that steam can escape.

6. Place the dishes on a baking sheet and bake for 20 minutes, or until the crust is golden brown and the filling is hot.

7. Allow to cool slightly, but serve warm with glasses of pinot noir.

OXTAIL *and* ALE PIE

THIS RECIPE IS A BIT OF A PROJECT; it requires time, love, and a little patience. But if it's flavor you're after, then this is a recipe you must try.

Oxtail is not a very popular cut of meat these days—you will likely have to place a special request for it with your butcher—but there is a lot of goodness and nutrition to be extracted from this inexpensive cut. When cooked the right way, I think it produces far more flavor and rich juices than any steak. It's well worth the advance planning.

Cooking the oxtail with top-quality dark Irish ale at a low temperature for more than four hours results in meat that is rich and extremely tender. This kind of slow cooking is about taking a modest cut and turning it into a divine essence of beef flavor that has nearly been forgotten—the essence of traditional Irish cooking.

Serves 4

2 tablespoons olive oil

½ cup (113 g) butter

3½ lb (1.5 kg) oxtail, cut in pieces by
    the butcher

Flour, for dusting

Sea salt and freshly ground black pepper,
    to taste

8 carrots, peeled and chopped

1 bunch celery, chopped

6 shallots, coarsely chopped

8 garlic cloves, sliced

4 fresh bay leaves

6 cloves

4 cups (1 liter) good-quality beef stock

1 cup (250 ml) Irish ale

1 recipe Puff Pastry (see page 165)

1 free-range egg yolk

1. Preheat the oven to 320°F (160°C).
2. Heat 1 tablespoon of the oil and the butter in a large, heavy-bottom saucepan over medium heat. Dust the oxtail with the flour seasoned with salt and pepper, and brown in the saucepan for about 5 minutes. Remove and set aside.
3. Turn the heat down to medium-low, then add the carrots, celery, shallots, and remaining oil. Let the vegetables sweat slowly until softened, about 10 minutes.
4. Add the garlic, bay leaves, cloves, beef stock, ale, and oxtail; season with salt and pepper to taste. Place the saucepan on a baking tray, or transfer the oxtail to an ovenproof dish or Dutch oven, and cover with a lid.

5. Place in the oven and slowly roast for 2½ to 3 hours, until the oxtail is caramelized and tender. Remove from the oven, and pour the mixture into a clean ovenproof baking dish.

6. Roll out the puff pastry on a floured surface to 1 inch thick. Drape the pastry lid over the oxtail to cover the baking dish, hanging over the edges slightly. Cut a criss-cross vent on top. Beat the egg yolk, and lightly brush on the pastry. Bake for 25 minutes, until the crust is golden and crisp.

7. Serve with a side of Classic Colcannon (see page 65) or Classic Champ (see page 67) and a nice glass of burgundy.

TATER TOT SHEPHERD'S PIE

SHEPHERD'S PIE WAS ONE OF MY FIRST FORAYS into the basics of Irish country cooking. Comforting and easy to make, dishes brimming with mutton and potato filled our freezer when Geoffrey was a toddler.

More recently, I began experimenting with ways to reinvent this classic pie. Inspired by craving a tater-tot hotdish (a Midwestern American casserole), I lined the top of my shepherd's pie with homemade tots, and it was much more fun than standard mash.

Serves 4

1 tablespoon sunflower or canola oil, plus more for frying

1 large onion, chopped

2 to 3 medium carrots, chopped

1 lb (450 g) ground lamb

2 tablespoons tomato purée

Splash of Worcestershire sauce

2 cups (500 ml) lamb or beef stock

FOR THE TOTS

4 large russet potatoes, baked and cooled

2 tablespoons all-purpose flour

2 teaspoons fine salt

1. Heat the oil in a medium saucepan over medium heat, then cook the onion and carrots for about 10 minutes, until softened. Turn up the heat, crumble in the lamb, and brown, pouring off any excess fat. Add the tomato purée and Worcestershire sauce; fry for a few more minutes until browned. Pour in the stock, bring to a simmer, cover, and cook for 20 minutes. Remove the cover and cook for another 20 minutes to reduce the liquid.

2. Meanwhile, peel the potatoes and shred them on the large holes of a box grater. Transfer to a large bowl, sprinkle in the flour and salt, and gently mix until combined.

3. Scoop 1½ tablespoons of the potato mixture into a short cylinder, about 1½ inches long and ¾ inch wide. Press the mixture in tightly and then press the tots onto a baking sheet, and repeat with the remaining potato mixture.

4. Line a second baking sheet with paper towels; set aside. Pour ¼ inch of oil into a large frying pan and set over medium-high heat until hot, about 5 minutes. Fry the tots in batches of 8 to 10 pieces (do not overcrowd the pan), turning once, until light golden brown on both sides, about 1 to 2 minutes per

batch. Using a slotted spoon, transfer the tots to the paper-towel-lined baking sheet, and season with salt. Repeat for all the tots.

5. Preheat the oven to 375°F (190°C).

6. Put the meat mixture into an ovenproof dish. Top with the tots to completely cover the meat. Bake for 20 to 25 minutes, until the tots are starting to turn golden brown and the mince is bubbling through at the edges. Serve with a salad of crisp garden greens.

Scullery NOTES | You can freeze tater tots for future use: Let the fried tots cool, then transfer them to an airtight container or ziplock bag. Arrange them in a single layer in the container or bag and place them in the freezer. You can also just pile the shredded potato on top of the filling and bake as directed.

LAVONDA'S BUTTERMILK PIE

YEARS AGO, I WAS GIVEN A SLICE of buttermilk pie at an American summer barbecue. The pie had been brought to the party by a guest who had recently relocated from Tennessee, and I was told it was a very old, classic family recipe. I never forgot that tangy vanilla flavor and creamy yet crumbly texture. Since moving to Ireland, I have been making my own butter, and having the daily surplus of buttermilk in my refrigerator means I've been dreaming of finding the perfect recipe for buttermilk pie.

Recently, a generous acquaintance—Lavonda Shipley from Chattanooga, Tennessee—kindly shared the recipe that she and her family enjoyed growing up. Her tried-and-true, authentic buttermilk pie recipe is straight from the American South, and it sure makes our taste buds whistle "Dixie."

This pie is so good, it really should be kept a family secret, but Lavonda has graciously allowed me to share this gem, and I implore you to try it.

Makes one 9-inch pie

1 recipe Basic Sweet Pie Crust
   (see page 164)

3 eggs

1½ cups (300 g) sugar, plus extra
   for dusting

1 teaspoon vanilla

⅓ cup (90 ml) buttermilk

½ cup (56 g) butter, melted and cooled

1 tablespoon flour

Pinch of salt

1. Preheat the oven to 350°F (175°C).
2. Line a 9-inch pie plate with the pie crust.
3. Using an electric mixer, blend the eggs, sugar, vanilla, buttermilk, butter, flour, and salt in a large bowl. Pour the mixture into the unbaked pie shell. Lightly dust sugar over the top and bake for 1 hour, or until firm and golden on top.
4. Remove from the oven and allow to cool before serving. It's lovely chilled in the summertime and warm in the wintertime.

PATSY PIES

I TRIED MY FIRST CORNISH PASTY on this side of the pond at a charming little food stall in Temple Bar, Dublin. It brought to mind a similar sort of pocket pie, also called a pasty, that I had eaten while visiting relatives on the Upper Peninsula of Michigan. I later found out that the original pasty comes from Cornwall, and the hearty U.S. version was brought over with the Cornish miners who came to work in the iron mines of the Midwest.

In our kitchen, we make a hybrid, using various Irish and sometimes non-Irish ingredients, and since you must abide by a certain recipe for your dish to be deemed a proper Cornish pasty, we simply refer to ours as Patsy Pies. In Ireland, Patsy is a popular nickname for those named Patrick or Padraig.

Research tells me that the original Cornish pasties were baked in a way that would make the pastry too hard to be eaten, almost like a portable case for the rich and savory meat-and-veg filling. The shell was simply there to protect and carry the filling. It has been said that a good pasty should be strong enough to withstand a drop down a mineshaft.

Makes 4 pies

FOR THE PASTRY

2 cups (500 g) bread flour, plus extra to dust

½ cup (115 g) lard

1½ tablespoons butter

1 teaspoon salt

¾ cup (213 ml) cold water

FOR THE FILLING

½ lb (250 g) skirt steak, diced into chunks

2 medium potatoes, peeled and diced

1 parsnip, peeled and diced

2 small onions, peeled and chopped coarsely

1 cup (250 ml) Irish stout

Sea salt and cracked black pepper, to taste

Butter, softened, to dot filling

1 egg, beaten with a little water

1. **MAKE THE PASTRY:** Put the flour in a mixing bowl and grate in the lard. Add the butter and salt, and rub the fat in with your fingers until the mixture resembles coarse bread crumbs.
2. Mix in just enough cold water to bring it together into a dough—you may not need the entire ¾ cup. (A food processor works well here.) The dough is ready when it comes cleanly away from the side of the bowl. Roll into a round ball, wrap with plastic wrap, and chill for 2 hours.
3. **MAKE THE PIES:** Dice the beef and vegetables into even-size cubes. Combine in a bowl with the Irish stout. Mix and season well with salt and pepper.

4. Roll out the pastry on a lightly floured surface to about ¼ inch thick; cut out circles to measure about 8 inches (20 cm) across.

5. Divide the filling between the pastry circles, spreading it on one half and leaving space around the edge. Top each filling with a small dot of butter. Brush the edges with the beaten egg, fold the crust over the filling, and pinch the edges together to seal. Crimp as desired, and cut a small vent in the top of each pie.

6. Preheat the oven to 400°F (200°C), and brush the pies with egg wash. Bake for 20 minutes until golden brown, then reduce the heat to 325°F (165°C) and cook for another 20 minutes. Juice will bubble through the vent when done.

FULL IRISH SLAB PIE

I AM A BREAKFAST PERSON BY NATURE, and the Irish pièce de résistance has to be the "full Irish": fresh free-range fried eggs, pork sausages, rashers (bacon, thick cut and very lean), sautéed mushrooms and broiled tomato halves, zesty baked beans, and savory black and white puddings with thick-cut toast. Luckily, my husband makes the best Irish breakfast ever, but I am biased.

When you are feeding a pack of hungry farmers, or visitors from abroad embarking on a pilgrimage to the ancient mountain of Croagh Patrick in County Mayo, this is the breakfast to serve—a full Irish breakfast baked beneath a slab of pie crust.

The somewhat madcap combination is positively beguiling and especially fortifying with strong coffee the morning after a late night of traditional music and sing-along.

Serves 12 generously

FOR THE CRUST

3¾ cups (468 g) all-purpose flour

1½ teaspoons sea salt

1½ cups (170 g) unsalted butter, very cold

¾ cup (177 ml) very cold water

FOR THE FILLING

1 lb (454 g) russett potatoes, peeled (if desired) and cut into ½-inch slices

4 medium (4- to 6-inch) sausages

4 large rashers

10 oz (284 g) fresh mushrooms, sliced

2 tomatoes, sliced

4 scallions, thinly sliced

One 14-oz (400-g) can baked beans, undrained

6 large eggs

1 teaspoon kosher or coarse sea salt, plus more to taste

Freshly ground black pepper, to taste

1 large egg yolk

1 teaspoon water

1. MAKE THE PASTRY: Place the flour and salt in a large mixing bowl. Rub in the butter with your fingers until the mixture resembles coarse bread crumbs. Do not overmix, or the butter will begin to melt from the heat of your fingers. Add the water and mix until a dough is formed. Divide the dough into two balls. Cover with plastic wrap, and refrigerate for 30 minutes or overnight.
2. Preheat the oven to 375°F (190°C). Line the bottom of a 10-by-15-by-1-inch baking sheet or jelly roll pan with parchment paper; set aside.

3. **PREPARE THE FILLING:** Place the potatoes in a medium saucepan and cover with cold water. Bring to a boil, then reduce to a simmer and cook for 7 to 10 minutes, until the potatoes are tender but not falling apart. Drain.

4. Brown sausages and rashers in a skillet over medium heat.

5. **ASSEMBLE THE PIE:** On a lightly floured work surface, roll one half of the dough into an 18-by-13-inch rectangle, working quickly to keep the dough as cold as possible, and using enough flour that it doesn't stick to the surface.

6. Drape the rolled dough onto the prepared baking sheet, leaving an overhang around the edges of the sheet; trim this extra dough to a ¾-inch overhang.

7. Layer the vegetables, baked beans, and cooked meats evenly over the bottom pie crust, and crack the eggs evenly over the filling. Season with salt and pepper.

8. Roll the second ball of dough into a 16-by-11-inch rectangle. Place this over the filling and cut several vents in the top. Fold the bottom crust's overhang under the edges, sealing them together.

9. Beat the egg yolk and water, and brush it over the crust.

10. Bake the pie until the crust is golden and the filling is set, about 40 to 45 minutes. Remove from the oven and transfer to a wire rack; cool for 2 to 3 minutes before cutting into squares to serve.

Scullery **NOTES** | If you have premade the pie crust and stowed it in the freezer, this dish is easy to assemble when you have guests. If you have more time, you can cut rolled dough into strips and weave them together over the filling to form a lattice pie top. This pie is best eaten on the day it is made.

BLACK CURRANT, LEMON VERBENA, *and* VANILLA GLAZED PIE

IN IRELAND, BLACK CURRANT is a wildly popular ingredient and can come in the form of cordials, fruit squashes, jams, and preserves, but unless you grow them yourself, the raw fruit is hard to come by.

This recipe was inspired by a visit to our favorite local restaurant, The Mustard Seed in Ballingarry, County Limerick. The charming and ebullient proprietor, Dan Mullane, served me a glass of fresh black currant cordial with soda and sprigs of lemon verbena. The amethyst-colored refreshment was out of this world.

The lemon verbena paired so beautifully with the cordial that I decided to experiment with a vanilla bean and lemon verbena glaze over fresh-picked black currants. The result was a splendidly tangy (but not tart), velvety vanilla pie bursting with berry flavor in a cornmeal crust that comfortably cradles its filling. NOTE: The glaze for this recipe must be made at least two hours or up to a day in advance.

Males one 9-inch pie

FOR THE GLAZE

2 cups (142 g) (or handfuls) fresh lemon verbena leaves, washed

1 vanilla bean

3 cups (675 g) sugar

½ cup (125 ml) water

FOR THE CRUST

2½ cups (312 g) all-purpose flour

¼ cup (30 g) cornmeal (medium ground)

3 tablespoons sugar

¾ teaspoon salt

½ cup (56 g) plus 6 tablespoons unsalted butter, chilled and cut into ½-inch cubes

¼ cup (28 g) solid vegetable shortening, cut into ½-inch cubes

4 tablespoons (or more) ice water

FOR THE FILLING

5 cups (750 g) fresh black currants

¾ cup (180 ml) lemon verbena glaze

2 cups (450 g) superfine sugar

¼ cup (30 g) cornstarch

Milk, for glazing

1½ tablespoons raw sugar, for dusting

1. **MAKE THE GLAZE:** Put all of the glaze ingredients into a saucepan and heat slowly, just until the sugar dissolves and creates a thick syrup. Remove from the heat; set aside to cool and steep for 2 hours, or longer if you can (the longer you steep it, the more pronounced the flavor). Strain out the lemon verbena leaves and vanilla bean. Set aside.

2. **MAKE THE CRUST:** Blend the flour, cornmeal, sugar, and salt in a food processor. Add the butter and shortening; pulse until the mixture resembles coarse bread crumbs. Add the ice water and blend just until moist clumps begin to form. Gather the dough into a ball, divide it in half, and flatten each half into a disk. Wrap the disks separately in plastic wrap, and chill for at least 1 hour.

3. **MAKE THE FILLING:** Combine the black currants, lemon verbena glaze, sugar, and cornstarch in a large bowl; toss to blend. Let stand at room temperature until juices begin to form, about 30 minutes.

4. **MAKE THE PIE:** Preheat the oven to 400°F (200°C). Place a rimmed baking sheet in the bottom of the oven. Roll out one dough disk between two sheets of generously floured parchment paper to form a 12-inch round. Peel off the top sheet of parchment paper; invert dough into a 9-inch glass pie plate. Carefully peel off the second sheet of parchment paper. Gently press the dough into the pie dish, sealing any cracks as needed and leaving an overhang around the sides.

5. Spoon the filling into the pie crust.

6. Roll out the second dough disk between another two sheets of generously floured parchment paper to form a 12-inch round. Peel off the top sheet of parchment paper. Carefully and evenly invert the dough on top of the filling. Peel off the second sheet of parchment paper.

7. Trim the overhang of both crusts to 1 inch. Fold under and press to seal. Crimp the edges. Cut slits in the top crust to allow steam to escape during baking, Lightly brush the top crust (not the edges) with milk, and sprinkle with raw sugar.

8. Bake the pie for 15 minutes. Reduce the temperature to 350°F (175°C), and continue baking until the crust is golden brown and the filling is bubbling thickly through the slits, about 1 hour and 15 minutes.

9. Remove from the oven and cool completely on a wire rack.

10. Serve with scoops of ice cream, custard, or whipped cream.

PEGGY'S APPLE TART
on a Plate

THE OLD SAYING GOES, "There is nothing more American than apple pie," but it was a slice of Irish apple tart that won my heart. I was never a big fan of apple pie. I much preferred creamier or berrier versions, so when my mother-in-law offered me a slice one autumn afternoon, I hesitated. Then I thought, *I don't want to seem contrary, do I?* And that began my love affair with the Irish apple tart.

Now, this isn't just any ordinary tart. It uses the age-old tradition of baking with an ordinary flat plate as opposed to the deep pie dish that we are accustomed to in the States.

I made only one zingy tweak to Peggy's classic recipe by adding a tiny bit of cinnamon and freshly grated ginger to the filling.

Makes one 10-inch tart

FOR THE FILLING

2½ to 3 cups (285–342 g) baking apples, peeled, cored, and thinly sliced

½ cup (112 g) superfine sugar

2 teaspoons cinnamon

Squeeze of lemon juice

1 tablespoon grated fresh gingerroot

FOR THE TART CRUST

3½ cups (500 g) all-purpose flour

⅔ cup (120 g) superfine sugar

Pinch of salt

1½ cups (320 g) unsalted butter, cold and cut in pieces

1 egg

2 egg yolks

1 teaspoon vanilla extract

1. Preheat the oven to 350°F (175°C).
2. To prepare, mix all the filling ingredients together in a bowl and let sit for 30 minutes.
3. Meanwhile, put the flour, sugar, and salt in a bowl. Rub in the butter in with your fingers until the mixture resembles coarse bread crumbs. Make a well in the middle, and add the egg, egg yolks, and vanilla. Stir with a fork to incorporate the flour evenly, then quickly bring the dry and wet ingredients together with your hands.
4. On a floured surface, knead the dough for a few minutes. Divide it in half, and roll each half into a ¼- to ½-inch thick circle.

5. Place the bottom crust in a 9-inch pie plate. Fill with the apples. Place the top crust over the filling and crimp the edges. Make three slits in the top crust.

6. Bake for about 1 hour, or until the crust is golden brown and the filling is bubbling. Remove from the oven, let cool slightly, and serve warm.

Scullery
NOTES

Serve this tart with fresh whipped cream.

CHAPTER 8

Country Suppers

O N OUR FARM, SUPPERTIME (DINNERTIME IN THE STATES) IS CALLED "TEA" AND IS SERVED AFTER THE COWS HAVE BEEN MILKED AND THE DAILY WORK IN THE FARMYARD IS DONE. THIS COULD BE ANY TIME FROM 6:30 TO 8 P.M., DEPENDING ON HOW MUCH WORK THERE IS TO DO EACH DAY.

This country supper, also known as "high tea," has long been considered the working man's dinner, a meal that would be eaten at home after a hard day at work, served in the evening, and washed down with mugs of strong black tea. It is also a time to chat about the events of the day and hash out the farm plan for tomorrow.

Since the main meal of the day on the farm is midday dinner (known elsewhere as lunch) and usually consists of a large, hot meal, the country supper is a tidy meal. I love it because you don't leave the table with a heavy feeling and bedtime is only a few hours away.

Supper always feels like a bit of a picnic to me, and I've loved learning my mother-in-law's simple, traditional recipes for this meal while adding in some classic American ingredients.

IRISH COUNTRY SALAD

I'LL NEVER FORGET the first time I visited the farm and met my future Irish family. After all the grand introductions and formal-ish conversation in the sitting room, I was politely asked if I would like a bite to eat, and despite the fact that I was completely famished, I eloquently replied, "Sure, just a little something would be nice, thank you."

We made our way to the kitchen where Peggy presented me with a comforting country plate, which traditionally includes mashed potato salad, cole slaw, slices of boiled ham, fresh tomato slices, and a slice of warm brown soda bread with farmhouse butter. Peggy and I nibbled away at this while swapping sentimental stories and having a good laugh or two. Afterward, we shared a warm pot of tea before I had to retire early. Jet lag had prevailed.

MASHED POTATO SALAD

I LOVE THIS POTATO SALAD, which is essentially a cold champ salad—very refreshing.

Serves 4

6 medium white potatoes, peeled and quartered

1 cup (240 g) mayonnaise

1 cup (240 g) sour cream

1 tablespoon finely chopped green onion

1 tablespoon finely chopped fresh chives

1 teaspoon finely chopped flat-leaf parsley

Salt and pepper, to taste

1. Place the potatoes in a large pot of cold water and bring to a boil for 20 minutes, or until tender. Drain and let sit for 5 to 10 minutes to cool. Transfer the potatoes to a large bowl, and add the mayonnaise, sour cream, green onion, chives, parsley, salt, and pepper. Lightly mash all ingredients together.

COUNTRY COLE SLAW

THIS IS A SIMPLE SLAW that can be served on the country plate but is also good as a sandwich filling.

Serves 4

1 large carrot

¼ head white cabbage

2 tablespoons mayonnaise

2 tablespoons plain yogurt
(see Farmhouse Yogurt, page 29)

1 tablespoon apple cider vinegar

Cracked black pepper, to taste

1. Peel and grate the carrot on a box grater. Using a sharp knife, remove the core from the cabbage; peel off the outer, softer leaves. Finely slice the cabbage into thin lengths.

2. In a large serving bowl, whisk together the mayonnaise, yogurt, apple cider vinegar, and black pepper into a thin dressing.

3. To serve, add the shredded cabbage and grated carrot to the serving bowl, and mix until loosely coated with the dressing.

Scullery NOTES | If you're preparing the ingredients ahead for mixing at a later time, place the grated carrot and cabbage into a ziplock freezer bag, seal, and put the bag in the bottom crisper drawer of your fridge.

BREAD, CHEESE, *and* CHIVE PUDDING

THIS PUDDING WAS CREATED on a rainy evening in June when we had visitors arrive out of the blue. I had just come in from helping in the milking parlor and had planned on putting together simple grilled cheese sandwiches and salad for tea when the doorbell rang. Friends who had been touring the countryside said they stumbled upon our place and thought it would be nice to pop in and say hello.

Naturally, I invited them in and offered up supper and a warm cup of tea. It is not unusual to have "callers" come by unnannounced; in fact, it is common to call at a neighbor or friend's house for a cup of tea and to catch up on gossip and discuss the weather. (Something that took a while for me to get used to!)

Having already started assembling the cheese sandwiches, I decided on the fly to serve something more substantial. I slid the sandwiches into a pie plate, poured beaten eggs over the top, and slipped it into a hot oven while we sipped our second pot of tea. The resulting pudding was substantial, like a big custardy dish of *croque-monsieur,* minus the ham.

Serves 2

4 slices crusty white bread

1 cup (115 g) grated sharp cheddar cheese

4 eggs, beaten

½ cup (125 ml) milk

Salt and pepper, to taste

½ cup (50 g) grated Parmesan cheese

2 tablespoons freshly chopped chives

1. Preheat the oven to 350°F (175°C). Lightly grease a 9-by-13-inch baking dish or pie pan.
2. Make two sandwiches by placing cheddar cheese between 2 bread slices and pressing together. Cut each sandwich in half and place in the baking dish.
3. Mix together the eggs, milk, salt, and pepper and ¼ cup of the grated Parmesan; pour the mixture over the sandwiches. Sprinkle with the remaining grated cheese and chives. (NOTE: Sandwiches do not need to be totally covered in egg mixture, but the egg should be absorbed with only a little left in the bottom of the dish.)
4. Bake for 20 to 25 minutes, or until golden brown, checking frequently to prevent burning.

Scullery NOTES | Cut the sandwiches into triangles for a more traditional-looking bread pudding. Serve with a fresh, crisp garden salad.

IRISH FARMER CHEESE SOUFFLÉ

HAVE NO FEAR, THIS SOUFFLÉ has a few steps but is technically quite easy. The cream has been infused with herbs and spices, so the recipe has a particularly memorable, savory boost of flavor.

Makes eight 6-ounce (177-ml) ramekins or one 2-quart (17.75-liter) soufflé

5 tablespoons butter, plus extra for greasing the ramekins

1 cup (240 ml) heavy cream

1 cup (240 ml) milk

1 small carrot, peeled and diced

1 small onion, quartered

4 to 5 black peppercorns

1 lemon thyme sprig with flowers, if in season, a few flat-leaf parsley stalks, and 1 bay leaf

½ cup (60 g) all-purpose flour

5 large organic eggs, separated

1 cup (110 g) farmer cheese, crumbled

¾ cup (75 g) Gruyère cheese, finely grated

½ cup (50 g) mature Parmesan or Coolea cheese, finely grated

Generous pinch of salt, cayenne, freshly ground black pepper, and nutmeg

2 teaspoons fresh lemon thyme leaves and flowers, for garnish

1. Preheat the oven to 450°F (230°C). Brush the bottom and sides of six 3-inch-deep ramekins (or six soup bowls) with melted butter; set aside.
2. Pour the cream and milk into a saucepan, add the carrot, onion, peppercorns, and fresh herbs. Bring slowly to a boil over low heat, then remove from the heat and set aside to infuse for 10 minutes. Strain, discarding the flavorings.
3. Melt the butter, stir in the flour, and cook for 1 or 2 minutes. Whisk in the strained cream and milk, bring to a boil, and whisk until the sauce thickens. Remove from the heat and cool slightly. Add the egg yolks, farmer cheese, Gruyère cheese, and most of the Parmesan or Coolea cheese (reserving some for the topping). Season with salt, peppers, and nutmeg. Taste and correct the seasoning if needed.
4. Whisk the egg whites until stiff peaks form, and fold them gently into the mixture to make a loose consistency. Spoon into the prepared dishes, scatter the lemon thyme leaves on top, and sprinkle with the reserved Parmesan or Coolea cheese.
5. Bake for 12 to 15 minutes (9 to 11 minutes for the individual soufflés), or until the sides and top are nicely puffed up and golden—the center should still be creamy. Garnish with lemon thyme leaves and flowers, and serve immediately.

Scullery **NOTES** This soufflé is excellent served alongside a crispy salad of fresh baby kale and herbs. If you can't find lemon thyme, fresh oregano, sage, or caraway is lovely as well.

DUCK EGG MAYONNAISE

"EGG MAYONNAISE" is a thing here in Ireland, but not the thing you think it is. It's well known in America, but under a different name, like chips versus crisps or chips versus French fries.

Egg mayonnaise is the Irish version of deconstructed egg salad. The eggs are boiled and sliced in half. Homemade mayonnaise is drizzled over the eggs, and they are served on a bed of mixed greens. It's just delicious, and to my eye, much more attractive than egg salad.

I tend to use duck eggs in this dish for their richness and large size, but large hen eggs work just as well.

Serves 6

6 duck eggs

4 tablespoons mayonnaise

1 teaspoon lemon juice

½ teaspoon minced garlic

Freshly ground pepper

2 cups (142 g) mixed greens

Smoked paprika for garnish

1. Place the eggs in a pan of cold water. Bring to a boil for 7 minutes, then remove from the pan and allow to cool.
2. Make the dressing by whisking together the mayonnaise, lemon juice, garlic, and pepper in a small mixing bowl.
3. Divide the mixed greens between six salad plates.
4. Peel the eggs carefully, slice each from top to bottom, and place the halves on the mixed greens. Liberally drizzle the mayonnaise dressing over the eggs. Sprinkle with the smoked paprika.
5. Serve with brown bread and tea.

Scullery **NOTES** | If the peel is not coming away from the boiled eggs easily, try refrigerating them (dry) for 10 to 15 minutes. This makes the shell easier to separate from the egg.

IRISH RAREBIT

FOR MY IRISH VERSION OF WELSH RAREBIT (broiled ham and cheese on toast), I prefer
Limerick ham. Traditionally, Limerick ham is smoked over juniper branches and prepared by soaking it
in cold water overnight, then boiling it in cider, and roasting it on a very high heat to crisp the fat. This
preparation renders an exquisite and unique flavor, and it is well worth seeking out if you can. If not, any
good-quality roasted or boiled ham will do.

These petite toasts are deceptively rich and filling, yet they are easy to prepare—perfect after a long
day of minding heifers and calves.

Makes 8 thick slices

Eight ½-inch-thick slices crusty bread

1 tablespoon unsalted butter

1 tablespoon all-purpose flour

¼ cup (60 ml) whole milk

1½ tablespoons Irish ale (8 Degrees Brewing or Dungarvan Brewing Company are terrific, if available)

1 cup (100 g) grated Wexford white cheddar (or other sharp cheddar)

Zest and juice of 1 lemon

½ tablespoon whole-grain mustard

1 medium free-range egg, beaten

8 slices Limerick ham

Freshly ground black pepper, to taste

1. Toast the bread until lightly golden on both sides; set aside.
2. Melt the butter in a saucepan over low heat. Add the flour and stir briskly for 1 minute. Remove the pan from the heat, and gradually add the milk, stirring constantly, until smooth and creamy. Return to the heat, bring back to a boil, then stir in the ale, cheese, lemon zest and juice, and mustard. Remove from the heat and stir in the egg.
3. Lay a slice of ham on each bread slice, then top with a spoonful of the cheese mixture. Broil for 3 to 4 minutes, or until melted and golden.
4. Season with freshly ground black pepper.

Scullery
NOTES

Serve the rarebit with a green salad and a glass of cider.

POTTED SMOKED TROUT

MORE OFTEN THAN NOT, if we are all working late in the farmyard, I will put together a peasant-style picnic spread for supper and call it a night. These suppers may comprise a loaf of soda bread; fresh butter; an array of cheeses; garden-fresh greens; and a can of salmon or, if we are lucky, potted smoked trout.

We like Goatsbridge Smoked Trout from Thomastown, County Kilkenny. Our friends Mag and Ger Kirwan have been farming rainbow trout for three generations at Goatsbridge, fished from the clear fast waters of the little Arrigle River. If you can't access Goatsbridge, any smoked trout will do in this scrumptious recipe.

Makes two 10-oz (280-ml) ramekins

1 cup (250 g) salted butter	Pinch of mace
2 to 3 shallots, diced	2 teaspoons lemon zest
1 small garlic clove (optional)	18 oz (500 g) hot-smoked trout
⅛ teaspoon horseradish	Small bunch of chives, finely chopped

1. In a small saucepan, melt the butter over medium heat, skimming off white solids to clarify. Add the shallots and garlic (if using), and cook for 2 to 3 minutes, until the shallots are soft. Add the horseradish, mace, and lemon zest; cook for another minute. Remove from the heat and let cool.
2. Portion the trout into two individual ramekins, and sprinkle lightly with the chives. Spoon the butter mixture over each ramekin, coating the trout completely. Cover with plastic wrap, and chill in the fridge for 24 hours before serving.
3. Serve at room temperature with crispy baguette toasts.

Scullery **NOTES** | Make it a picnic by adding a selection of serve-yourself salads and sliced cheeses to complement the potted trout.

POTATO *and* SPRING LEEK
with ADOBO SOUP

LONG AGO THE IRISH CLEVERLY FIGURED OUT that if you simply sauté any vegetable, boil it in a nice stock, purée, and add a touch of cream, you'll always have a velvety soup masterpiece. While I will always love a good matzo ball soup from a New York deli, a crock of spicy Cincinnati-style chili, or my grandmother's homemade chicken noodle soup, Irish soups and chowders have completely won me over.

Potato and leek soup is a classic Irish combination, and I especially love it prepared with freshly foraged wild spring leeks from the woods and infused with chipotle for a smoky kick.

Serves 6

1 tablespoon olive oil

1 brown-skinned onion, sliced

8 oz (225 g) potatoes, diced

2 medium leeks, thinly sliced

1 chipotle pepper in adobo sauce, finely chopped

4 cups (1.5 liters) vegetable or chicken stock

Salt and freshly ground black pepper, to taste

2/3 cup (150 ml) heavy cream or crème fraîche

1. Heat the oil in a large saucepan. Add the onion, potatoes, leeks, and chipotle pepper. Cook for 3 to 4 minutes, until the vegetables start to soften. Add the vegetable stock and bring to a boil. Season well with salt and pepper, and simmer until the vegetables are tender.

2. Pulse with a hand blender or in a blender until smooth. Reheat in a clean pan, stir in the cream, and heat through.

3. Pour into bowls, and serve with Best Brown Bread (see page 41).

Scullery **NOTES** | Garnish the soup with wild spring leek flowers, chili pepper–infused oil, and cracked black pepper.

TARTINE *of* PRAWN

with Marie-Rose Sauce

WHEN I MOVED TO IRELAND, my shrimp days appeared to be over. Here, prawns reign supreme, and you'll even find the essence of prawn in potato chips. An open-faced sandwich of prawns with a creamy cocktail sauce on brown bread is commonly found on pub menus across the countryside. Recreating it for supper at home is easy and delicious.

I like to serve this sandwich with a liberal smear of sauce on both slices of bread with prawns placed on top, but you can mix the prawns with the sauce and make a salad spread, if you prefer.

Serves 2

4 tablespoons mayonnaise

4 tablespoons crème fraîche

1½ tablespoons ketchup

Dash of Tabasco sauce

Dash of Worcestershire sauce

1 tablespoon lemon juice

2 slices Best Brown Bread (see page 41)

6 large Atlantic prawns, cooked and peeled

Handful of herbs or wild arugula,
    for garnish

1. In a medium mixing bowl, whisk together the mayonaisse, crème fraîche, ketchup, Tabasco and Worcestershire sauces, and lemon juice until well combined. Taste and add more Tabasco sauce, Worcestershire sauce, or lemon juice as necessary.
2. Lay the slices of bread on plates. Smear a liberal amount of sauce on each slice. Place 3 prawns on each slice. Garnish with herbs or arugula.

Scullery
NOTES | Leftover Marie-Rose sauce can be stored in the fridge for up to two weeks.

DOWN *and* DURTY BAKED EGGS

THERE IS A FAMOUS IRISH PUB and restaurant called Durty Nelly's in nearby Bunratty, County Clare. If we have guests who want to visit Bunratty Castle, famous for its folk park and medieval music banquets, we will usually stop at Durty Nelly's for a pint during the visit.

Legend has it that in the misty history of the Bunratty countryside, there lived a buxom lady known as Durty Nelly. Times were hard in Ireland, but Durty Nelly was wily and always found a way to make ends meet. She was the keeper of the toll bridge over the River Owengarney, which flowed outside her window on its way to join the Shannon. Everyone who sought to cross the bridge would have to pay their dues to Nelly; those who could not pay in cash, paid in kind with the presentation of a chicken, a few eggs, a piece of home-cured bacon, or even (so it's said) a bit of comfort for the lady herself.

Durty Nelly was also renowned for her *shebeen*, a special corner of the house overlooking the river where she kept a jar of whiskey on hand to warm the bellies of exhausted journeymen. She went on to invent a special moonshine that was said to have healing properties, and people came from far and wide to partake in the elixir.

On a whim, I named these eggs, which are baked in chili sauce and Ballymaloe tomato relish, after Durty Nelly's sweet and spicy enterprising spirit.

Serves 4

1 tablespoon olive oil

1 medium red onion, chopped

1 garlic clove, sliced

1 red chili pepper, finely chopped

One 14-oz (400-g) can chopped tomatoes

½ cup Ballymaloe Country Relish
  (see the Resources section)
  or a tomato chutney of your choice

2 tablespoons tomato chili jam

4 eggs

1. Preheat the oven to 400°F (200°C).
2. Heat the oil in a cast-iron or ovenproof pan. Add the onion, garlic, and chili pepper, and cook for 5 minutes, until softened. Stir in the tomatoes, relish, and jam; simmer for 8 to 10 minutes, until thick.
3. Using the back of a large spoon, make 4 wells in the sauce, then crack an egg into each one. Place in the oven for 15 minutes, or until the eggs are baked to your liking.
4. Remove from the oven, sprinkle with fresh herbs, and serve with crusty bread.

Scullery
NOTES | This spicy sauce can be frozen for one month.

BANGERS *and* MASH

MASHED POTATOES WITH MEATY SAUSAGES and a rich mushroom and onion gravy is the ultimate comfort food, especially after spending several consecutive days on the farm while winter's gale winds are blowing.

The word *banger* comes from the fact that sausages, particularly the kind made during World War II under rationing, were made with water, so they were more likely to explode under high heat if not cooked carefully.

They say that modern sausages do not have this attribute, but I have had some bangers make some pretty big pops on my stovetop over the years.

Serves 4

Olive oil, for cooking

1 lb (450 g) Irish sausages (bratwurst is a good substitute)

FOR THE MASH

3 potatoes, peeled and cut into chunks

Salt and pepper, to taste

4 scallions, finely chopped

2 tablespoons unsalted butter

¼ cup (60 ml) buttermilk

2 tablespoons whole milk

FOR THE GRAVY

1 tablespoon unsalted butter

1 small onion, sliced

2 cups (200 g) sliced fresh mushrooms

½ cup (118 ml) Irish stout

2 cups (412 ml) canned beef broth

1 tablespoon Worcestershire sauce

1½ teaspoons cornstarch

¼ cup (60 ml) water

1. Heat the olive oil in a large skillet over medium heat and add the sausages. Slowly cook each side until brown and crisp and the center is no longer pink. Set aside.
2. **MAKE THE MASH:** Place the potatoes in a medium saucepan and cover with enough water to cover them. Cook over medium-high to high heat. When the water comes to a boil, season with salt. Cook until the potatoes are fork-tender, about 25 to 30 minutes.
3. Drain the potatoes, and add the scallions, butter, buttermilk, milk, and salt and pepper. Mash to the desired consistency. Check the seasoning, and add more salt and pepper as needed.
4. **MAKE THE GRAVY:** Melt the butter in a large skillet over medium-high heat. Add the onion and mushrooms and cook until softened, about 10 minutes. Pour in the Irish stout, scrape the bottom of the pan, and let reduce, about 1 minute. Add the beef broth and Worstershire sauce.

219

5. In a separate bowl, mix the cornstarch and water to form a roux; add to the skillet. Cook over medium-high heat until the gravy has reduced to the desired thickness.

6. To serve, put the mashed potatoes on a plate, place the bangers on top of the mash, and pour the gravy over the top.

Scullery
NOTES

Garnish this dish with chopped green onions. You can also add chopped, blanched kale, chard, or collard greens to the mash, and get your greens that way.

CHAPTER 9

Sunday Lunch

MY FIRST SUNDAY ROAST AT THE FARM WAS AN ALL-AFTERNOON EVENT. PEGGY MADE A BEAUTIFUL ROAST GOOSE WITH ALL THE TRIMMINGS, AND WE FINISHED THE MEAL WITH FOUR DIFFERENT DESSERTS. IT WAS CASUAL YET DECADENT, A BALANCE I STILL ASPIRE TO, ALTHOUGH I THINK IT IS A TRAIT THAT DEVELOPS NATURALLY OVER TIME WHEN YOU HAVE PEGGY'S COMBINATION OF A GENEROUS HEART AND THE CARE THAT COMES AFTER YEARS OF COOKING FOR FAMILY AND APPRENTICES EVERY DAY.

The traditional family Sunday roast is a special ritual on the farm. It is served on Sunday afternoon and usually consists of roasted meat and roasted or mashed potatoes with accompaniments such as pudding (or popovers), stuffing, vegetables, and gravy. At its heart, this meal is basically a less grand version of a traditional holiday dinner, such as for Thanksgiving or St. Patrick's Day.

The purpose of Sunday lunch is to savor and retreat; we rest from farmwork to spend quality time together as a family. It is important to reflect and relax, even though this time must be sandwiched between milking the cows. It is often too easy to simply carry on working—even more of a reason I encourage our Sunday lunch tradition.

Since each of our individual family units lives in a separate home on the farm, we take turns hosting the Sunday lunch. Sometimes, we will treat ourselves and go out for the meal as a family; luckily, many restaurants in Ireland have a proper roast on the menu for Sunday lunch as well.

Over the years, I have put together my own Sunday lunch menus: some are traditional, and some have more of an obvious American twist. Here are complete menus for five of our favorites.

MY MOTHER-IN-LAW GIFTED ME WITH AN OLD Irish cookery schoolbook from the 1950s with various notes on how to plan and prepare menus. It's called *All in the Cooking,* and fortunately it's just been brought back into print. I love to refer to it when planning a special meal or even a Sunday roast if it's for a larger group. I find the following notes from *All in the Cooking* very helpful.

MENU PLANNING NOTES

In compiling a menu, there are a few points which must be remembered, and these apply whether the meal is to be elaborate or simple.

1. The number of people to be catered for and the type of meal required.
2. Food value of the meal should be carefully balanced to supply individual needs.
3. Select dishes the raw materials of which are in season—they are then cheaper and have a better flavor.
4. Provide mainly hot dishes during the cold weather and a selection of cold dishes during hot weather.
5. Arrange the dishes so that each succeeding dish is distinct in mode of cooking, flavor, appearance and garnish.
6. Consider the help available, and include some dishes that can be prepared beforehand if necessary.

QUANTITIES TO ALLOW PER HEAD:

Meat:	With bone, 6–8 oz per person
	Without bone, 4 oz per person
	Steak, 6–8 oz per person
	Cutlets, 2 cutlets per person
	Chicken: 1 for 4–5 persons
Potatoes:	6–8 oz per person
Vegetables:	4 oz per person
Sauce:	4–5 helpings from ½ pint
Puddings:	Milk, ¼ pint per person
	Steamed, 1 oz per person

CARVING GUIDE:

1. A general knowledge of the anatomy of the joint is necessary and the position of the various cuts.
2. Before cooking, do as much jointing as possible without spoiling the appearance of the meat.
3. Before serving, all skewers and pieces of twine, etc., must be removed.
4. The dish on which the joint is served should be large enough to do the carving with ease, and to hold a certain amount of the slices as well.
5. If the carving is to be done at the table, the dish must be placed in the right position, and the carver's chair must be high enough to facilitate doing the work with ease.
6. All meat, except saddle of mutton, must be cut across the grain.
7. The carving must be neat, and the slices straight and uniform, not jagged. Bad carving is most wasteful.
8. In distributing the slices, the different cuts must be shared out fairly.

A WILD SPRING LAMB FEAST

Wildflower and Herb Rubbed Roasted Leg of Lamb
Hasselback Rosemary Potatoes
Braised Garden Greens
Lemon Thyme Gravy
Mint Sauce

WILDFLOWER *and* HERB RUBBED
ROASTED LEG *of* LAMB

I LOVE TO INCORPORATE as many edible wild herbs and flowers into dishes as I possibly can. They taste delicious, look pretty, and often have healing attributes as well. This leg of lamb was inspired by a visit to the west of Ireland, where sheep graze on hills of heather, grass, and nettles. Adding heather to the herb rub gives the skin a distinctly sweet flavor when roasted. Remember to use gardening gloves when handling nettles, as they can sting!

Serves 6

One 5- to 7-lb leg of lamb, Frenched with inner bone removed by butcher for easier carving

FOR THE HERB RUB

½ cup (10 g) chopped fresh curry leaves, plus more for garnish

¼ cup (5 g) finely chopped thyme

½ cup (10 g) finely chopped rosemary

¼ cup (5 g) freshly chopped mint leaves

¼ cup (5 g) heather flowers, crushed

¼ cup (5 g) young stinging nettle leaves, finely chopped

¼ cup (5 g) minced fresh garlic

2 tablespoons lemon zest

2 tablespoons Irish Atlantic sea salt

1 long stem rosemary

1. Pulse the herbs, heather flowers, nettle leaves, garlic, lemon zest, and salt in a food processor until they form a paste.
2. Remove the butcher's string from the lamb and slash the top-side fat in criss-cross fashion. Slather the top of the lamb with the wildflower and herb paste, being sure to rub it into the slash marks. Place the rosemary stem on top and retie the butcher's string. Wrap in plastic wrap and place in the refrigerator overnight.
3. Take the lamb out of the refrigerator an hour before roasting time, and allow it to sit at room temperature.
4. Preheat the oven to 350°F (175°C).
5. Cover the lamb with foil and place it on a wire rack inside a large roasting pan. Pour 1 cup of water into the roasting pan and place it in the oven. Roast for 1 hour, then remove the foil. The internal temperature should be at least 125°F (51°C). Cook for 1 more hour for a medium-rare roast (135°F [57°C]), and 30 more minutes for well done (155°F [68°C]). Baste with juices regularly throughout roasting time.
6. Remove from the oven and transfer the lamb to a plate. Let it rest while you make gravy with the reserving drippings.

Scullery **NOTES** | You can substitute arugula flowers, nasturium, or chive blossoms for the heather in this recipe.

HASSELBACK ROSEMARY POTATOES

I WAS INTRODUCED TO Hasselback spuds by my friend and Irish cookbook author Donal Skehan. They originally hail from Sweden but can be found on many Irish menus. Donal says the trick to slicing them thin without going all the way through is to place each small potato in the dip of a wooden spoon while slicing. The knife hits the spoon before it splits the potato.

Serves 4 to 6

6 pounds (3 kg) (about 18) medium, oval-shaped potatoes

3 tablespoons butter

5 tablespoons olive oil

Sea salt, to taste

1. Preheat the oven to 425°F (220°C).
2. Put each potato, in turn, in the bowl of a wooden spoon, and cut across at about ⅛-inch (3-mm) intervals. Put the baking pan on the stove with the butter and oil, and heat until sizzling. Roll the potatoes in the pan so they are completely covered with butter and oil. Sprinkle each potato with salt. Place in the oven and cook for about 70 minutes, until fork-tender.
3. Remove from the oven, transfer the potatoes to a warmed plate, and serve with the roast lamb.

BRAISED GARDEN GREENS

EACH SPRING I plant several varieties of greens. They are easy to grow and yield great quantities. Depending on the season, spinach, kale, mustard and collard greens, chard, beet, and radish greens are all fantastic for this simple yet flavor- and nutrient-packed recipe.

Serves 4

4 tablespoons olive oil

About 12 cups (900 g) chopped and well-packed mixed greens, including kale, collard, mustard, or greens of your choice

3 cloves garlic, minced

⅛ teaspoon sea salt

¼ teaspoon red pepper flakes

1. Heat the oil in a large skillet over medium-high heat. Add the greens, stirring to coat, and cook until they are barely wilted. Add the garlic, salt, and red pepper flakes; stir to combine. When the greens are tender, remove from the pan with a slotted spoon, and serve.

Scullery NOTES | A great trick when harvesting fresh garden greens is to fill the kitchen sink with water and a few capfuls of vinegar; add the greens to loosen any insects or debris. Rinse well before preparing.

LEMON THYME GRAVY

THIS GRAVY WAS CREATED when I wandered out to the garden to find that only lemon thyme was available; I had already snipped all of the regular thyme, and there wasn't any new growth. The lemon brightens up the flavor in a smooth, subtle way. If you don't have access to lemon thyme, you can use any kind of thyme in this recipe.

Makes 3 cups (720 ml)

---

4 tablespoons unsalted butter

4 tablespoons all-purpose flour

1 tablespoon fresh lemon thyme, finely chopped

1 cup (235 ml) reserved pan juices from cooked lamb

2 cups (470 ml) reduced-sodium lamb or vegetable broth

Sea salt and freshly ground pepper, to taste

---

1. Melt the butter in a skillet over medium-high heat until sizzling hot. Slowly stir in the flour; reduce heat to medium. Cook about 2 minutes, stirring constantly, until the flour is light brown. Stir in the lemon thyme. Slowly whisk in the pan juices and broth; season with salt and pepper. Cook for 2 to 3 minutes, stirring constantly, until the liquid returns to a boil and begins to thicken.
2. Serve hot.

MINT SAUCE

I HAVE A FOREST OF MINT growing in the garden at all times, so making mint sauce is a sure way to make the most of the harvest. Find fresh mint from the grocer or the farmers' market or, even better, grow your own for this sauce.

Makes ½ cup (165 g)

---

1 cup (25 g) fresh mint leaves, finely chopped

Pinch of salt

1 level tablespoon superfine sugar

4 tablespoons boiling water

4 tablespoons sherry vinegar

---

1. Place the mint leaves in a bowl and sprinkle with salt. Add the sugar, pour the boiling water over the leaves, stir, and leave to cool.
2. Stir in the vinegar and taste. Add more water or vinegar, and adjust the seasoning as needed.
3. Serve with the lamb roast.

Scullery NOTES | Garden Apple Mint Jelly (see page 101) is also wonderful with this roast.

A PROPER, LINGERING, ROAST BEEF LUNCH

Standing Rib Roast of Beef

Pudding Popovers

Roughed-Up Roasties

Carrot, Turnip, and Cumin Purée

Red Wine Beef au Jus

Garden Horseradish Aioli

STANDING RIB ROAST *of* BEEF

ROAST BEEF IS THE KING of Sunday lunches. The rich, layered flavor of this cut of beef is both satisfying and extravagant. I relish each bite and cherish the leftovers.

We are predominantly a dairy farm, but we also raise beef cattle for ourselves, so we know where the meat comes from and how it has been raised and fed, which makes this meal even more special. The honey also comes from the farm and adds an exquisite woodland flavor to the beef. Always use top-quality beef and honey for this recipe.

Serves 4 to 6

One 5-lb (2.5-kg) rib roast of beef, bone-in

½ bunch fresh rosemary (about 5 sprigs)

1 heaping teaspoon sea salt, plus more to taste

1 heaping teaspoon white or black peppercorns

¼ cup (60 ml) olive oil

3½ tablespoons unsalted butter, room temperature

2 tablespoons honey

1. Take the beef out of the fridge about 30 minutes before you cook it so it is room temperature before roasting.
2. Preheat the oven to 475°F (246°C), and put your largest, sturdiest roasting pan in to heat.
3. With a mortar and pestle, grind the leaves from 2 of the rosemary sprigs into a paste with the salt and peppercorns. Add 1 tablespoon olive oil, then rub this paste all over the beef.
4. Place the beef in the hot roasting pan, fatty side up, and roast, uncovered, for 50 minutes for rare to medium rare (internal temperature 130°F [54°C]), 10 minutes more for medium (150°F [65°C]).
5. Remove from the oven, but leave the oven on. Carefully transfer the roast to a plate. Dot half the butter on top of the meat, then use the remaining rosemary sprigs to brush the honey all over the meat. Cover with a double layer of foil and a tea towel, and let it rest for 30 minutes. Set the rosemary sprigs aside but do not discard them.
6. When you are ready to carve the beef, remove the towel and foil. Carve, and pour any juices that collect on the plate into a small, heatproof dish; place the dish in the oven to warm. Use the rosemary sprig brushes you saved to paint the various cuts of meat with the flavorful juices left on the plate.
7. Serve the roast beef with a hearty dollop of creamy Garden Horseradish Aioli (see page 235).

PUDDING POPOVERS

WHILE YORKSHIRE PUDDINGS, or "pudding popovers" as I like to call them, are an exquisite accompaniment to a proper Sunday roast beef dinner, they are even more revelatory at 3 A.M. after pulling a calf from a struggling maiden heifer (part and parcel to Irish dairy farming life).

Makes 12 popovers

4 large eggs

1½ cups (350 ml) whole milk

½ teaspoon coarse salt

1¼ cups (156 g) all-purpose flour

4 tablespoons vegetable oil
  (or beef drippings)

2 tablespoons cold water

1. Pour the eggs and milk into a large mixing bowl, and add the salt. Whisk thoroughly with an electric hand beater or hand whisk. Let stand for 10 minutes.
2. Gradually sift the flour into the milk mixture, and whisk again to create a lump-free batter resembling thick cream. If there are still lumps, pass the batter through a fine sieve. Let the batter rest at room temperature for a minimum of 30 minutes.

3. When you are ready to bake the popovers, heat the oven to the highest temperature possible, but do not exceed 450°F (230°C) or the fat may burn.

4. Place ½ teaspoon of the vegetable oil in each section of a 12-cup muffin pan, and heat in the oven until the fat is smoking.

5. Add the cold water to the batter and whisk well. Fill each section of the pan one-third of the way with batter, and return the pan quickly to the oven.

6. Bake until the popovers have risen and are golden brown, approximately 20 minutes. Do not open the oven while they are baking, or they could fall.

7. Remove from the oven, pop the puddings out of the pan, and repeat the baking process until all of the batter is used up.

8. Serve with beef or pot roast. The popovers keep in an airtight container in the fridge for one week and frozen for one month.

ROUGHED-UP ROASTIES

THESE ROASTED POTATOES are crunchy on the outside and supersoft and floury on the inside, and they can be found on dinner tables across Ireland. The first time I bit into a goose-fat-roasted spud that I had grown in our own garden, I nearly cried tears of joy. Be sure and use a floury potato and goose, duck, or beef drippings for the authentic Irish experience.

Serves 4 to 6

4½ lb (2 kg) large floury potatoes (such as russet or Golden Wonder), peeled and quartered

2 tablespoons semolina

½ cup (75 ml) olive oil (or beef, goose, or duck fat drippings)

Fresh rosemary sprigs, to garnish

1. Drop the potatoes into a large pan of boiling salted water, and cook for 6 minutes. Drain the potatoes, return them to the pan, and sprinkle with the semolina. Shake the potatoes in the dry saucepan with the lid on to rough up the edges so they will crisp up well in the oven.

2. Preheat the oven to 400°F (200°C). Heat the oil in a roasting pan on the stovetop. Toss the potatoes in the fat to coat well. Place the pan in the oven and bake for 50 minutes or until golden brown, basting with the hot oil 2 to 3 times.

3. Remove the potatoes from the oven, garnish with rosemary sprigs, and serve.

CARROT, TURNIP, *and* CUMIN PURÉE

ANOTHER POPULAR SIDE DISH for the Irish Sunday lunch is a blended root mash. Usually prepared with carrot, potato, and either rutabaga or turnip, this creamy mix is a winner with children and grown-ups alike.

Serves 6

2 lb (1 kg) carrots, peeled and sliced

2 lb (1 kg) turnips (or rutabagas),
  peeled and sliced

½ cup (113 g) butter

Salt and pepper, to taste

2 teaspoons cumin

2 tablespoons brown sugar

½ cup (120 ml) half-and-half

Mint leaves, for garnish

1. Place the carrots and turnips in a pan of cold salted water, and bring to a boil. Cook until soft, then drain the water from the pan. Using an electric mixer or a potato masher, mash vegetables with the butter, salt, pepper, cumin, brown sugar, and half-and-half.
2. Garnish with mint leaves, and serve.

Scullery
NOTES | Do not peel the turnip with a vegetable peeler;
it is very easy to get cut doing this, speaking from experience.

RED WINE BEEF JUS

THIS SIMPLE YET INTENSELY FLAVORFUL JUS, or juice from the beef, is excellent on the day of roasting and, if there are any leftovers, makes a sensational dipping sauce for hot beef sandwiches the next day.

Makes 4 cups (960 ml)

2 cups (480 ml) red wine

4 cups (960 ml) beef stock

1 tablespoon chopped fresh thyme leaves

Salt and pepper, to taste

1. Place the roasting pan on top of the stove over two burners set on high heat. Add the wine to the beef roast drippings in the pan, and cook over high heat until reduced, scraping the bottom of the pan with a wooden spoon to deglaze. Add the stock, and cook until the liquid is reduced by half. Whisk in the thyme, and season with salt and pepper.
2. To serve, ladle over carved roast beef slices. The jus can be stored in the refrigerator for up to a week.

GARDEN HORSERADISH AIOLI

WE ALWAYS SEEM TO HAVE heaps of horseradish in our garden, which means plenty of prepared horseradish in the larder. This aioli is richer than the prepared sauce, but that makes it even more special.

Serves 4 to 6

1 egg yolk

1 teaspoon Dijon mustard

½ teaspoon salt, plus more to taste

1 teaspoon garlic purée

½ cup (118 ml) olive oil

½ cup (118 ml) canola oil

2 tablespoons lemon juice

2 tablespoons freshly grated horseradish

Freshly ground black pepper, to taste

1. In a medium mixing bowl, whisk together the egg yolk, mustard, ½ teaspoon salt, and garlic purée. Slowly drizzle in the oils, whisking constantly until the aioli is the consistency of mayonnaise. Stir in the lemon juice and horseradish, and season with salt and pepper to taste.
2. Serve with roast beef. Store in an airtight container for up to a week in the refrigerator.

OUR MAGNIFICENT ODE *to* 'MERICA MEAL

Buttermilk Fried Chicken

Big Mess o' Greens

Bread Sauce

Southern-Style Baked Beans

Jo Jo's

BUTTERMILK FRIED CHICKEN

IRONICALLY, THIS CLASSIC AMERICAN-STYLE DISH is by far the most requested Sunday lunch on our farm. Everyone enjoys eating foods that are novel to them, and when serving fried chicken to a group of hungry Irish farmers, you can't go wrong.

Since we raise our own free-range poultry, we have the luxury of using farm-raised chicken for this meal. Our fresh buttermilk makes it ridiculously succulent, but buttermilk from the supermarket will work just as well.

While there is a lot of preparation for this recipe, it is the result of passionately testing many varieties of fried chicken formulas shared by friends from the American South. This combination of brining and flavorful coating is the one that finally put a smile on everyone's face. Chickpea flour is the secret to its lovely crunch.

*Serves **6***

FOR THE BRINE

5 lemons, cut in half

20 bay leaves

1 bunch (4 oz) chervil

1 bunch (1 oz) thyme

1 bunch tarragon

½ cup (170 g) honey

1 head garlic, cut in half through the center

¾ cup (140 g) red peppercorns

2 cups (285 g) sea salt

1 gallon spring water

½ gallon (900 ml) buttermilk

FOR THE COATING

5 cups (625 g) all-purpose flour

1 cup (125 g) chickpea flour

¼ cup (50 g) garlic powder

¼ cup (50 g) onion powder

1 tablespoon plus 1 teaspoon smoked paprika

1 tablespoon plus 1 teaspoon cayenne pepper

1 tablespoon plus 1 teaspoon kosher salt

1 teaspoon freshly ground black pepper

Two 3- to 4-lb (1.4–1.8 kg) chickens, cut into pieces

Peanut or canola oil, for deep-frying

1 quart (475 ml) fresh or cultured buttermilk

Kosher salt and freshly ground black pepper, to taste

---

1. **MAKE THE BRINE:** Combine all the brine ingredients in a large pot over high heat, cover, and bring to a boil. Boil for 1 minute, stirring to dissolve the salt. Remove from the heat and let cool completely, then chill before using. The brine can be refrigerated for up to three days.

2. **MAKE THE CHICKEN:** Pour the brine into a container large enough to hold the chicken pieces. Add the chicken, and refrigerate for 10 to 12 hours.

3. Remove the chicken from the brine, and rinse under cold water, removing any herbs or spices that stick to the skin. Pat dry with paper towels.

4. Fill a pot or deep saucepan with at least 2 inches of oil and heat to 320°F (160°C).

5. Combine all the coating ingredients in a large bowl. Pour the buttermilk into another bowl, and season with salt and pepper.

6. Coat the thighs and drumsticks in the flour mixture, dip in the buttermilk, and do a final dredge in the flour mixture. Carefully lower the thighs and drumsticks into the hot oil. Adjust the heat as necessary to return the oil to the proper temperature. Fry for 2 minutes, then carefully move the chicken pieces around in the oil and continue to fry, monitoring the oil temperature, and turning the pieces as necessary for even cooking, until the chicken is a deep golden brown, cooked through, and very crisp (for 11 to 12 minutes). Remove from the frying pan and place on a cooling rack.

7. Turn up the heat, and wait for the oil to reach 340°F (170°C). Meanwhile, coat the chicken breasts and wings. Carefully lower the chicken breasts into the hot oil and fry for 7 minutes, or until golden brown, cooked through, and crisp. Transfer to a cooling rack, sprinkle with salt, and turn skin-side up. Cook the wings for 6 minutes, or until golden brown and cooked through. Transfer the wings to the rack, and turn off the heat.

8. Arrange the chicken on a serving platter and let rest for 7 to 10 minutes after cooking so it has a chance to cool down.

Scullery
NOTES | If the chicken has rested for longer than 10 minutes, put it on a tray in a 400°F (200°C) oven for 1 to 2 minutes to ensure that the crust is crisp and the chicken is hot.

BIG MESS O' GREENS

WE ALWAYS HEAR THAT it's not good to boil vegetables too long because you cook the nutrients out of them, but this side dish uses the greens *and* the liquor left from cooking. Here at the farm, I won't serve a fried chicken Sunday lunch without a big mess of garden-fresh greens.

Serves 4 to 6

FOR THE STOCK

6 slices bacon, chopped

3 cups (750 ml) vegetable stock

1 or 2 smoked ham hocks (or pork neckbones)

1 large onion, chopped

1 or 2 jalapeño peppers, chopped

1 tablespoon cider vinegar

1 teaspoon salt

2 teaspoons sugar

½ teaspoon black pepper

FOR THE GREENS

2 or 3 bunches fresh turnip or collard greens (about 2 lb [1 kg] or 8–10 cups)

3 to 4 mustard or kale leaves

1. In a large stockpot, fry the bacon until the fat is rendered; remove meat. Add the vegetable stock to the bacon grease and bring to a boil. Add the ham hocks, onion, jalapeños, cider vinegar, salt, sugar, and black pepper.
2. Return to a boil and simmer on medium-low heat for 45 minutes. Transfer the ham hocks to a plate, let cool to the touch, and remove any meat from the bones. Add the meat back to the pot, and discard the bones.
3. Clean the greens thoroughly, and drain well. Remove the tougher stalks as needed; tender stalks can be cooked and eaten. Chop the greens coarsely. Add to the pot with the meat and stock; bring to a boil, then reduce the heat to low and simmer for 30 minutes. Turn the heat as low as possible while still maintaining a simmer, and continue cooking, stirring occasionally, for 1 hour. Serve the greens in the juices.

BREAD SAUCE

TRADITIONAL IRISH BREAD SAUCE is an unusual pairing for fried chicken, but my reasoning was that since this sauce goes best with poultry—usually roast turkey or chicken—why wouldn't it work with buttermilk fried chicken? A no-frills sauce made with an unusual combination of onion, cloves, black peppercorns, and milk is a savory and somewhat sweet addition to this Sunday lunch platter.

1 large onion	1 teaspoon sea salt
15 to 18 whole cloves	¾ cup (110 g) freshly white bread crumbs
1 bay leaf	¼ cup (50 g) butter
8 black peppercorns	2 tablespoons heavy cream
2 cups (570 ml) whole milk	Freshly ground black pepper, to taste

1. Cut the onion in half and stick the cloves in its flesh. Place the clove-studded onion, along with the bay leaf, peppercorns, and milk in a saucepan over medium heat. Add the salt, and bring to a boil.
2. Remove the pan from the heat, cover, and leave in a warm place to infuse for 2 hours or more.
3. When you're ready to make the sauce, remove the onion, bay leaf, and peppercorns; set them aside. Stir the bread crumbs into the seasoned milk, then add 2 tablespoons of the butter. Put the saucepan on a very low heat, stirring now and then, until the crumbs have puffed up and thickened the sauce, about 15 minutes.
4. Remove from the heat. Replace the clove-studded onion, bay leaf, and peppercorns in the saucepan, and again leave it in a warm place until the sauce is needed.
5. Just before serving, remove the onion and spices. Reheat over low heat, then beat in the remaining butter and the cream. Taste to check the seasoning, and add salt and pepper as needed. Pour into a warm serving vessel.
6. Serve alongside fried chicken and greens. This sauce will keep for a week in the fridge.

SOUTHERN-STYLE BAKED BEANS

OKAY, THESE MAY NOT BE 100 percent made from scratch, but they are so tangy and delicious and save you about six hours of cooking time. So you'll be delighted you made them!

1 large onion, diced	¼ cup (50 g) light brown sugar
4 cups (440 g) baked beans (homemade or store-bought)	4 tablespoons ketchup
3 tablespoons prepared yellow mustard	1 tablespoon lemon juice
¼ cup (50 ml) maple syrup	½ lb (225 g) smoked bacon strips, cut into ½-inch pieces

1. Preheat the oven to 350°F (175°C).
2. In a Dutch oven, mix together the onion, beans, mustard, maple syrup, light brown sugar, ketchup, and lemon juice. Top with the bacon pieces. Cover and bake for 45 to 60 minutes. Alternatively, you can put it in a slow cooker on low for 4 to 6 hours. Leftovers will keep in an airtight container in the refrigerator for one week.

JO JO'S

JO JO'S ARE MY PERSONAL FAVORITE version of potato wedges. They are dredged in flour and seasonings and baked in a hot oven, then browned under the broiler to finish.

Serves 4 to 6

1 tablespoon butter, melted

1 tablespoon olive oil

3 russet potatoes, peeled and
    cut into 6 to 8 wedges each

1 teaspoon seasoning salt

2 tablespoons all-purpose flour

¼ teaspoon cayenne pepper

1. Preheat the oven to 400°F (200°C).
2. Mix the butter and olive oil in a bowl. Brush the mixture onto the potatoes.
3. Combine the seasoning salt, flour, and cayenne pepper in a resealable plastic bag. Add the potatoes to the bag, and shake to coat.
4. Place the potato wedges on a nonstick baking sheet and bake for 20 minutes. Turn and bake for 10 more minutes. Turn on the broiler and broil for 5 to 7 more minutes, or until browned.
5. Serve hot.

A COMFORTING ROAST PORK
with CIDER GRAVY LUNCH

Roast Loin of Pork with Crackling Crust

Onion, Apple, and Sage Dressing

Cider Gravy

Stewed Apple

Maple Roasted Parsnips

Skin-On Buttermilk Mash

ROAST LOIN *of* PORK *with* CRACKLING CRUST

ROAST PORK is a regularly requested dinner on the farm. My mother-in-law also used to prepare a stuffed pork tenderloin that was always stunning, with just the right blend of savory herbs. I love this roast loin of pork with its crispy crackling served with an apple and sage dressing and robust cider gravy.

Serves 4 to 6

5 lb (2.25 kg) loin of pork, chined (see Scullery Notes)

1 small onion, peeled

Sea salt and freshly milled black pepper, to taste

1. Preheat the oven 475°F (246°C).
2. Score the skin of the pork all over in thin strips, bringing the blade of the knife about halfway through the fat beneath the skin. Place the pork in a roasting pan, skin-side up. Cut the onion in half, and wedge the two pieces slightly under the meat. Sprinkle about 1 tablespoon sea salt evenly over the pork, pressing it in as much as you can.
3. Place the pork on a high shelf in the oven, and roast for 25 minutes. Reduce the heat to 375°F (190°C) and cook for 35 minutes per pound (for example, a 5-lb loin would cook for just under 3 hours). There's

no need to baste the pork as there's enough fat to keep the meat moist, with an internal temperature of at least 160°F (70°C).

4. When the pork is cooked, remove it from the oven and transfer it and the onion to a plate. Let it rest in a warm place for at least 30 minutes before carving.

5. Prepare the Cider Gravy (see page 245).

6. Serve the pork carved into slices, giving everyone some crackling and spoonfuls of Stewed Apple (see page 245).

Scullery **NOTES** | This cut is best bought on the bone, but the butcher must chine it for you—that is, loosen the bone yet leave it attached so it can easily be cut away before carving.

ONION, APPLE, *and* SAGE DRESSING

THIS DRESSING IS A STAPLE in Irish country kitchens, and the leftovers (if there are any!) are excellent in a pork roast sandwich the next day.

Serves 4 *to* 6

2 tablespoons extra virgin olive oil, plus extra for oiling the pan	Salt and freshly ground black pepper, to taste
¼ cup (28 g) butter, softened	2 tablespoons mixed herbs (see page xv)
1 fresh bay leaf	¼ cup parsley leaves, chopped
4 celery stalks, chopped	8 cups (800 g) cubed white or whole-wheat bread
1 medium to large yellow onion, chopped	4 cups (1000 ml) chicken or vegetable stock
3 apples, cored, quartered, and chopped	

1. Preheat the oven to 400°F (200°C).

2. Preheat a large skillet over medium-high heat. Add the olive oil and butter to the skillet. When the butter has melted, add the bay leaf, celery, onion, and apples. Season with salt, pepper, and mixed herbs; cook for 5 to 6 minutes, or until the vegetables and apples begin to soften.

3. Add the parsley and bread cubes to the pan and combine. Moisten the stuffing with chicken stock until all of the bread is soft but not wet. Remove the bay leaf and let the stuffing cool either in the pan or in a bowl.

4. Brush a baking dish with olive oil. Spread the stuffing in the dish, and bake until set and crisp on top, about 15 to 20 minutes.
5. Serve hot with the pork loin and cider gravy.

CIDER GRAVY

THIS VELVETY AND RICH cider-spiked gravy is an irresistible accompaniment to roast pork.

Serves 4 to 6

2 tablespoons all-purpose flour	1 cup (250 ml) vegetable stock
1 to 2 teaspoons coarse-grain mustard	¼ cup (60 ml) heavy cream (optional)
1 cup (250 ml) hard cider	Salt and freshly ground black pepper, to taste

1. After the pork has cooked and been removed, along with the onion, from the pan, pour out any excess fat. Put the pan over medium heat and whisk the flour vigorously into the meat juices. Slowly add the mustard, cider, and vegetable stock; cook for about 3 to 4 minutes, whisking constantly, until slightly thickened. Add the cream (if using), and season with salt and pepper.
2. Pour into a gravy boat, and serve warm.

STEWED APPLE

IN THE AUTUMN ON THE FARM, the apples are collected and made into pies or "stewed" into a sauce. My mother-in-law, Peggy, always served a dish of this applesauce with pork.

Serves 4 to 6

1 lb (500 g) cooking apples, peeled, cored, and quartered	¼ cup (50 g) superfine sugar
	1 tablespoon water

1. Slice the apples and place in a medium pan with the sugar and water. Cover the pan and put it on the stove over medium heat. When it comes to a boil, put the timer on for 5 minutes and leave to cook. Stir after about 4 minutes; the apple slices will be dissolved and fluffy. Cook for a further 1 to 2 minutes, or until the apple is cooked, but a few chunks are still visible. Remove from the heat, and taste the mixture, adding more sugar if required.
2. Let cool, then spoon into an airtight container, and refrigerate for up to one week.

MAPLE ROASTED PARSNIPS

MAPLE SYRUP ADDS just the right amount of sweetness to the already sweet parsnips and, I find, is the perfect side dish for roast pork and potatoes.

Serves 4 to 6

2 lb (1 kg) parsnips, peeled and sliced into quarters	½ cup (118 ml) olive oil
	3 tablespoons maple syrup

1. Preheat the oven to 400°F (200°C).
2. Blanch the parsnips in salted boiling water for 3 minutes. Arrange them in a roasting pan, pour the oil over them, dribble with the maple syrup, and mix together.
3. Roast until tender, about 25 minutes.

Scullery NOTES | Be careful as you taste test: the sugar content of the parsnips, more so than their syrup, makes them blistering hot right out of the oven.

SKIN-ON BUTTERMILK MASH

THE BUTTERMILK in these mashed potatoes adds an extra flavor boost that we all love. And keeping the skins on reminds me of America.

2 lb (1 kg) red potatoes (preferably organic), unpeeled

1 cup (250 ml) buttermilk

¼ cup (57 g) unsalted butter, softened

½ teaspoon freshly ground black pepper

Sea salt, to taste

1. Cut the unpeeled potatoes into 1-inch pieces, then place in a large saucepan. Cover generously with cold salted water (1 teaspoon salt for every 5 cups water) and simmer, partially covered, until the potatoes are tender, 10 to 15 minutes.
2. Meanwhile, heat the buttermilk, butter, and pepper in a small saucepan over medium heat until the butter is melted.
3. Drain the potatoes well in a colander and return to the pan. Mash with a potato masher, and, while still hot, stir in the milk mixture. Season with salt.

CHAPTER 10
New Traditions

WARNING: This chapter contains 500,000-plus calories!

WHEN ADAPTING TO A NEW COUNTRY, THE LINEUP OF HOLIDAY CELEBRATIONS IS BOUND TO CHANGE. IN MY CASE, THIS HAS MANIFESTED IN VARIOUS WAYS—SOME PROFOUNDLY JARRING (THE ABSENCE OF FIREWORKS ON THE FOURTH OF JULY) AND SOME PRETTY EASY TO SWALLOW (PLUM PUDDING). THERE ARE NEW NATIONAL HOLIDAYS TO CELEBRATE, A DIFFERENT WAY OF OBSERVING SHARED HOLIDAYS, AND DYED-IN-THE-WOOL FAMILY TRADITIONS TO HONOR. THUS, I HAVE BEEN OBLIGED TO LEARN NEW AND INDIGENOUS WAYS OF COOKING AND PREPARING FOOD FOR SUCH FESTIVITIES.

Still, I always put on a special Thanksgiving spread, despite usually having to do so the weekend before or after the holiday to accommodate Irish family and friends, and I try to throw an Easter egg–decorating children's party each year, complete with duck eggs (the only white eggs readily available). But that is where my former American holiday traditions cease on this side of the pond. Over the years, I have come to fully embrace the ways of Ireland when it comes to holiday merrymaking.

Without a doubt, on either side of the Atlantic, the king of all holidays is Christmas. American and Irish Christmases share many traditions, such as Santa Claus, Catholic midnight mass, hanging stockings on Christmas Eve, and generally eating to excess. What came as a surprise to me, but really shouldn't have, is that farm animals don't celebrate Christmas. The cows and chickens are eating, drinking, milking, and laying as usual. Which means everyone still has to work—even on Christmas morning!

Here are some of my favorite new, tried-and-true food traditions that I have grown to love over the years.

McDONNELL FAMILY CHRISTMAS PUDDING

CHRISTMAS CAKE AND CHRISTMAS PUDDING are staples in Irish homes around the country during the holiday season. Both are prepared with pound after pound of dried fruit and equal amounts of flour and fat. The Christmas cake is beautifully iced with marzipan and white fondant, then lavishly decorated with sparkly bits of edible glitter and gold leaf.

Christmas pudding, on the other hand, can be prepared over many weeks leading up to Christmas. It is made with suet, dried fruits, and booze. The ingredients are stirred up in a basin, steamed for five hours, then left in the pantry and fed with brandy each week until Christmas Day, when it is then steamed for another two hours. The hot, crumbly, savory-sweet pudding was new to my palate, but once it was topped off with a generous scoop of rum raisin ice cream, I was sold for life.

Serves 6 to 8

SPECIAL TOOLS: Two 4-cup (1.2 liter) pudding basins, ramekins, or custard dishes

4 cups (400 g) white bread crumbs

Pinch of salt

1 cup (225 g) superfine sugar

2 teaspoons mixed spice (see page xv)

½ cup (100 g) mixed candied peel

½ cup (100 g) raisins

2⅓ cups (275 g) currants

½ cup (100 g) golden raisins

1 tablespoon glacé cherries

2 cups (450 g) chopped suet or vegetable shortening

3 large eggs

1 cup (200 ml) Irish stout

½ cup (100 ml) Irish whiskey

1. One week before Christmas, mix the bread crumbs, salt, sugar, mixed spice, peel, fruit, and suet together in a large bowl. Mix well, then pour in the stout and whiskey. Cover the bowl with a tea towel and place in a cool, dry place.
2. Stir the mixture every day to meld the flavors of the ingredients.
3. On the day before serving, beat the eggs well and stir them into the melding mixture, making sure all the ingredients are combined.
4. Lightly grease the pudding basins and spoon in the batter. Pat the batter down on top.

5. Measure out circles of parchment paper and foil to the size of each basin plus 2 inches. Put a circle of parchment paper and then foil over the top of each basin, making sure there is an overhang, and tie securely around the lip of each basin with string.

6. Put the basins in a large steamer over boiling water and cover with a lid. Boil for 7 hours, topping up the boiling water from time to time, if necessary. If you do not have a steamer, put the basins in a large pan on inverted saucers as a base. Pour in boiling water to a third of the way up the sides of the basins.

7. Remove from the water and cool. Change the parchment paper and foil covers for fresh ones and tie up as before. Store in a cool cupboard until Christmas Day.

8. To serve, steam for 2 hours to reheat. Serve portions with brandy butter, rum sauce, rum raisin ice cream, or homemade custard.

Scullery
NOTES

Garnish this pudding with fresh holly leaves and berries, or flambé it with Irish whiskey or brandy for festive charm.

AUTUMN MICHAELMAS ROAST
with PEGGY'S POTATO STUFFING

MICHAELMAS, KNOWN IN IRELAND as *Fomhar na nGeanna,* falls on September 29, the feast of Saint Michael the Archangel. It is commonly associated with geese, because the birds that are hatched in spring and put out to grass in May are plump and ready for market at this time.

Years ago, most farms in Ireland reared geese. My sister-in-law's mother once told me that geese were great guards for the farmyard and garden, and no farm in our area would have been without a pair of geese when she was growing up. They would alert families to visitors, welcome or not, with their unmistakable honk.

The Michaelmas goose is traditionally stuffed with potato and apple stuffing and roasted slowly, every now and then pouring off the fat to be reserved for roast potatoes. Goose fat is perfect for many other non-cooking purposes, such as shining shoes.

This recipe uses my mother-in-law Peggy's potato stuffing instead of the traditional potato and apple. Peggy's version soaks up the gorgeous goose fat while providing a lush, herby flavor to the bird as well.

Serves 8

9- to 11-lb (4- to 5-kg) oven-ready goose, with giblets	6 sweet apples, cored and cut into 8 pieces, plus more for garnish
3 cups (350 g) Peggy's Potato Stuffing, prepared (see page 258)	1¼ cups (295 ml) dry white wine

1. Preheat the oven to 400°F (200 °C). Prick the skin of the goose all over with a sharp skewer or fork; pull the inside fat out of the bird and reserve.
2. Spoon the potato stuffing into the neck end of the goose, then truss with strong cotton or fine string. Weigh the bird and cover in tinfoil. Put it on a wire rack placed in a roasting pan. Roast for 15 minutes per pound (450 g), plus 15 minutes at the end, basting frequently.
3. Thirty minutes before the end of the cooking time, drain off the fat and discard. Add the apples and wine to the pan. Place the bird on top, standing on the roasting rack. Remove the foil and cook, uncovered, for the last 30 minutes, then serve.

Scullery NOTES | Garnish this roast with fresh-cut bay leaves and apple slices.

PEGGY'S POTATO STUFFING

ONE OF MY FAVORITE RECIPES that my late mother-in-law, Peggy, prepared was her savory potato stuffing. She only made it on special occasions. As straightforward as it may be, potato stuffing always seemed exotic yet heartwarming, a dish that I had never encountered back home.

I wasn't the only one who looked forward to Peggy's stuffing; each serving always brought a comforting smile to all the faces around the table. This is Peggy's tried-and-true recipe. I hope you enjoy it as much as we do.

Serves 6

5 large russet potatoes, boiled or steamed, and coarsely mashed (do not overcook)

4½ tablespoons butter

1 large onion, finely chopped

1 to 2 tablespoons mixed herbs (see page xv)

Salt and pepper, to taste

1. In a large mixing bowl, combine the potatoes, butter, and onion. Add the mixed herbs, and season with salt and pepper. Mix all the ingredients thoroughly. Use to stuff a goose, duck, or turkey before roasting.

Scullery **NOTES** | This stuffing is particularly good in a large roast goose or duck, but in our house, Peggy would also traditionally stuff the carcass of a turkey with potato stuffing and the turkey breast with bread stuffing.

LITTLE CHRISTMAS ROAST DUCK *with* TARRAGON-LEEK BREAD STUFFING

NOLLAIG NA MBAN (PRONOUNCED "NUL-LAIG NAH MON"), or Women's Christmas, is a traditional Irish holiday celebrated here on the farm with great pride and joy. The holiday, which falls on the day of the Epiphany or the first Sunday in January, is still a strong tradition, especially in the southwest of Ireland. It is so-called because Irish men are required to take on all the household duties for the day. Most women hold parties or go out to celebrate the day with their friends, sisters, mothers, and aunts. Bars and restaurants serve mostly women and girls on this night. Children are encouraged to buy presents for their mothers and grandmothers. We usually have a lovely dinner made at the farm prepared by Granddad, who also does all the cleaning for the day as well. While some people think this holiday does not fall in line with modern times, I personally find it endearing and sweet, and it could certainly be celebrated around here more than once a year!

Serves 4 to 6

FOR THE STUFFING

1 tablespoon olive oil

1 leek, chopped

½ cup (125 g) sliced Granny Smith
    or Golden Delicious apples

½ cup (125 g) fresh white bread crumbs

Grated rind of 1 lemon

3 tablespoons chopped tarragon

1 teaspoon chopped garlic

1 cup (300 ml) chicken stock

Salt and pepper, to taste

1 egg, lightly beaten

FOR THE DUCK

One 5- to 6-lb (3-kg) duck

2 tablespoons lemon juice

2 tablespoons honey

Salt and pepper, to taste

1. Preheat the oven to 425°F (220°C).
2. **MAKE THE STUFFING:** Heat the olive oil in a pan over medium heat, and fry the leek until soft, fragrant, and translucent, 5 to 10 minutes. Stir in the apples, bread crumbs, lemon rind, tarragon, garlic, and chicken stock. Season with salt and pepper. Mix in the egg to bind the stuffing together.

3. **PREPARE THE DUCK:** Dry the duck with paper towels, and prick all over with a fine skewer. Fill the cavity of the duck with the stuffing, truss, and set on a wire rack placed in a roasting pan.

4. Mix together the lemon juice and honey; smear over the duck with your fingers. Sprinkle with salt and pepper.

5. Place in the hot oven for 10 minutes, then lower the temperature to 375°F (190°C) for a further 2 to 2½ hours. Baste the bird several times during cooking.

6. Remove from the oven and let rest for 15 minutes before carving.

Scullery
NOTES | Use the duck-fat drippings to make a lovely duck gravy or roasted potatoes.

IRISH WEDDING CAKE

DURING THE PLANNING OF OUR WEDDING in Ireland, we met with our cake designer to discuss flavors and to do a bit of taste testing. Before serving us, she read down her list aloud: "Chocolate and raspberry, white sponge with mango filling, Bailey's chocolate cake, . . ." My mouth was watering. Finally, she said, "Irish cake for the top tier." I stopped her and curiously inquired, "Oo, what is Irish cake?" She replied matter-of-factly, "The top tier is always prepared as an Irish fruitcake." My eyes grew wide with disbelief, while she and Richard just sat smiling and nodding their heads. Everyone gets a slice of the sweet cake and then a dense sliver of the top-tier fruitcake. Whatever is left of that tier is then meant to go in the freezer to eat on the christening of your first child. Who knew?

This recipe is for the top-tier fruitcake only. Traditionally, it would be iced with almond marzipan and covered with fondant (which I consider the best part). Since fondant requires a host of other kitchen skills, I recommend seeking out a store-bought version if you'd like to go whole hog. If not, you could also ice the cake with a luxurious buttercream. This stunning cake recipe is from my great friend and cake decorator extraordinaire, Claire Shields, and the design is inspired by our very own Irish wedding cake.

Serves 12

IRISH WEDDING CAKE (TOP TIER)

1¼ cups (160 g) all-purpose flour

2½ teaspoons baking powder

1¾ teaspoons salt

1 cup (145 g) raisins

1 cup (145 g) golden raisins

1 cup (145 g) currants

½ cup (75 g) candied cherries

½ cup (75 g) candied peel

½ cup (75 g) slivered or chopped almonds

1 cup (200 g) dark brown sugar

1 cup (113 g) butter,
    softened but not melted

¼ cup (85 g) molasses

Juice of 1 small lemon

Juice of 1 small orange

3 extra-large eggs

1½ teaspoons almond extract

½ teaspoon cinnamon

½ teaspoon nutmeg

¼ teaspoon ground cloves

¼ teaspoon ground ginger

¼ teaspoon allspice

¼ cup (50 ml) Irish whiskey,
    plus extra for drizzling

1. Preheat the oven to 325°F (165°C). Line an 8-inch round cake pan with a double layer of parchment paper on the sides and bottom; sandwich a layer of cooking spray in between to hold them in place. The paper at the sides must be taller than the pan to allow for the cake to rise.

2. In a medium bowl, sift together the flour, baking powder, and salt. In a large bowl, mix together the fruits, candied peel, almonds, and ¼ cup of the flour mixture to coat everything.

3. In a separate bowl, cream together the dark brown sugar and the softened butter. Whip in the molasses and the lemon and orange juices. In another bowl, beat together the eggs and almond extract, and blend into the butter mixture.

4. Sift the remaining flour, salt, and spices together, and add to the floured fruit and nut mixture. Add the butter and egg mixture, and mix in the ¼ cup whiskey. Stir well until all the ingredients are well mixed.

5. Pour the batter into the pan and smooth with a spatula, leaving a shallow well in the center, as this will take longer to bake. Bake in the center of the oven at 325°F (165°C) for 50 minutes. Turn the heat down to 300°F (150°C) and continue to bake, checking frequently, for 3 to 4 hours. The cake is done when a knife inserted into the center comes out clean.

6. Remove from the oven, and let the cake cool completely before removing it from the pan. Trim off the top so the cake is level for assembly. Wrap the cooled cake in a sheet of waxed paper, christening it with a splash of Irish whiskey, which will quickly be absorbed, before closing the paper. Wrap the entire package in aluminum foil. Refrigerate for at least two weeks before icing. Sprinkle with small amounts of whiskey every few days to moisten and mellow.

Scullery NOTES | You can buy marzipan and fondant icing in cake decorating and specialty baking stores. The longer the cake sits, the better the flavor on the wedding day. It can rest for up to a month before serving.

ST. PATRICK'S DAY BACON
and CABBAGE POT STICKERS
(with Soy Dipping Sauce)

IN THE IRISH COUNTRYSIDE, the spirit of St. Patrick's Day really lives on. My husband and his family still pick shamrock clovers to pin on their lapels for the day, and now I am a part of that special tradition as well.

I will never forget my first St. Patrick's Day experience after moving to Ireland. Everything in the little village nearest to us was closed on the day—the post office, the bank, a good number of shops. About the only place with open doors was the church; it was not only a national holiday, but a religious one as well.

My mother-in-law invited us to the farmhouse for dinner, and I could hardly contain my excitement about having my first authentic Irish corned beef and cabbage. We sat down at the dinner table while Peggy brought out generous plates of roasted pork loin with mashed potatoes covered in a white creamy parsley sauce accompanied by a bit of boiled cabbage on the side. I was stunned. Where was the corned beef, and why on earth was there so little cabbage?

I explained to my new family that in America, most people eat corned beef and cabbage on St. Patrick's Day. My father-in-law looked at me like I was mad and then calmly reasoned, "We do not eat corned beef, t'wouldn't be the nicest." I could tell by the look in his eye that corned beef was not held in the same esteem as the beautiful chunk of pork loin, known as "bacon" here in Ireland. I felt at once surprised and embarrassed.

Over the years, our Paddy's Day celebrations have evolved. We have begun a ritual of going for a long walk on the farm and visiting one of the few fairy forts (circular mound dwellings from ancient times) still exisiting on the land for a picnic. I bring all the fixings, and we sit under an ivy-covered tree and nibble away, all the time being on the lookout for fairies.

Since I always like to try something a little different from roast bacon and cabbage, one year I made an Asian-style potsticker dumpling with pork, cabbage, and parsley sauce. I borrowed the dumpling wrapper recipe from my friend and blogger, Molly Yeh (http://mynameisyeh.com) and went to town with traditional ingredients. A couple of hours later, we walked out the door with a basket of dumplings, dipping sauce, chopsticks, and a flask of tea. With a picnic like that, who needs corned beef and cabbage?

Makes 20 medium-size dumplings

FOR THE WRAPPERS

2 cups (250 g) all-purpose flour,
plus more for dusting

1½ teaspoons kosher salt

½ cup (120 ml) boiling water

½ cup (120 ml) cold water

FOR THE FILLING

¾ cup (300 g) cabbage, roughly chopped

½ teaspoon sea salt

½ teaspoon grated fresh gingerroot

3 tablespoons finely chopped kale

⅓ lb (150 g) shredded boiled ham
(or Irish bacon)

⅛ teaspoon ground white pepper
(or freshly ground black pepper)

½ tablespoon soy sauce

½ tablespoon Chinese rice wine
(or dry sherry)

1 teaspoon sesame oil

FOR THE SLURRY

1 tablespoon cornstarch

½ cup (120 ml) water

Sunflower oil, for frying

FOR THE DIPPING SAUCE

2 tablespoons sesame oil

½ cup (115 g) scallions, chopped

¼ cup (60 ml) brown rice vinegar

¼ cup (60 ml) soy sauce

1. MAKE THE WRAPPERS: In a medium bowl, combine the flour and salt. Gradually stir in the boiling water until the mixture is mealy. Gradually add the cold water, and stir until the mixture comes together into a dough.

2. Knead the dough on a floured surface, adding more flour as necessary, until the dough becomes smooth. Transfer to a clean bowl, cover with a damp towel, and let rest while you make the filling.

3. MAKE THE FILLING: Put the cabbage in a food processor and pulse until finely minced. Transfer to a large bowl and sprinkle with the salt. Let sit for 10 minutes.

4. Pulse the ginger, kale, ham, pepper, soy sauce, rice wine, and sesame oil in a food processor to mix well. Set aside.

5. Squeeze the water out of the cabbage and into the sink. Place the dry cabbage in a dry bowl and add the ham mixture. Fold together with your hands.

6. MAKE THE DUMPLINGS: Roll out the dumpling dough into a circle and cut out wrappers with 2-inch round cookie cutters. Set aside.

7. Mix together the cornstarch and water for the slurry in a small bowl. Take one dumpling wrapper, and spoon about 1 tablespoon of the ham mixture into the middle. Dip one finger into the slurry, and paint the edges of the dumpling wrapper. Fold the bottom side of the wrapper over the filling and press into a half-moon shape. Place on a baking sheet, cover loosely with plastic wrap, and repeat with the rest of dumplings. Make sure the dumplings do not touch each other on the sheet.

8. When all the dumplings are assembled, you can cook immediately or cover with plastic wrap and refrigerate for up to several hours. To cook, half-fill a large pot with water and bring to boil. Gently

slide in one-third of the dumplings. When the water returns to a boil, turn the heat down and simmer gently for 6 to 8 minutes. Remove the dumplings with a slotted spoon, and repeat with remaining dumplings.

9. Coat the bottom of a frying pan with the sunflower oil and place over medium heat until hot. Fry dumplings until they are golden on each side.

10. **MAKE THE DIPPING SAUCE:** Heat the sesame oil in a saucepan until it smokes. Add the scallions, then the brown rice wine vinegar and soy sauce. Mix well, then take off the heat and pour into a bowl for dipping.

Scullery
NOTES | Salting and squeezing the water out of the cabbage is essential. It prevents your dumplings from being waterlogged and soggy.

IRISH PANCAKES

PANCAKE TUESDAY is another name for Shrove Tuesday, Fat Tuesday, or (at our farm) simply an ex-cuse to eat pancakes all day. Pancake Tuesday is a not a national bank holiday, but it is widely recognized throughout Ireland. Pancakes and doughnuts are associated with the day before Lent begins, because they are a way to use up rich foodstuffs such as eggs, milk, and sugar before the forty days of fasting. The liturgical fasting emphasizes eating plainer food and refraining from food that would give pleasure. Give me an excuse to eat pancakes or doughnuts all day, and I will take you up on it, no questions asked.

Irish pancakes are daintier than the gigantic fluffy buttermilk variety in the States. They are more like crepes that can be filled with loads of yummy surprises: lightly sweetened with a drizzle of lemon and a pinch of sugar; richly slathered with chocolate or toffee sauce and fresh cream; spread with raspberry or strawberry preserves and sprinkled with confectioner's sugar; generously lined with smooth Nutella; savory and filled with soft cheese and boiled ham; potatoey with a bit of sour cream and stewed apple . . . The list goes on and on, and they are all divine.

Makes about 12 pancakes

1 cup (125 g) all-purpose flour	1 tablespoon melted butter
Pinch of salt	1¼ cups (300 ml) whole milk
1 egg	

1. Sift the flour and salt into a mixing bowl; make a well in the center. Crack the egg into the well; add the melted butter and half the milk. Gradually stir the liquid into the flour with a wooden spoon, until all of the ingredients have been incorporated; beat well to make a smooth batter. Stir in the remaining milk, and let stand for about 30 minutes. Stir again before using.

2. To make the pancakes, heat a small heavy-bottom frying pan until very hot, then turn the heat down to medium. Lightly grease with oil and ladle in enough batter to coat the base of the pan thinly (about 2 tablespoons), tilting the pan so the mixture spreads evenly.

3. Cook over medium heat for 1 to 2 minutes, or until the batter looks dry on top and begins to brown at the edges. Flip the pancake with a spatula or fish slice, and cook the second side.

4. Turn onto a plate, smear with a little butter, sprinkle with sugar, and splash with a squeeze of lemon juice. Enjoy!

MAD MAY EVE TEA CAKES

EACH MAY EVE, I plan a special little tea party in the garden for whoever will come. These easy-to-make tea cakes are a fun take on traditional chocolate-covered marshmallow tea cakes. If you are short on time, you can substitute any packaged round tea biscuit or cookie for the base.

Makes about 30 tea cakes

FOR THE COOKIE BASE

1 cup (100 g) whole-wheat flour

½ cup (50 g) all-purpose flour

Pinch of salt

1 teaspoon baking powder

¼ cup (50 g) golden superfine sugar

4 tablespoons unsalted butter, cold

2 to 3 tablespoons whole milk

FOR THE MARSHMALLOW

3 large free-range egg whites

¾ cup (150 g) golden superfine sugar

6 teaspoons golden syrup
(or light corn syrup)

Pinch of salt

Seeds from ½ vanilla bean

½ cup (160 g) raspberry or blackberry jam
(or marmalade)

FOR THE CHOCOLATE COATING

1 cup (150 g) milk chocolate, chopped
(or chips)

⅓ cup (75 g) dark chocolate

2 teaspoons vegetable oil (or coconut oil,
if you prefer)

1. **MAKE THE BISCUIT BASE:** Preheat the oven to 350°F (175°C).

2. In a large mixing bowl, sift together the flours, salt, baking powder, and sugar. Rub in the butter with your fingers until the mixture resembles coarse bread crumbs. Add the milk, and stir everything together to form a smooth ball. You may need a little more or less milk—the dough should be smooth and pliable but not sticky.

3. Pat the dough into a flat oval, then dust the work surface with flour. Roll the dough to approximately ⅛ inch thick. Using a 2½-inch round cookie cutter, cut out small rounds. Place on parchment paper, and chill in the fridge for 10 minutes; this should stop them from shrinking when baking.

4. Bake the biscuits for 15 minutes or until crisp. You don't want a soft texture; a crisp base is needed for the tea cake.

5. **MAKE THE MARSHMALLOW FILLING:** Place the egg whites, sugar, golden syrup, salt, and vanilla seeds in a large, heatproof bowl set over a pan of simmering water (make sure the bottom of the bowl doesn't touch the water). While it is heating, beat the mixture with an electric hand mixer for 6 to 8 minutes until it is smooth, silky, and double in volume. The trick is to have a good, stiff marshmallow texture so that it holds when piped, without overcooking. A thick whipped-cream consistency is ideal.

6. Spoon the marshmallow into a piping bag.

7. Spread each biscuit with ¼ to ½ teaspoon jam, then pipe a 1-inch dollop of marshmallow on top. Leave the biscuits to set at room temperature for 2 hours.

8. **MAKE THE COATING:** When ready to assemble, line a couple of trays with a silicone mat or parchment paper. Melt the chocolates and oil in a heatproof bowl over a pan of simmering water. Set aside to cool slightly.

9. To coat the cookies, dip each one in the chocolate, then hold upside down to allow the excess to drip off. Very quickly turn right-side up and place on the prepared trays. Leave all the tea cakes to set at room temperature, about 1 hour.

10. Serve with glasses of milk or cups of hot tea.

Scullery **NOTES** | These tea cakes keep best at room temperature in an airtight container for one week. If you put them in the refrigerator, the chocolate will discolor.

MAY EVE IS THE EVENING BEFORE MAY DAY (April 30). Legend has it that on this night a certain type of sorcery transpires in which female evildoers called *pishogues* (pronounced "pish-ohh-g") come around and do their best to make people's lives miserable in the Irish countryside. A pishogue would do things such as surreptitiously place eggs, bread, meats, and other foods on someone's land, and doing so would somehow take the riches from that farm and transfer them to the pishogue's estate.

Now, these pishogues were real people—neighbors, churchgoers—and everyone knew who they were. Real people who were known to be sort of possessed and forced into doing dreadful acts. This pishoguery put the fear of God into people, and villagers began sprinkling holy water on their homes, livestock, farmyards, and machinery to ward off this evil on May Eve.

No May Eve would be complete without a story involving the ubiquitous "love potion." Yes, coaxioriums were popular on this evening as well. Allegedly, if a woman made an advance on a man and was rejected, she would slip him a potion and he'd come around.

My absolute favorite bits of holiday folklore are stories of women who had the power to turn into hares. They would morph into wild hares and get into all kinds of mischief, then return home and have a cup of tea as if nothing had happened. Often, someone would come across a lady's dress and shoes lying near a hedge, and they would take no notice, assuming that she had likely changed into a hare and was just out gallivanting in the field.

While this all seems far-fetched, many of these accounts have credible witnesses and are steeped in traditions that have withstood the test of time. Here in our village of Kilcolman, we sprinkle holy water to be safe and all I can say is, what's good for the gander . . .

OYSTER STUFFING *for* AMERICAN THANKSGIVING

AMERICAN THANKSGIVING IS ALWAYS A BIG HIT at our farmhouse. Each year, I carefully plan a harvest menu using as many ingredients from the farm as possible. We invite family and friends and generally serve the traditional stuffed turkey, mashed potatoes, cranberry sauce, and pumpkin pie, but I always like to add a few surprises depending on what is left in the garden as well.

One Thanksgiving, a fellow American expat living in Dublin joined us at the farm. She made an unforgettable oyster stuffing that we have adopted as a new Thanksgiving tradition ever since. Here's my take on it.

Serves 8 to 10

11 cups (about 400 g) crusty bread cut in ½-inch cubes

6 slices bacon, coarsely chopped

6 tablespoons unsalted butter, melted, plus more for greasing the pan

6 shallots, thinly sliced

1 leek, thinly sliced

4 celery stalks, thinly sliced

40 medium (about 1 lb) oysters, shucked, with 1 cup (250 ml) of the liquor reserved

1 cup (250 ml) chicken stock

¼ cup (50 ml) sherry

⅓ cup (15 g) chopped flat-leaf parsley

2 tablespoons chopped thyme leaves

2 tablespoons chopped sage leaves

1 teaspoon sweet marjoram, chopped

1 tablespoon fennel seeds

½ teaspoon hot pepper sauce

Sea salt and freshly ground black pepper, to taste

1. Preheat the oven to 300°F (150°C). Butter a 2-quart oval baking dish; set aside.
2. Arrange the bread cubes on a baking sheet in a single layer and bake, stirring occasionally, until dried but not browned, about 15 minutes. Remove from the oven and let cool.
3. Cook the bacon in a 12-inch skillet over medium-high heat, stirring frequently, until it is crisp and the fat has rendered, about 10 minutes. Add 4 tablespoons of the melted butter. Add the shallots, leek, and celery; reduce the heat to medium and cook, stirring occasionally, until the vegetables are soft, about 10 minutes.
4. Add the oyster liquor, chicken stock, sherry, parsley, thyme, sage, marjoram, fennel seeds, hot pepper sauce, and salt and pepper. Bring to a boil over high heat and cook, stirring occasionally, for 5 minutes. Scrape the mixture into a large bowl, and stir in the bread cubes and oysters. Set aside to allow the flavors to come together for 10 minutes.

5. Raise the oven temperature to 400°F (200°C). Transfer the oyster mixture to the prepared baking dish and cover with foil. Bake for 30 minutes. Remove the foil, drizzle with the remaining butter, and continue baking until golden brown and crusty, about 15 minutes more.

6. Serve immediately.

Scullery
NOTES | Fresh oysters are best, but if you are in a pinch, canned or jarred oysters in liquor will work as well.

'Tis Different: My First Irish Thanksgiving

SURPRISINGLY, THE FIRST BIG HOLIDAY THAT I experienced in Ireland was an American one. I was coming over to visit Richard during the week of Thanksgiving and felt I couldn't miss out on the celebration. Richard's parents were away, so on the guest list were two young farm apprentices; a quiet Irish couple who were friends of the family; Richard's grandmother, Mary; and his brother, David. No one knew what to expect, not even me.

The farm provided a fresh homegrown turkey to roast, which was so juicy and succulent it made me wonder what type of turkey imposters I'd eaten previously. We could only make one trip to the grocery store, so I had to be sure I didn't forget anything—once we were back at the farm, we would certainly not be driving forty-five minutes to town if we needed a stick of butter. I hadn't prepared myself for the differences in measurements, so with a snail-paced Internet connection, I had to recalibrate all of my recipes using the metric equivalents in grams, kilos, and

milliliters. Instead of using familiar measuring cups, I got intimately acquainted with a kitchen scale. There were more than a few tears, but I was delighted when everything turned out perfectly.

There we were, all seated in front of our heaping plates of turkey with all the trimmings, when my future brother-in-law kindly inquired, "So, is Thanksgiving a Jewish holiday?" It occurred to me later that he was probably trying to work out if I was Jewish, not if Thanksgiving was Jewish. I smiled and answered in my deeply Midwestern, somewhat Fargo-esque dialect, "Oh, no, no, no," followed by a more sophisticated, "As a matter of fact, Thanksgiving is an American holiday celebrated by all, um, creeds." He looked at me, took a bite of turkey, chewed, swallowed, and then asked with a raised eyebrow, "What is it all about then?"

My mind went blank, and all I could think of was the scene from *A Charlie Brown Thanksgiving* where the Peanuts gang string up popcorn and Snoopy gets into a fight with a folding chair. Put on the spot, I didn't have a good answer. I was suddenly representing all of America, and I couldn't answer a simple question about the origins of Turkey Day. Mortified, I made a mental note to Google Thanksgiving and memorize every last historical fact. Then Richard stood up and asked, "Who wants cranberry sauce?" I was saved by the sauce.

When it was time for dessert, I enthusiastically dished out my perfect pumpkin pie, which had been painstakingly baked in my mother-in-law's metric kitchen using organic puréed pumpkin that I had strategically (and probably illegally) packed in my suitcase along with two bags of fresh Ocean Spray cranberries. I never thought for a moment that anyone could *not* like pumpkin pie. I presumed that they wouldn't want anything else for dessert, and I couldn't give them a choice because as I learned, there is no apple pie when you discover you are short a stick of butter.

I served Richard's grandmother first. She had a funny look on her face and asked me,

"What kind of tart is this again?" I shared all the ingredients and told her, "It is especially loved because we only have it once a year." Richard's grandmother was ninety years old and had a kind of chutzpah that comes with time. She knew what she liked and didn't like by then, and everyone knew this about her. We all dug in. I looked around the room and mostly saw smiles. I was delighted and relieved.

Then, at the top of the table, I spied Mary pushing a bite-size piece of pie around her plate. She had barely touched it. I asked her how she liked it, and with a gentle smile on her face she carefully replied, "'Tis different." I went along with it, saying that I suppose it *is* an acquired taste. Eventually she finished her piece, and we all retired to the sitting room for the rest of the evening.

A few years after Grandma passed away, I was informed that she actually thought my pumpkin pie tasted "rotten." It was explained that she meant rotten in the kindest sense of the word; that the flavor and texture combination was simply not to her liking.

HALLOWEEN BARMBRACK

ON THE FARM, we bake a barmbrack, a fruit-filled tea bread, each year. It is also a Halloween tradition; a token is baked into it to be used as a form of fortune-telling. The eater may find a ring (predicting impending marriage); a button or thimble (portents of bachelor- or spinsterhood, respectively); or a coin (presaging wealth). In earlier (and less culturally sensitive) times, items may have included a rag or dried pea (for poverty) or a matchstick (for impending death). These days, the tokens aren't always included, but I enjoy adding the trinket to the mix just for fun. If you buy a brack at the supermarket or bakery that is labeled "Halloween Brack," there will still be a ring or another token hidden inside, so you must mind yourself when biting into a slice!

Makes one 8-inch round loaf

3 cups (445 g) all-purpose flour	1¼ cups (300 ml) milk
1 teaspoon grated nutmeg	2 eggs, beaten
½ teaspoon salt	1½ cups (220 g) golden raisins
¼ cup (28 g) butter	1½ cups (220 g) currants
1½ tablespoons active dry yeast	1 cup (145 g) candied fruit peel
2 tablespoons sugar	1 toy ring or charm wrapped in waxed paper

1. Grease an 8-inch round cake pan; set aside.
2. In a medium bowl, sift together the flour, nutmeg, and salt. With a pastry cutter, blend in the butter until it resembles coarse bread crumbs. In a separate bowl, combine the yeast with 1 teaspoon of the sugar. Add the remaining sugar to the flour mixture and blend well.
3. In a saucepan over medium heat, heat the milk to just below boiling, allow to cool, then add to the yeast and sugar. Stir in all but 1 tablespoon of the eggs (reserve this for glazing), and add to the dry ingredients. Knead lightly to produce an elastic dough. With a wooden spoon, fold in the fruit, the candied peel, and the trinket. Pour the batter into the prepared cake pan. Cover with a clean cloth and leave in a warm place to rise (it should double in size in about 1 hour). Preheat the oven to 400°F (200°C).
4. Brush the top of the brack with the reserved beaten egg to glaze. Bake until golden, or until a skewer inserted in the center comes out clean, about 50 to 60 minutes.

EACH OCTOBER, IRELAND WELCOMES THE tradition of the festival of Samhain (pronounced "saw-wen"), which is said to hold the origins of Halloween. Samhain had three distinct elements. First, it was an important fire festival, celebrated over the evening of October 31 and throughout the following day when ceremonial fires would be lit.

Second, it was a festival not unlike the modern New Year's Day in that it carried the notion of casting out the old and moving into the new. To Irish pagan ancestors, it marked the end of the pastoral cycle, when all the crops would have been gathered and placed in storage for the long winter ahead and when livestock would be brought in from the fields and selected for slaughter or breeding.

But it was also, as the last day of the year, when the souls of the departed would return to their former homes and when potentially malevolent spirits were released from the Otherworld and became visible to mankind.

CHAPTER 11

Puddings, Cakes, and Confections

PUDDING WAS A CONFUSING CONCEPT TO ME DURING MY FIRST YEAR IN IRELAND. WAS IT A SAVORY POPOVER SERVED WITH ROAST BEEF AND GRAVY? OR JUST PLAIN DESSERT? WAS IT BREAD AND BUTTER PUDDING? IT CERTAINLY WASN'T THE CUSTARDY, POWDERED INSTANT MIX I KNEW FROM CHILDHOOD.

Turns out, pudding is a couple of things here in Ireland. From what I eventually gathered, the word *pudding* itself is actually derived from the French term *boudin*, meaning "tiny sausage case." In Ireland, pudding can be a savory, mealy sausage: black pudding is a blood sausage, and white pudding is a meat sausage made with fat, suet, and oats instead of blood. James Joyce once proclaimed, "White pudding and eggs and sausages and cups of tea! How simple and beautiful was life after all!" in *A Portrait of the Artist as a Young Man.* As much as I love that quote, I sadly have never felt affection for puddings, black or white.

But give me the popover variety covered in gravy served alongside slices of tender roast beef, and I'm one happy farmer.

A seeming contradiction, *pudding* is also a generic word for dessert in Ireland. Perusing a dessert menu titled "Puddings" that is full of cakes, confections, and sweets brings tremendous satisfaction to this all-American soul.

A whole new world of pudding opened up to me when I moved to this Irish farm, and I'm certainly not complaining. Here are a few of my favorites.

SMOKY DARK CHOCOLATE PORTER CAKE

A FEW YEARS AGO I SNUCK A BOTTLE of a supersmoky American home-brewed craft porter beer back home to Ireland. I found a recipe for porter cake in an old folder at the farm and swiftly decided to put that special American beer to use.

Porter cake is a tradition in Ireland that began when some clever baker decided a porter would make a perfect addition to the dark, robust flavor of the popular fruitcake. For my variation, I kept the mixed spice, left out the fruit, and added superdark chocolate. The end result is a rich, velvety, smoky chocolate cake that carries the porter flavor evenly throughout. I've iced it in chocolate espresso buttercream, but it doesn't need frosting, especially if you are serving it with a scoop of ice cream or a dollop of fresh cream.

You can use any porter or stout for this recipe, but Knockmealdown Porter by 8 Degrees Brewing in Cork is perfect. A chocolate stout would also be superb if you can find it.

Makes 1 cake (two 9-inch layers or four 3-inch layers)

---

3 oz (85 g) unsweetened dark chocolate (75% cocoa solids), chopped

14 tablespoons salted butter, room temperature

1¼ cups (350 ml) extra-smoky porter (or regular or chocolate stout)

1¼ cups (250 g) superfine sugar, plus 3 tablespoons

2¼ cups (280 g) all-purpose flour

2 teaspoons baking powder

1 teaspoon mixed spice (see page xv)

½ teaspoon baking soda

½ teaspoon salt

3 large eggs, separated

---

1. Position the rack in the center of the oven, and preheat to 350°F (175°C). Butter and flour two 9-inch round springform cake pans with 1½-inch-high sides or four 4½-inch springform minicake pans. Line the bottom of each pan with a round of buttered and floured parchment paper.

2. Put the chocolate, butter, and beer in medium metal bowl. Set the bowl over a saucepan of barely simmering water, and stir until the mixture is melted and smooth. Remove the bowl from the saucepan and let cool slightly.

3. In a medium bowl, whisk the sugar with the flour, baking powder, mixed spice, baking soda, and salt to blend. Add the egg yolks, one at a time, to the lukewarm melted chocolate mixture, beating until well blended after each addition. Beat in the flour mixture, in two additions, just until incorporated.

4. Using clean, dry beaters, beat the egg whites and remaining 3 tablespoons of sugar in another medium bowl until stiff but not dry. Fold one-third of the egg whites into the cake batter to lighten, then fold in the remaining egg whites in two batches.

5. Divide the batter between the prepared cake pans, and smooth the tops with a spatula.

6. Bake for about 30 minutes, until a tester inserted in the centers comes out clean. Transfer the cakes to wire racks and cool in the pans for 20 minutes. Release the spring form and invert the cakes onto the racks, remove the parchment paper, and cool completely.

7. Place one cake layer on a cake plate and spread the frosting (recipe follows) on top. Place the remaining cake layer on top. Spread the top and sides of the cake with the remaining frosting, swirling to coat in a decorative fashion. (If the frosting becomes too soft, refrigerate it to firm it up.) Cover the cake with a cake dome and refrigerate overnight. Bring the cake back to room temperature before serving.

DARK CHOCOLATE ESPRESSO BUTTERCREAM

Makes about 1 cup (225 g)

4 oz (114 g) unsweetened dark chocolate (75% cocoa solids), chopped

2 teaspoons instant espresso powder

3 tablespoons milk

1 cup (227 g) butter, softened

½ teaspoon vanilla extract

⅛ teaspoon salt

4 cups (500 g) confectioner's sugar

1. Place the chocolate in a medium, heatproof bowl. Set the bowl over a saucepan of barely simmering water, and stir until melted and smooth.

2. In a glass measuring cup, dissolve the instant coffee in the milk.

3. With an electric mixer, beat the butter, vanilla, and salt in a large mixing bowl for 3 minutes. Beat in the melted chocolate until blended, scraping the side of the bowl occasionally. Gradually beat in the confectioner's sugar until light and fluffy. Beat in the coffee mixture, 1 tablespoon at a time, until the mixture reaches spreading consistency.

4. This frosting can be made a day in advance. Store in an airtight container in the refrigerator, and bring back to room temperature before icing the cake.

COFFEE-WALNUT CAKE

IN THE UNITED STATES, "COFFEE CAKE" connotes a whole different creation than it does in Ireland. American coffee cake is not an iced cakey cake at all; it is often a cinnamon streusel, Bundt-shaped pastry traditionally served alongside coffee. I still remember the poppyseed coffee cake that my grandmother sourced from her local Eastern European bakery and always, always had on hand whenever we visited.

So, at first, I didn't know what to make of the Irish idea of coffee cake, which is basically a coffee-flavored sponge layer cake slathered in sweet coffee-caramel flavored icing. But, over time, this cake has become one of my favorites.

Makes one 8-inch layer cake

FOR THE SPONGE

½ cup (54 g) walnut pieces

1 cup (225 g) superfine sugar

1 cup (227 g) soft unsalted butter
(plus some for greasing)

1⅓ cups (166 g) all-purpose flour

4 teaspoons instant espresso powder

2½ teaspoons baking powder

½ teaspoon baking soda

4 large eggs

1 to 2 tablespoons milk

FOR THE BUTTERCREAM FROSTING

3¼ cups (468 g) confectioner's sugar

¾ cup (170 g) unsalted butter, softened

2½ teaspoons instant espresso powder,
dissolved in 1 tablespoon boiling water

10 walnut halves, finely chopped, for garnish

1. **MAKE THE CAKE:** Preheat the oven to 350°F (175°C). Butter two 8-inch springform pans, and line the bottom of each with parchment paper; set aside.

2. Put the walnut pieces and sugar in a food processor, and pulse to a fine powder. Add the butter, flour, espresso powder, baking powder, baking soda, and eggs; process to a smooth batter. Add the milk through the funnel with the motor still running, or just pulsing, to loosen the batter; it should have a soft consistency, so add more milk if you need to.

3. Divide the mixture between the lined pans, and bake for 25 minutes, or until the sponge has risen and feels springy to the touch. Remove the cakes from the oven, and cool in their pans on wire racks for about 10 minutes. Turn them out on the racks and peel off the parchment paper.

4. When the sponges are cool, make the buttercream.

5. MAKE THE BUTTERCREAM: Pulse the confectioner's sugar in the food processor, then add the butter and process to make a smooth icing. Add the dissolved espresso powder while it's still hot, pulsing to blend into the buttercream.

6. If you are mixing by hand, sift the confectioner's sugar and beat it into the butter with a wooden spoon. Then add the hot coffee.

7. ICE THE CAKE: Place one cake layer upside down on a cake stand or serving plate. Spread about half the icing on top. Place the second layer, right-side up (so the two flat sides of the cakes meet in the middle), on top, and cover the top and sides with the remaining icing.

8. This cake is meant to be a bit rustic, so however the frosting goes on is fine. Sprinkle the finely chopped walnuts on top of the icing and all around the edges.

Scullery
NOTES Serve the cake with Sweet Cream Ice Cream (see page 23) for an extra-special treat.

FARMHOUSE *TRES LECHES* CAKE

THIS DENSE AND CREAMY DAIRY CAKE is indeed made using milk in three different forms: whole, evaporated, and condensed. When I first developed this recipe, I wanted to try and use all three milks fresh from the farm, even the seemingly complicated evaporated and condensed milks, so I learned how to prepare each from scratch.

While it does take a fair bit of time, both evaporated and condensed milk are very simple to make, and the flavor is far superior to any canned version from the supermarket.

The preparation of this cake is very similar to that of angel food cake, except the recipe includes the egg yolks as well. It is important to sift the flour at least three times and keep all ingredients really airy throughout the mixing process. If you have children, this is fun to make with them as it involves poking holes in the cake with a toothpick, which kids have loads of fun doing.

I encouraged our little farmer, Geoffrey, to assist me in everything from manning the mixer to the pricking and, finally, pouring the *tres leches* over the cake. Let's just say, he is very proud of "his milk cake."

Makes one 8-inch 2-layer cake

Unsalted butter, for greasing the pans

1½ cups (187 g) all-purpose flour, plus more for coating the pans

1 tablespoon baking powder

¼ teaspoon ground cinnamon

6 large egg whites

1½ cups (300 g) granulated sugar

3 large egg yolks

2½ teaspoons vanilla extract, divided

½ cup (120 ml) whole milk

1 cup (237 ml) Evaporated Milk (see page 27)

2 cups (480 ml) heavy cream

1 cup (237 ml) Sweetened Condensed Milk (see page 26)

1 tablespoon dark rum

---

1. Preheat the oven to 350°F (175°C). Butter and flour the bottoms and sides of two 8-inch cake pans; set aside.

2. Whisk together the flour, baking powder, and cinnamon in a large bowl. In another bowl, beat the egg whites with an electric mixer until stiff peaks form, 7 to 8 minutes. Gradually beat in the sugar. Add the egg yolks, one at a time, beating to blend between additions. Beat in 2 teaspoons of the vanilla. Add the flour mixture in three additions, alternating with the milk in two additions (you begin and end with the flour mixture). Pour the batter into the pans; smooth the top.

3. Bake for 25 minutes. Reduce the temperature to 325°F (165°C), and continue baking until the cake is golden brown and the middle springs back when pressed, 20 to 25 minutes. Remove from the oven,

and let the cake cool in the pans for 15 minutes. Invert onto a wire rack set inside a rimmed baking sheet.

4. Whisk together the remaining ½ teaspoon vanilla, Evaporated Milk, 1 cup of the heavy cream, Sweetened Condensed Milk, and rum in a medium bowl. Poke holes all over the top of the cake with a skewer. Slowly drizzle half of the sauce over the cake, letting the liquid soak in before adding more. Let sit for 10 minutes.

5. Invert a plate on top of each cake. Lift the rack and gently invert the cake onto the plate. Drizzle the remaining sauce, including any liquid collected in the baking sheet, over the cake. Whip the remaining cream and frost the stacked cakes with it.

Scullery
NOTES

Icing this cake with whipped cream is optional. It is excellent either way!

FARMHOUSE BUTTERMILK BEIGNETS

A BEIGNET IS A FRITTER of choux paste covered in confectioner's sugar. Who can resist a little fried dough plunged into confectioner's sugar? No one on this farm, I can tell you! Using fresh buttermilk instead of cultured or evaporated adds fluffiness. These are best eaten immediately (is there any other way?), but they will keep for a week if stored properly.

While some say the word *beignet* comes from the Celtic word *bigne,* meaning "to raise," beignets are mostly associated with New Orleans, Louisiana, where people have flocked to Café Du Monde for decades to indulge in these fabulous French fritters.

Makes 20 beignets

¾ cup (180 ml) whole milk

1½ cups (375 ml) buttermilk

4 teaspoons active dry yeast

2½ tablespoons sugar

3½ cups (445 g) strong bread flour,
    plus extra for flouring the work surface

½ teaspoon baking soda

¼ teaspoon salt

Peanut or vegetable oil, for frying

Confectioner's sugar, to serve

1. Heat the whole milk in a small saucepan over medium-high heat until small bubbles form on the surface. Remove from the heat, add the buttermilk, and pour into a stand mixer fitted with the whisk. Whisk in the yeast and sugar; set aside for 5 minutes.

2. Add the flour, baking soda, and salt; mix on low speed, using the dough hook, until the dry ingredients are moistened, 3 to 4 minutes. Increase the mixer speed to medium and continue mixing until the dough forms a loose ball but is still wet and tacky, 1 to 2 minutes longer.

3. Cover the bowl with plastic wrap and set the dough aside in a warm place for 1 hour.

4. Pour 3 inches of oil into a large pot, and heat to a temperature of 375°F (190°C) over medium heat, about 20 minutes.

5. Line a plate with paper towels and set aside.

6. Turn the dough out on a lightly floured work surface. Sprinkle the top of the dough with flour, gently press to flatten, fold it in half, and tuck the ends under to create a rough-shaped round. Dust again and roll out to a ½-inch- to ⅓-inch-thick circle.

7. Let the dough rest for 1 minute, then cut into 2-inch squares with a chef's knife or a pizza wheel (you should get about 20 beignets).

8. Gently stretch a beignet lengthwise, and carefully drop it into the oil. Add a few more, and fry for 2 to 3 minutes, until puffed and golden brown, turning them often with a slotted spoon. Do not crowd the pot. Transfer to the prepared plate to drain while you cook the rest.

9. Serve warm, sprinkled liberally with confectioner's sugar, with hot coffee on the side.

Scullery NOTES | The beignet dough can be made up to 8 hours in advance. Line a baking sheet with oiled parchment paper. After cutting the dough, place the beignets on the paper and put another oiled sheet of parchment paper, oiled-side down, on top. Wrap the entire baking sheet with plastic wrap and refrigerate. The beignets can be fried straight from the refrigerator.

FARMHOUSE RICE PUDDING

ONE OF MY MOTHER-IN-LAW'S FAVORITE DESSERTS was a simple creamy, dreamy rice pudding with a spoonful of orchard jam. It took me a few tries to create a working recipe, and eventually I realized that a simple, old-fashioned baked version yields the perfect consistency to please everyone on the farm. Still creamy but with a golden, caramelized skin on top that everyone fights over, this recipe is easy to bang up and serve any day of the week.

Serves 6

1¾ cups (410 g) Evaporated Milk (see page 27)	⅓ cup (40 g) golden granulated or superfine sugar
2 cups (570 ml) whole milk	1 whole nutmeg
4 oz (110 g) pudding or arborio rice	2 tablespoons (25 g) butter
	1 cup (225 g) of your favorite jam (optional)

1. Preheat the oven to 300°F (150°C). Lightly butter a 9-inch round, ovenproof baking dish.
2. Mix together the Evaporated Milk and whole milk in a bowl. Put the rice and sugar in the baking dish, pour in the liquid, and stir well. Grate the whole nutmeg over the surface, then dot the butter on top in little pieces.
3. Bake on the center shelf of the oven for 30 minutes, then slide the shelf out and stir the mixture well. Bake for another 30 minutes, then stir again. Bake for another hour without stirring.
4. At the end of the cooking time, the rice grains will be swollen, with pools of creamy liquid all around them, and a caramelized coating on top. Allow to cool slightly. Slather the top with jam, if you like, and serve.

Scullery **NOTES** | If you cover the pudding completely with a layer of jam, it will be freshest if eaten within two days; otherwise, it will last for one week in the fridge.

QUEEN *of* PUDDINGS

USING MERINGUE IN IRISH DESSERTS was common years ago, as eggs were easier to come by than other more elaborate ingredients such as chocolate, nuts, exotic fruits, or marzipan. The same could be said for using jam and other conserves for sweet treats. Whatever the reason or heritage, this classic breadlike pudding is utterly delicious.

I discovered the Queen of Puddings when visiting a small cottage café in the southwest of Ireland while entertaining farm visitors for a weekend. I ordered the dessert for the name alone but fell hard for the sweet, jammy cake covered in a canopy of pillowy meringue. The recipe calls for raspberry jam, but I generally choose whatever preserves are in the larder. Marmalade makes for a particularly delicious combination too.

The Queen of Puddings is sweet but also very light in flavor and texture: the perfect dessert to end a quiet Sunday family lunch or to serve at a girly afternoon tea party or picnic.

Serves 4 to 6

Zest of 1 lemon	1 cup (85 g) bread crumbs
1½ cups (425 ml) milk	3 eggs
2 tablespoons butter	3 tablespoons raspberry jam
½ cup (100 g) sugar	

1. Preheat the oven to 350°F (175°C). Butter an 8-inch ceramic or Pyrex pie plate; set aside.
2. In a large saucepan, simmer the lemon zest and milk over medium heat for 5 minutes. Add the butter and ⅓ cup (67 g) of the sugar; cook until the sugar dissolves and the butter is melted. Stir in the bread crumbs and leave to cool.
3. Beat the egg yolks and mix into the bread crumb mixture a little at a time.
4. Pour the mixture into the prepared pie plate, and bake for 20 minutes, or until the custard is set.
5. Beat the egg whites and the rest of the sugar with an electric mixer until stiff peaks form.
6. In a small saucepan, heat the jam until melted.
7. Remove the pudding from the oven, pour the jam over it, then spoon the meringue over the whole thing, swirling the surface into peaks.
8. Return to the oven and bake until light brown, approximately 15 to 20 more minutes.

Scullery
NOTES | Use a piping bag to press out pretty pointed dollops of meringue for a striking presentation.

SMOKY *and* SALTY BUTTERMILK VANILLA FUDGE

MY MOTHER ALWAYS MADE CHOCOLATE FUDGE for the holidays, but since I preferred vanilla or butter pecan, I usually went without. After coming home with a box of the best vanilla fudge from a visit to Martha's Vineyard, I knew I had to try to make my own at home. Using scratch-made cultured buttermilk, my vanilla fudge comes out tangy and not too sweet. The smoked sea salt gives it that toasty campfire flavor that reminds me of bonfires on a New England beach.

Makes about 20 squares

2 cups (400 g) granulated sugar

1 cup (237 ml) Cultured Buttermilk (see page 9)

½ cup (115 g) unsalted butter, cut into pieces

1 tablespoon honey

1 teaspoon vanilla extract

1 teaspoon vanilla bean seeds

⅛ teaspoon smoked sea salt, plus more for decorating

1. Line a 9-by-5-inch loaf pan with parchment paper, leaving a generous overhang on the long sides; set aside.
2. Heat all the ingredients in a medium saucepan over medium-high heat, stirring occasionally, until the butter and sugar are melted, about 3 minutes. Bring to a simmer and cook, stirring occasionally, until the mixture reaches 238°F (114°C) on a candy thermometer, 8 to 10 minutes (the mixture will be pale gold and smell faintly of toffee).
3. Carefully pour into a medium bowl and, using an electric mixer on medium-high speed, beat until cool and thickened (it will be stiff and matte), 5 to 8 minutes.
4. Scrape the fudge into the prepared pan; smooth the top and sprinkle with smoked sea salt.
5. Let sit at least 1 hour before cutting into pieces.

Scullery NOTES | Fudge can be made up to one week ahead of time. Store it tightly wrapped at room temperature until ready to serve.

SWEET CARAWAY SEED CAKE

FOR AS LONG AS I CAN REMEMBER, I have had a crush on caraway. Maybe it's because when I was growing up, there was always a loaf of rye in the bread box, and caraway seeds were also sprinkled on various suppertime dishes, such as pan-roasted pork chops or poached fish. The distinct aniselike flavor is delicious and always brings back fond memories of home.

When I noticed this classic seed cake recipe turning up in many of the old Irish cookbooks I have been collecting, I put it on my must-make list. I could not wait to sink my teeth into a slice and see how caraway would fare in a sweet cake. And lo and behold, it is the perfect balance of sweet and savory—and delicious.

Serves about 8

¾ cup (175 g) butter, softened

1½ cups (175 g) superfine or granulated sugar

3 large eggs

About 1 tablespoon milk or water

½ teaspoon vanilla extract

1½ cups (225 g) all-purpose flour

½ teaspoon baking powder

1 tablespoon fresh caraway seeds

1. Preheat the oven to 350°F (175°C). Line the base of a 7-inch springform pan with parchment paper; set aside.
2. Cream the butter in a mixing bowl with a wooden spoon. Add the sugar and beat until light and fluffy. Whisk the eggs, milk or water, and vanilla together, and gradually add to the creamed butter and sugar. Fold in the flour in batches; mix the baking powder in with the last addition of the flour. Gently mix in the caraway seeds. Pour into the prepared cake pan.
3. Bake for 50 to 60 minutes. The cake is done when a toothpick comes out clean. Remove it from the oven, and let cool in the pan on a wire rack.
4. Cool completely before slicing.

Origins of Caraway Seed Cake

CARAWAY SEED CAKE IS A VARIATION OF ONE of the most popular cakes made in Ireland, the Madeira. It is similar to American pound cake but lighter and flakier; since a full pound of flour, butter, and eggs are *not* used, it is moist and sweet in all the right ways. Madeira is considered a sponge cake and is the base of many traditional Irish cakes, including the traditional birthday cake, which is simply a Madeira made with citrus peel, gingerroot, and golden raisins. Other variations on the Madeira are cherry; golden raisin; rice (using rice flour); chocolate; Excelsior (coconut); Athassal (tricolored with almond, chocolate, and vanilla); jam sandwich (layered with raspberry jam); ginger; Genoa (fruit peel with sliced almonds on top); poppy seed; and, of course, the classic Christmas fruitcake.

According to my mother-in-law, Madeira cake was originally made to be nibbled by the ladies as they sipped their Madeira or port wine. This nibbling has been going on in Ireland since the eighteenth or nineteenth century, and it certainly doesn't look like it's going anywhere anytime soon. Give this recipe a try, and have it on hand when friends call over for a cuppa and some chit-chat on a crisp autumn afternoon.

FARMHOUSE SPRING PUDDING

FOR MY FIRST EASTER IN IRELAND, I was kindly invited to dinner at the farm. I remember my mother-in-law, Peggy, had prepared a glorious roast dinner that we all feasted on, while the sun shone through the windows and the birds chirped and sang outside.

I had decided to bring along a dessert to share. My recipe for rhubarb-strawberry crumble was a spring staple in my mother's kitchen. I was a bit nervous, as it was the first time I'd made anything for my husband's family since the previous Thanksgiving, when my pumpkin pie was met with varying degrees of admiration.

After we finished our main course, the desserts were brought out, mine being part of a larger selection. Everyone chose a little bit of everything. Luckily, the crumble went over very well and was liked by everyone, including Richard's grandmother, who thought it was "beautiful." This crumble has been requested several times for our Easter celebration and is now a seasonal farm staple.

My Farmhouse Spring Pudding was adapted as a variation of my family recipe for rhubarb-strawberry crumble. In an effort to make it even more Irish, I made the topping more like the traditional Irish Eve's pudding-style, cake-topped, cooked fruit dessert.

Serves 4 to 6

FOR THE FRUIT BASE

1½ cups (225 g) diced rhubarb

1½ cups (225 g) strawberries

½ cup (100 g) sugar

1½ teaspoons vanilla bean seeds

1 tablespoon orange juice, freshly squeezed

FOR THE TOPPING

3¼ tablespoons unsalted butter

¼ cup (50 g) superfine sugar, plus more for dusting

2 teaspoons lemon zest

1 large egg, beaten

⅔ cup (85 g) all-purpose flour

1 teaspoon baking powder

½ teaspoon salt

1 or 2 tablespoons milk

1. Preheat the oven to 350°F (175°C). Grease a 1-quart baking dish with butter; set aside.
2. Combine the rhubarb, berries, sugar, vanilla bean seeds, and juice. Set aside for 1 hour.

3. Cream together the butter, sugar, and lemon zest until light and fluffy, about 5 minutes. Slowly add the egg, and beat until well blended. Sift together the flour, baking powder, and salt; fold into the butter mixture. Add enough milk to reach a dropping consistency.

4. Pour the fruit mixture into the prepared baking dish. Spread the batter over the fruit. Bake in the center of the oven for about 25 to 30 minutes, until the topping is golden brown. Remove from the oven, and dust liberally with superfine sugar. Best eaten the same day, but will keep for one week in the fridge.

RICH CHOCOLATE BUTTERMILK CAKE

CONFESSION: CHOCOLATE IS NOT MY FAVORITE CAKE. I have always been partial to vanilla or fruity flavored cakes and would choose those over chocolate every time. On the flip side, everyone else on this farm is addicted to chocolate. Over the years, I have come to the conclusion that a farmer's affinity for chocolate can be attributed to energy-craving exhaustion. Nevertheless, it is the family favorite, so I decided early on that I would have to perfect a chocolate cake that we all would love. I wanted to create a creamy, mellow, supermoist chocolatey-but-not-overpoweringly-so chocolate layer cake. The test was on. I started with a sour cream chocolate cake, then tried crème fraîche and even cream cheese. While a couple of those tasted nice, not until I incorporated buttermilk did I discover the ideal formula. This is a rich, dense, somewhat tangy cake with a superbuttery chocolate buttercream icing and creamy deep chocolate ganache. It is well suited for chocolate-loving family and friends, but it is also a treat for those who claim they aren't absolutely crazy for chocolate.

Makes one 9-inch layer cake

FOR THE CAKE

1¾ cups (218 g) all-purpose flour

2 cups (400 g) granulated sugar

¾ cup (90 g) unsweetened cocoa powder

1½ teaspoons baking soda

¾ teaspoon salt

2 large eggs

1 cup (237 ml) buttermilk

½ cup (113 g) butter, melted

1 tablespoon vanilla extract

1 cup (237 ml) hot coffee (or 2 teaspoons instant coffee in 1 cup boiling water)

FOR THE CHOCOLATE FILLING

7 oz (200 g) dark chocolate (at least 70% cocoa solids), chopped

17 tablespoons unsalted butter, softened

4 egg yolks

1¼ cups (156 g) confectioner's sugar, sifted

FOR THE CHOCOLATE GANACHE

5 oz (140 g) dark chocolate (about 52% cocoa solids), chopped

1¼ cups (300 ml) heavy cream

FOR DECORATION (OPTIONAL)

Chocolate curls

Unsweetened cocoa powder and confectioner's sugar, for dusting

1. **MAKE THE CAKE:** Preheat the oven to 350°F (175°C). Grease and flour two 9-inch round baking pans (or line with parchment paper circles); set aside.

2. In the bowl of a stand mixer fitted with the paddle attachment, stir together the flour, sugar, cocoa, baking soda, and salt. Add the eggs, buttermilk, melted butter, and vanilla; beat until smooth, about 3 minutes. Remove the bowl from the mixer, and stir in the hot coffee with a rubber spatula. The batter will be very runny.

3. Divide evenly between the two pans, and bake on the middle rack of the oven for about 35 minutes, until a toothpick inserted in the center comes out clean with just a few moist crumbs attached.

4. Remove from the oven and let cool 15 minutes in the pans. Run a butter knife around the edges of each cake. Place a wire cooling rack over the top of each pan and flip the cakes; gently thump on the bottom of the pans until the cakes release.

5. **MAKE THE FILLING:** Melt the chocolate in a heatproof bowl over a saucepan of barely simmering water. Set aside to cool slightly. In a large mixing bowl, cream the butter with an electric mixer for at least 10 minutes at high speed, until pale and fluffy. Add the egg yolks and confectioner's sugar, and beat vigorously for another 5 minutes. Once the mixture is thoroughly combined, remove 2 tablespoons and stir them into the cooled, melted chocolate. Then slowly pour the melted chocolate down the side of the mixing bowl (to prevent the eggs from scrambling), folding it in quickly and gently until fully combined and smooth.

6. **MAKE THE GANACHE:** Once the cakes are cooled, put the chocolate in a large bowl. Bring the cream to a boil, then pour it over the chocolate, and stir until it melts. Set aside to cool. With a hand mixer, beat the cooled chocolate until it barely forms soft peaks; make sure not to overbeat it, or it will become too stiff to spread.

7. **ASSEMBLE THE CAKE:** Split the cakes in half horizontally with a sharp serrated knife. Spread the chocolate filling onto each layer (except the top one) and sandwich the layers together. Frost the cake with the chocolate ganache. Decorate with chocolate curls, and dust with cocoa powder and confectioner's sugar, if you wish.

NAOMI'S MIDNIGHT TREACLE PUDDING

EVEN THOUGH—OR PERHAPS *BECAUSE*—I'm now a farmer's wife and mother to a young son, I still crave a getaway on the rare occasion I'm free. Luckily, I have a lovely group of international friends whom I meet for coffee and cake—and every once in a while, a night out on the town.

One such friend is Naomi Sparks, who would often graciously host me overnight since we live such a distance from the city. We have spent many a night sitting in her kitchen, reading cookbooks until 4 A.M. after coming home from a long evening of dinner and dancing in Limerick City.

Once Naomi offered to "whip up a midnight treacle pudding" when we arrived back at her place very late and very hungry. She started measuring sugar, butter, flour, eggs, and milk and stirring up a storm. She popped the mix into a microwave-safe bowl. Within fifteen minutes, a proper-looking pudding with two spoons sat in front of us. We dug in and devoured it. The flavor and texture of this recipe is a soft, spongy cake with lovely, gooey syrup throughout—like a giant fluffy pancake soaked in syrup.

I don't normally recommend microwave baking, but in this case, I couldn't resist.

Makes one pudding cake

½ cup (100 g) sugar

8 tablespoons butter, softened,
   plus more for greasing the bowl

1 scant cup (100 g) all-purpose flour

2 teaspoons baking powder

1 teaspoon salt

2 eggs

2 tablespoons milk

4 tablespoons golden syrup
   (or light corn syrup)

1. With an electric mixer, blend together the sugar, butter, flour, baking powder, salt, eggs, and milk in a large mixing bowl.
2. Butter the bottom and sides of a 2-pint plastic or glass pudding basin, ramekin, or custard dish with butter. Pour the golden syrup into the bottom of the basin, then pour in the batter. Microwave on high for 5 minutes. Let sit for at least 1 minute.
3. Turn the cake out onto a plate. Serve immediately with custard or a dollop of whipped cream. Do not let it sit too long, or it will lose its cakelike texture and become rubbery. As Naomi recommends, certainly don't bother keeping some for the next day. It must be eaten immediately.

Scullery **NOTES** | Naomi says, "If you're posh, serve this in bowls with cream or custard. But if it's good friends or family, just turn the pudding out onto a plate, arm everyone with a spoon, and attack."

RICHARD'S "PROPER" IRISH COFFEE

WHEN RICHARD AND I WERE FIRST DATING, he took me to a quaint little restaurant in Kerry on a rainy, cold evening. We shared a dazzling meal that started off with a rich and zesty Dingle crab and roasted new potato salad, followed by a succulent loin of local free-range pork served with stewed apple and sage stuffing. After dinner, Richard ordered an Irish coffee for me. Until then, I'd never tried one. When he could see how delighted I was by this creamy, whiskey-spiked coffee, he proudly claimed that he made "*the* best Irish coffee," and one day he would show me. I figured since he grew up near Foynes, County Limerick, the celebrated birthplace of Irish coffee, perhaps it was true.

Years later, on our first Christmas together, Richard offered to make Irish coffees after the meal. He painstakingly laid out all the ingredients and carefully prepared each of us a cup, explaining each step as he prepared the drink: "Never let the cream drop into the middle of the coffee, always let it glide off the back of the spoon onto one side of the glass for an even coating." It was perfect, the best I've ever had.

The ingredients for Irish coffee don't vary much from person to person or place to place, nor does the process. The trick is all in the weight of the hand as you pour. I don't make an Irish coffee anything like Richard's. And I've never had one nearly as good. So, give it a go. You may have a natural flair for it.

Makes 1 *cup*

6 oz (175 ml) hot, fresh-brewed strong coffee	1 jigger (40 ml) Irish whiskey
1 teaspoon brown sugar	Heavy cream, lightly whipped

1. Pour hot water into a heatproof cup or glass to warm it, then pour out the water. This will also prevent your glass from cracking.
2. Fill the glass about three-quarters full with the coffee, add sugar, and stir until it is fully dissolved. Add the Irish whiskey.
3. Top with freshly whipped cream using Richard's "proper" method: Put a dollop of whipped cream on the back of one spoon. With a second spoon, push the cream very slowly down the back of the first spoon, allowing it to slide gently onto the coffee, being careful not to break the coffee's surface. (This takes some practice.)
4. Enjoy while hot!

CLAIRE'S FRANGIPANE

MY FRIEND CLAIRE ALWAYS HAS SOMETHING SWEET and almond-flavored on hand to go with a cup of tea in her kitchen. She is one of those women who can whip up an amazing meal for ten while looking after three small children, a puppy, and a smattering of craft projects and assembling an ornate fondant cake—all while looking like Gwyneth Paltrow. If she weren't so kind and generous, you'd have it in for her.

When Claire first served me a slice of her frangipane for an afternoon tea, I had never eaten a cake that was . . . well, the best word I can think of to describe it is *moreish*. *Moreish* is an Irish colloquialism that means something that you just can't get enough of, and I could eat Claire's frangipane until the cows come home.

Frangipane is a crumbly, almond sweetened cake, often used in a classic jam-and-almond Bakewell tart that features an almond cake layer slathered in jam, but it absolutely sings on its own. Supereasy and quick, Claire's version is a perfect treat for last-minute guests.

Makes one 8-inch cake

¾ cup (150 g) sugar

⅔ cup (150 g) butter

2 eggs

1 cup (150 g) almond flour

¼ cup (33 g) all-purpose flour (optional)

1. Preheat the oven to 350°F (175°C). Grease an 8-inch springform pan, and line the bottom with parchment paper; set aside.
2. Beat the sugar and butter together in a stand mixer fitted with the paddle attachment until light and fluffy, about 5 minutes. Add the eggs, one at a time, then slowly pour in the flours and blend well.
3. Pour the batter into the prepared pan and bake for 30 to 40 minutes.
4. Remove from the oven, dust with sugar, and cool. Slice and serve with a dollop of cream or just on its own.

Scullery **NOTES** | I have made this recipe omitting the all-purpose flour (with no substitution) for a gluten-free version, and it is just as terrific.

CHAPTER 12

Country Kids

LIVING IN THE IRISH COUNTRYSIDE IS ESSENTIALLY A CHILD'S FANTASY. WHAT WE READ IN OUR YOUNG SON'S BOOKS AND SEE IN HIS FAVORITE FILMS—CHARMING CASTLES, ENCHANTED FORESTS, SWEET CALVES, WOOLLY LAMBS, HUGE TRUCKS, TINKERING TRACTORS, GALLOPING HORSES, CROWING ROOSTERS, LAYING HENS, FEISTY FARM CATS, BUSY BUILDING SITES, PRICKLY HEDGEHOGS, RUNNING HARES, AND RED FOXES WITH BIG FLUFFY TAILS—ARE ALL IN GEOFFREY'S BACKYARD.

Kid-friendly treats are equally magical. Children are spoiled for choice with Ireland's best-loved kid's classics—cookies of every style, from chocolate-dipped to snappy ginger nut, fluffy coconut-'n-cream, and the butteriest of buttery shortbread. In fact, many children learn to enjoy a cup of tea with their cookies from a young age in Ireland—our son included, which never fails to make me smile.

I just love putting a spin on some of the favorites we enjoy at the farm. Because adding a mile of meringue to a classic banoffee pie, putting the snickerdoodle in griddle scones, and making a campfire toad in the hole is a whole lot of fun. And fun can only make children's food better, right?

MILE-HIGH BANOFFEE PIE

BANOFFEE PIE, the iconic caramel cream pie with bananas and whipped cream, is a toothsome masterpiece found at most cafés and on the dessert carts of many Irish restaurants. I like to think of it as the pie version of bananas Foster.

As the story goes, the pie was invented by Ian Dowding and Nigel Mackenzie at The Hungry Monk restaurant in Jevington, East Sussex, England, in 1972. It featured soft caramel toffee layered with bananas and topped with whipped cream. They called the dish "Banoffi," and it proved so popular with their customers that they couldn't take it off the menu.

In the spirit of Americana, I've changed the topping to meringue and stacked it up sky-high. Kids take one look at the cartoonlike height of this favored dessert and go bananas for it.

Makes one 9-inch pie

FOR THE PASTRY

3¼ cups (400 g) all-purpose flour,
   plus more for rolling

14 tablespoons cold butter,
   cut into small pieces

1 egg white, for brushing

FOR THE FILLING

3 tablespoons butter

1 cup (175 g) light unrefined cane sugar

1⅓ cups (300 ml) whole milk

3 tablespoons cornstarch, sifted

4 egg yolks

2 bananas, peeled and sliced into coin
   shapes

Cocoa powder or chocolate shavings
   (optional)

FOR THE MERINGUE

5 egg whites

1 cup (200 g) superfine sugar

1. **FOR THE PASTRY:** Tip the flour into a bowl, then rub in the butter with your fingertips until it resembles bread crumbs. Add 4 to 6 tablespoons cold water, bit by bit, until a dough is formed. Knead briefly on a floured surface. Shape into a ball, wrap in plastic wrap, and chill for 30 minutes.
2. Preheat the oven to 400°F (200°C). Roll the pastry on a floured surface into a circle large enough to line a 9-inch pie tin with a slight overhang. Cover with tin foil and fill with baking beans. Place on a baking tray and bake for 15 minutes before carefully removing the foil and beans.
3. Brush liberally with egg white, place the pastry case back in the oven for 10 minutes or until golden, then remove from the oven and trim the edges. Turn the oven down to 300°F (150°C).

4. **FOR THE FILLING:** Melt the butter in a saucepan over low heat and stir in the sugar until dissolved completely.

5. In a small bowl, add milk to the cornstarch and stir into a smooth paste.

6. Pour the milk and cornstarch paste into the butter mix, slowly bring to a boil, and simmer for 2 to 3 minutes, stirring continuously, until thickened. Leave to cool slightly.

7. In a separate mixing bowl, beating all the time with a whisk, pour ½ the milk/cornstarch/butter mixture onto the egg yolks, then pour back into the rest of the milk/cornstarch mixture on the stove, stirring constantly.

8. Bring to a boil and simmer for 2 to 3 minutes, or until thick. Turn off the heat, but leave the mixture in the pan—it should be warm when topped with the meringue.

9. **FOR THE MERINGUE:** Whisk the egg whites with an electric mixer until they are stiff. Sprinkle in half the sugar and whisk again until stiff and shiny, adding the remaining sugar, 1 tablespoon at a time, and whisking until stiff again.

10. **ASSEMBLE THE PIE:** Place a layer of banana slices into the pastry shell, then spoon in the warm caramel filling.

11. Lightly sprinkle with cocoa powder or shavings if you wish.

12. With a wooden spoon, spoon and swirl the meringue over the top to make a dome shape.

13. Bake for 35 minutes on a low oven rack until the meringue is golden and crisping up. Remove the pie from the oven and allow to cool before eating.

Scullery **NOTES** | Leftovers keep for a week in the refrigerator, but the pie is best eaten on the day it is prepared.

SNICKER-GRIDDLE SCONES

GRIDDLE SCONES ARE THE ORIGINAL SCONES, developed well before baking powder was a common leavener and scone-baking moved to the oven. In Ireland, this would have meant using a griddle on top of a wood-burning stove, a traditional technique that my sister-in-law's mother will still use from time to time.

I had my first taste of a griddle scone while visiting a neighboring farm the first year after I moved to the Irish countryside. While we were sitting in her kitchen sipping a welcome cup of coffee after feeding the lambs, my new friend pulled out a mixing bowl, made up some scone dough, and fried it on a hot griddle all in ten minutes flat, never missing a beat of the gossip she was sharing. She cut the cakelike scone into four wedges and served them straight from the pan. We slathered our hot slices with butter and honey and slurped our coffee amid conversation and our children climbing at our feet.

Since we always love snickerdoodle cookies when traveling stateside, I experimented with cinnamon, and these scones have since become a Saturday morning staple in our kitchen. If you prefer a more traditional Irish griddle scone, simply omit the spice.

Makes 12 scones

1 cup (200 g) all-purpose flour

2 teaspoons baking powder

1 teaspoon salt

1 teaspoon ground cinnamon

1½ tablespoons butter

2 tablespoons light unrefined cane sugar

1 egg

⅓ cup (75 ml) whole milk

2 tablespoons butter, for frying

Butter and honey or maple syrup, to serve

1. In a large mixing bowl, whisk together the flour, baking powder, salt, and cinnamon. Rub the butter in with your fingers until the mixture resembles coarse bread crumbs. Add the sugar and stir well.
2. In a separate bowl, beat the egg, then pour in the milk. Gradually pour the egg mixture into the flour mixture, stirring first with a spoon, then with your hands, to make a soft but not sticky dough. Turn it out on a floured work surface, and knead until smooth.
3. Divide the dough into three equal portions. With a rolling pin, roll into circles that are about ½ inch thick. To make the scones, either use scone cutters or cut into triangles.

4. Heat a heavy-bottom frying pan over medium heat and melt the butter. Cook the scones in batches for a couple of minutes on each side, until golden brown.

5. To serve, spread with butter and drizzle with honey or maple syrup.

Scullery
NOTES

Sorghum syrup is lovely on these scones as well!

DARK CHOCOLATE-ORANGE
BISCUIT CAKE

PERHAPS THE MOST POPULAR, best-loved, easy-to-make family recipe, the chocolate biscuit cake is many an Irish mummy's go-to sweet treat. But it's not just for children. I have seen chocolate biscuit birthday and celebration cakes, including, most famously, the wedding cake for Prince William and Kate Middleton.

This no-bake treat is chilled in the refrigerator and can easily be frozen so you can have it on hand when unexpected callers drop by for a chat. I love adding Jaffa cakes, a chocolate-covered orange cake-like cookie found in Ireland and the United Kingdom, to the mixture. A creamy and crunchy sliver goes equally well with a big glass of cold milk or a cuppa tea.

Makes three 10-inch logs

2 cups (300 g) digestive biscuits

1 cup (100 g) rich tea biscuits
(or shortbread)

1⅓ cups (100 g) candied orange peels
covered in dark chocolate (or Jaffa cakes,
if available), roughly chopped

½ cup (100 g) unsalted butter, melted

2 cups (300 g) chopped dark chocolate
(60–75% cocoa solids)

One 14-oz (400-g) can condensed milk

Confectioner's sugar, to serve

1. In a large mixing bowl, roughly crush the digestive and rich tea biscuits. Add the candied orange peel, and stir in the melted butter.
2. Melt the chocolate in a large bowl over a saucepan of simmering water, then stir in the condensed milk. Pour this mixture over the biscuits and stir well to combine.
3. Put a large double layer of plastic wrap on a clean work surface that has been wiped with a damp cloth (this will help the film to stick). Spoon one-third of the biscuit cake mix down the center of the film; you need a rough log shape about 10 inches long and 2 inches wide.
4. Wrap the log in the plastic wrap, pushing against the work surface to make it tight. Once it is completely covered, hold the ends of the plastic wrap and roll the log as if it were a rolling pin, to help tighten the wrap. Tie the ends of the plastic wrap into a knot. Repeat this twice with the rest of the batter to make a total of three logs. Chill the logs for at least 8 hours in the refrigerator, or preferably overnight.

5. To serve, unwrap a log and sprinkle it with confectioner's sugar, then slice carefully using a hot knife.
6. The logs can also be frozen in an airtight wrapping or container and will keep for one month. Thaw to room temperature, slice, and serve.

Scullery **NOTES** | This can also be prepared in a cake pan and cut into squares. Biscuit cake makes a great hostess gift or contribution to a school bake sale.

If you have trouble sourcing digestive biscuits, honey graham crackers could be used instead, giving the cake a different flavor.

OAT-MILLET-CHIA-BANANA FLAPJACKS

ONE DAY AFTER LUNCH AT A LOCAL CAFE, I made my way up to the cash register to pay the bill.

"Would you like anything else?"

I pointed to the large glass cookie jar next to the till. "Sure, may I have two of these gorgeous-looking granola bars, please?"

"Two flapjacks for takeaway?" the clerk said.

Puzzled, I shook my head. "Oh, no, the granola bars in the cookie jar."

"Those yokes? They are flapjacks," she replied.

"Wait, what? Flapjacks are pancakes in America."

With that lilting Irish irony, she said, "Well, flapjacks are flapjacks in Ireland."

"Really?"

She grinned. "Really. And they'll sure put you in fine fettle."

Eventually I figured out that flapjacks are *not* flapjacks, and a "fine fettle" means good health or good humor. The flapjacks I took home were devoured before the end of the day—a fine fettle indeed.

You can experiment with your own favorite nuts, seeds, oils, fruits, and other healthy grains. Flapjacks are a versatile snack to nibble with tea, after feeding calves or taking a run, and are superfantastic for the lunchbox.

Makes 12 flapjacks

⅓ cup raw honey

¾ cup (200 g) unsalted butter

1 medium-ripe or soft banana, mashed

1 teaspoon cinnamon

2 cups (330 g) organic porridge oats

1 cup (115 g) organic millet flakes, plus more for topping

½ cup (55 g) chia seeds

Pinch of sea salt

---

1. Preheat the oven to 350°F (175°C). Butter a 9-by-13-inch Swiss roll pan, and line the base with parchment paper; set aside.
2. Place the honey, butter, banana mash, and cinnamon in a large saucepan over low heat, stirring until the butter has melted completely.
3. Combine the oats, millet, chia seeds, and salt in a large mixing bowl. Pour over the banana and honey mixture, and stir to coat the oats mixture.
4. Pour into the prepared pan, and spread evenly to fill the pan, making sure the surface is flat. Sprinkle a small handful of millet flakes over the top.

5. Bake for 25 minutes, or until golden brown. Remove from the oven while the flapjack is still slightly soft; it will harden when it cools. Place the pan on a wire cooling rack, cut the flapjack into squares, and leave in the pan until completely cool.
6. Flapjacks will keep for up to one week in the bread box and a few days more if refrigerated.

FIONN'S SWEET CARROT PANCAKES

WHEN GEOFFREY WAS ABOUT FOUR YEARS OLD, I came up with a bedtime story for him about a small Irish boy named Fionn who lives on a farm and won't eat his vegetables. It starts like this:

Once there was a little boy named Fionn who lived on a farm, on a green, green island in the blue, blue sea. On Fionn's farm there was a handful of happy cows, a few clucky chickens, and a gigantic garden filled with the most tremendously tasty vegetables. But little Fionn did not like vegetables. He would not eat them. Never. Ever.

The tale naturally ends with Fionn's clever recipe for carrot pancakes. The inspiration for this saga was that I couldn't get our son to eat his vegetables until he started growing his own food in our garden. Nowadays, he can't get enough of his vegetables, but still, the only way he will eat carrots is in these pancakes. The batter creates delicious waffles as well.

Makes eight 6-inch pancakes or waffles

2 eggs

1½ cups (375 ml) buttermilk

1 cup (80 g) finely grated carrot

½ cup (40 g) grated orange zest, plus more for serving

2 cups (220 g) all-purpose flour

2 tablespoons sugar (or honey)

4 teaspoons baking powder

¼ teaspoon salt

Butter, for frying

Honey butter or maple syrup, for serving

1. In a large mixing bowl, whisk together the eggs, buttermilk, carrot, and orange zest.
2. In a separate bowl, combine the flour, sugar, baking powder, and salt; stir well. Mix the flour mixture into the egg mixture just until combined; do not overbeat. Let the batter rest for 10 minutes.
3. Heat and liberally butter a griddle or waffle iron. Ladle ½ cup (250 ml) of batter onto it. For griddle cakes, cook until the edges are golden and bubbles begin to break on the surface, then flip and cook for the same amount of time. To make waffles, pour the batter onto the waffle iron and bake until steaming stops, per the manufacturer's instructions.
4. Garnish with orange zest, and serve with honey butter, maple syrup, or a topping of your choice.

TOAD *in the* HOLE

WE AMERICANS HAVE ENJOYED pigs in a blanket for years, but I had never eaten a toad in the hole until I moved to Ireland. Both are breakfast sausages combined with a sort of pancake, and while I can understand the origins of the pig, I'm still not sure about the toad. Nevertheless, toad in the hole has become a breakfast favorite on the farm, and the children go mad for it every time I pull it out of the oven.

When Geoffrey asked if we could have a campfire breakfast on a summer Sunday morning, the best recipe I could think of was to bake up a batch of toads in the hole in tin camping cups. Lo and behold, it worked, and the three of us sat perched on tree stumps in the garden wood, feasting and singing camping songs until our toads were all gone.

Serves 4

1½ cups (188 g) all-purpose flour

1 scant teaspoon kosher salt

Pinch of freshly ground black pepper

3 eggs, beaten

1½ cups (375 ml) whole milk

2 tablespoons melted butter

1 tablespoon vegetable oil

4 medium-size (1 lb; 450 g) Irish or English sausage made with pork and bread crumbs, or good-quality pork or beef sausage links (in casings)

1. In a large bowl, whisk together the flour, salt, and pepper. Make a well in the center of the flour. Pour in the eggs, milk, and melted butter, and whisk into the flour until smooth. Cover and let stand 30 minutes.

2. Coat the bottom and sides of four tin coffee mugs, an 8-by-12-inch or 9-inch square casserole dish, or a 4-hole popover tin with vegetable oil. Place a rack in the bottom third of the oven. Put your empty dish(es) of choice on the rack, and preheat the oven to 425°F (220°C).

3. Meanwhile, heat the vegetable oil in a skillet over medium-high heat. Add the sausages and brown them on at least a couple of sides.

4. When the sausages have browned, pull out the oven rack and place the sausages in the dish(es). Pour the batter over the sausages. Cook for about 20 to 30 minutes, or until the batter is risen and golden.

5. Serve at once.

Scullery | Sweeten the pancake batter a bit for American palates by adding ⅛ cup sugar to the dry
NOTES | ingredients and then drench them in maple syrup immediately upon removal from the oven, just before serving.

KIDDIE ELDERFLOWER
HONEYSUCKLE COCKTAILS

I HAVE FOND MEMORIES OF SIPPING SHIRLEY TEMPLES (or as my dad would refer to them, "kiddie cocktails") as a child. So I came up with this little concoction after Geoffrey innocently requested a pint of cider "like Daddy has" at an afternoon garden party we were hosting. He was all dressed up and just wanted to drink what everyone else was having, so I created a long drink that was sweet and looked sophisticated but was alcohol-free.

Refreshing and fruity, the combination of musky elderflower-honeysuckle nectar and sparkling water is the perfect thirst quencher for a long summer day on the farm, and it doubles as a dazzling drink for farm dinners al fresco.

Makes 1 quart (1 liter)

5 lb (2.5 kg) granulated or superfine sugar

5½ cups (1.5 liter) water

2 unwaxed lemons

1 orange

20 fresh elderflower heads, stalks trimmed

10 honeysuckle flower heads, freshly picked

Ice, to serve

Club soda or 7-up, to serve

1. Put the sugar and water into the largest saucepan you have. Heat without boiling over low heat, stirring occasionally, until the sugar has dissolved.
2. Pare the zest from the lemons using a vegetable peeler, then slice the lemons into rounds. Repeat with the orange.
3. Once the sugar has dissolved, bring the pan of syrup to a boil, then turn off the heat. Fill a large mixing bowl with cold water. Add all the flower heads, and swish them gently to loosen any dirt or bugs. Lift the flowers out one at a time, gently shake off excess water, and transfer to the syrup along with the lemon and orange zest and slices; stir well. Cover the pan and leave to infuse for 24 hours.
4. Sterilize your glass bottle (see page 92).
5. Line a colander with a clean tea towel, and set it over a large bowl or pan. Ladle in the syrup, letting it drip through slowly. Discard the bits left in the towel. Use a funnel and a ladle to fill the sterilized bottle. The cocktail is ready to drink right away and will keep in the fridge for up to six weeks. Or you

can freeze it in plastic containers or ice cube trays and defrost as needed. It keeps in the freezer for up to a year.

6. To make the cocktail, fill a tall glass with ice cubes, pour in 3 tablespoons elderflower cordial, top with soda, stir, and serve. You may garnish the glass with elderflower blossoms, if you desire.

Scullery
NOTES | Do not use flowers that have been picked in the rain; curiously, the fragrance and flavor are not as pronounced with wet flowers. You can add a jigger of vodka to each glass to make grown-up cocktails.

BOOKMAKER'S *BANH MI*

ONCE A YEAR, we pack a picnic and head to the local steeplechase, a horse race that is run from one point to another over fences and rolling hills in the raw Irish countryside. The first recorded steeplechase match in Ireland went from Buttevant Church to St. Mary's Church, Doneraile, County Cork, in 1752. The riders raced from the steeple in one church to the steeple in the second church, hence the name *steeple-chasing*. These freestyle runs generally take place throughout spring, summer, and autumn around the country, on grass and on sand beaches, from coast to coast with young, powerful thoroughbreds crashing over willow-woven fences and leaving dust in their wake.

The children get really excited about these intimate races and are absolutely smitten by the rows of bookies, all filled with wit and vinegar, set up to take bets for each race. We leave the races each time feeling as if we've time-traveled to another era.

It is said that years ago the traveling bookmakers would prepare special sandwiches for their work on race days: a simple steak sandwich with mustard in a baguette, pressed down flat so as to fit into their luggage, and aptly named "the Bookmaker."

We have started our own traditional picnic sandwich. With quick-pickled vegetables, these are more like a Vietnamese *banh mi* than the original Bookmaker, but we put them in our pack and eat them just like the bookies of yore.

Serves 4

2 large filet or sirloin steaks

2 garlic cloves, peeled and finely chopped

One ¾-inch (2-cm) piece gingerroot, peeled and finely chopped

3 tablespoons olive oil

1 tablespoon black pepper

1 tablespoon fish sauce

1 teaspoon dark soy sauce

FOR THE PICKLED VEGETABLES

2 to 3 large kale or chard leaves, stemmed and chopped into fine strips (or 1 julienned carrot, if children prefer)

1 small radish, peeled and thinly sliced

Pinch of salt

1 to 2 tablespoons rice wine vinegar

2 tablespoons sugar

½ chili pepper, deseeded and finely sliced

1 teaspoon finely chopped garlic

FOR THE SANDWICH

4 tablespoons mayonnaise

2 tablespoons chili sauce

1 large French baguette (or crusty roll such as Vienna)

½ cucumber, cut into long, wide strips using a vegetable peeler

1 small red pepper, finely sliced

Handful of fresh coriander (cilantro) leaves

1 tablespoon sesame seeds

1. Place the steaks in a shallow dish. Mix the garlic, ginger, olive oil, black pepper, and fish and soy sauces in a bowl; pour over the meat. Marinate for 3 hours, or overnight.
2. Just before cooking the steak, mix the kale, radish, salt, rice wine vinegar, sugar, chili pepper, and garlic in a large bowl; toss together well.
3. In a separate bowl, stir together the mayonnaise and chili sauce; set aside.
4. Place a heavy-bottom frying pan over a high heat; allow it to get smoking hot. Add the steaks. Cook for 2½ to 3 minutes on each side for medium doneness, another minute on each side if you like your steak well done, and a minute less on each side if you like it rare. Remove the steak from the pan, and let it rest for 5 minutes.
5. Slice each steak on the diagonal into 5 slices. Slice the baguette lengthwise, and spread the chili mayonnaise on both sides.
6. Place the beef on the mayonnaise, then pile on the pickled vegetables, cucumber, red pepper, and coriander; sprinkle with sesame seeds. Top with the other half of the bread.
7. Wrap the sandwich in plastic wrap, and place in the refrigerator with a heavy object on top. Just before leaving for your picnic, slice the baguette into four pieces, rewrap in paper, and you're off to the races!

339

ACKNOWLEDGMENTS

First and foremost, thank you, Richard McDonnell, for turning up in Minneapolis on that freezing February night and stealing my heart. You have been tirelessly supportive and encouraging of my cooking and writing journey and have taught me so much about farming and how to live with grace in the Irish countryside. You humble and inspire me each day.

Thank you, Roost Books, for publishing this book, with special appreciation to Jonathan Green, for your support in the beginning. I would like to express my gratitude to Jennifer Urban-Brown, Daniel Urban-Brown, Shubhani Sarkar, and Julia Gaviria—thank you for your genius design, art direction, and copyediting. It was such a joy to work with you all.

Thanks especially to my editor, Rochelle Bourgault, for her patience, poise, and wisdom, but mostly for giving me the opportunity to be an author and for making this book so much better than I could have ever anticipated. I feel so lucky to be working with you.

Thanks to my agent, Sharon Bowers, for sending me "fan mail from a literary agent" and for pushing me to write my proposal and get my story and recipes out in the world. Thank you for always being available, always making me laugh, and always having the answer!

Thank you, Geoffrey McDonnell, for coming into this world and inspiring me to learn how to cook and grow our own food. It makes my heart swell when I think of you by my side in the garden and kitchen, always filled with awe and eager to learn. I hope you will grow up to be the "Farmer Chef" that you are aspiring to become.

I want to thank my late father, Alfred M. Wozney, who relentlessly told me from the time I was a toddler that I was special and could do anything my heart desired. Those words have catapulted me to be confident, take risks, and fearlessly try new things, including embarking on this crazy Irish journey. I wish you could be here to celebrate this book with us.

Thank you, Peggy McDonnell, who bestowed on me such a tremendous gift: a true understanding of cooking, baking, and preserving on an Irish farm. While Peggy was a great cook, she was also extremely modest. She honestly never thought of her cooking as exceptional. But we all knew better, and she inspired me every day. Thank you, Peggy, we miss you so much.

Thanks to my father-in-law, Michael, for being unconditionally supportive and patient with my "American ways" and for being so generous in sharing so much history and incredible Dunmoylan stories with me. I am never not in awe of you and the evolution of this farm and the family bonds it has held down the years.

Thank you, Mary Wozney, for your support and for sharing so many recipes with me that have healed my homesickness through the years.

Thanks to Elizabeth Becker, for listening and always pointing me toward a new way to look at things, for inspiring me to keep trying, and for recognizing my hard work with praise. You are incredibly special to me and my family.

To Rosanne McDonnell, thank you for graciously volunteering your time to help me with this book and for always being so very compassionate and encouraging.

Thank you, David McDonnell, for being encouraging and always sharing sound advice.

To my cousin Sheri Gagnon, thank you for tirelessly sharing my blog posts, photos, and stories on social media. Your support has meant the world to me!

Friends and Food Co-conspirators

Sonia Mulford, the best friend and work partner a girl could ask for. You've been there from the start and have helped me so much, both with moral support and with creative collaboration. I am indebted to you for your beautiful styling work on this book and for all of the brilliant years of friendship. Thank you.

Donal Skehan, who encouraged me to start food blogging in the first place. Thank you for urging me on this journey and for giving me your constant support and inspiration.

Thank you, Moya McAllister, for your brilliant photo editing assistance—I always learn so much from you.

To my blog readers, without whom this book would not exist. I am grateful for your continuing interest and frequent commentary. You are the reason I write. Thank you.

Thank you for your support and inspiration Cliodhna Prendergast, Susan Spungen, Stephanie Meyer, Amy Roark, Joy Estelle Summers, Claire and Conor Shields, Anne Marie Morrisey-Murphy and Riccardo Chianella, Nicky and Yannis Halas, Naomi and Trevor Sparks, Gitte and Robert Kennedy, Aoife McElwain, Joe McNamee, Mag and Ger Kirwan, Birgitta Curtin, Pat Whelan, Corey Taratuta, Liam Hughes, Meighan McGuire, Mike Hartzel, Michael Van Huffel, Jesse and Ariel Hayes, Cassie Scroggins, Carrie Shanahan, Charles Youel, Pamela Meier, David Howell, Todd Syring, Marilyn Ciepielinksi, Gregory Simmons, Joey Glassman, Todd LeDoux, Kristin Jensen, Brenda and Scott Smith, Caroline Hennessey, The Irish Food Blogger's Association, Tammy Kimbler, Sharon Hearne Smith, Helen James, Pat Whelan, Moya McAllister, Trish

Deseine, Aimee Bourque, Dianne Jacob, Elissa Altman, Nessa Robins, Mimi Thorisson, Marte Marie Forsberg, Beth Kirby, Ella McSweeney, Aoife Carrigy, Georgina Campbell, Sally and John McKenna, Donal Doherty, Suzanna Crampton, Pamela Meier, Sharon Noonan, Marion O'Connor, Celeste Norcia, and Ailbhe Phelan.

Contributors

Thank you, Claire Shields, for supplying me with your fantastic frangipane recipe, for the loan of dishes and cutlery, and for gorgeously re-creating our wedding cake. You are the best.

Naomi Sparks, thank you for that midnight pudding and all the memories we have. Miss you!

Thank you, Lavonda Shipley, for your beautiful buttermilk pie recipe and for all your help on our shoot when you visited the farm.

Thanks, Molly Yeh, for your amazing potsticker recipe and for being an all-around cheerleader!

Thank you, Niamh Shields, for your sensational blaas recipe and for so much blogging inspiration.

Recipe Testers

Many thanks to Maryellen Garvey, Nik Sharma, Tara Hinrichs, Kathleen P. Halloran-Jones, Deb Piepho, Lisa Nordquist, John Kaufman, Eva Arnold, Megan McCardle-Parsons, Kelly Hannan, Marcia Pilgeram, Susanne Stahl Kosec,

Andrea Driscoll, Josephine Ziegler, Claire Rea, Amanda O'Sullivan, Valentina Babkova, Lauren Fitzgerald, Louise Hopkins, Fiona Hickey, Ellen Townson, Gayle Malcolm, Anne Bennett-Brosnan, Lauren Turner, Beatriz Ageno, Tammy Kimbler, Molly Peterson, Cynthia Levine, Louise Hopkins, Corey Taratuta, Liam Hughes, Carla Gallagher, Missy Ledesma, Devyn Olson-Sawyer, Nicki McCracken, Alison Pearce, Gillian Blackburn, Joan Quigley, Kristin Jensen, Evin Bail O'Keefe, Sarah Ní Shúilleabháin, and Lauren Turner. A cookbook is only as good as its recipes, and your testing and feedback were positively invaluable to me.

Professional

Thanks to Mairead Lavery and the *Irish Farmers Journal* for giving me my first opportunity to write professionally. I am forever grateful.

To Jeff Gordinier, for spotting my blog and finding it worthy enough to share with your *New York Times* audience. I am extraordinarily thankful for your support.

To Pilar Guzman and Yolanda Edwards for inviting me to share "my Ireland" with you and be a part of your Condé Nast team. You have both deeply inspired me over the years, and it is such a tremendous honor to work with you.

Aisling O'Toole, Jo Linehan, Nathalie Marquez-Courtney, Aer Lingus, thank you for giving me the opportunity to share with your audience.

COMMON CONVERSIONS

INGREDIENTS

AGAVE SYRUP:
⅓ cup = 100 g

BAKING POWDER:
1 tablespoon = 11 g

BAKING SODA:
1 tablespoon = 11 g

CHOCOLATE CHIPS:
1 cup = 160 g

COCOA POWDER:
1 cup = 120 g

FLOUR, ALL-PURPOSE OR WHOLE WHEAT:
1 cup = 130 g

HONEY:
1 cup = 300 g; 1 tablespoon = 18 g

SALT, FINE:
1 teaspoon = 5 g

SALT, COARSE:
1 teaspoon = heaping 5 g

SUGAR, BROWN:
1 cup (packed) = 170 g

SUGAR, CONFECTIONER'S:
1 cup = 130 g

SUGAR, GRANULATED OR SUPERFINE:
1 cup = 200 g; 1 tablespoon = 12.5 grams

TREACLE, MOLASSES, OR GOLDEN SYRUP
(OR LIGHT CORN SYRUP):
1 cup = 280 g

PANS AND DISHES

4-inch tartlet mold =
10-cm tartlet mold

6-oz ramekin =
180-ml ramekin

8-inch square baking dish =
20-cm square baking dish

9-inch cake pan =
22-cm cake pan

9-by-5-inch loaf pan =
23-by-13-cm loaf pan

9-by-13-inch baking dish =
22-by-33-cm baking dish

10-inch tart or cake pan =
25-cm tart or cake pan

RESOURCES

Ballymaloe Cookery School. Situated on its own fully certified, hundred-acre organic farm, Ballymaloe's twelve-week certificate program is world-renowned. For information, go to http://cookingisfun.ie.

Ballyvolane House. For that perfect hedgerow martini, visit this historic Irish country house with its extraordinary warmth, style, and comfort. It provides luxury accommodation and salmon fishing on the river Blackwater, located in the North Cork countryside of southern Ireland. For reservations, go to http://bally volanehouse.ie.

Bob's Red Mill Flours. This is the go-to brand for whole-wheat flour (best brown bread) and other whole grains in the United States. The website is www.bobsredmill.com. In Ireland, Macroom Mills Flour and Dunany Organic Flours are available at Sheridan's Cheesemongers, www.sheridanscheese mongers.com/.

Burren Smokehouse. This is the place to go for top-class Irish smoked salmon; visit www.burren smokehouse.ie.

Dean and Deluca. For a selection of Irish artisan products available in the United States, you can order online at www.deananddeluca.com.

Food Ireland. A great stateside resource for Irish ingredients is www.FoodIreland.com.

Goatsbridge Farm. For trout caviar and smoked trout from Kilkenny, go to http://goats bridgetrout.ie.

Longueville House. A great supplier of apple brandy for apple fritters and beautiful ciders, this Georgian mansion hotel has apple orchards on the estate. Owner William O'Callaghan makes hard cider and apple brandy that is double-distilled in copper-pot stills, then aged four years in oak barrels. Order at http://longuevillehouse.ie.

Sheridan's Cheesemongers. For the best cheese in Ireland, visit Sheridan's. It features more than fifty Irish cheeses in a variety of styles from more than thirty artisan producers in the north and south. Sample before buying or head to the wine bar above the Galway shop for tasting platters to share. You can also order online at www.sheridanscheesemongers.com.

Turf from Ireland. We love the flavor and fragrance of turf-smoked meats. Order some real Irish turf, and add a small amount to your wood chip dust for the ideal flavor to come through. Visit www.turf fromireland.com.

INDEX OF RECIPES

INDEX

ABOUT THE AUTHOR

Imen McDonnell is a food and lifestyle columnist for the *Irish Farmers Journal* and a contributing writer to *Condé Nast Traveler* and *Irish Country Magazine*. In a former life, she spent her days working in broadcast production in New York, Minneapolis, and Los Angeles. She now resides with her husband and son on their family farm in rural Ireland and shares stories of farm life and food on her popular blog *Farmette* (http://farmette.ie). Imen's modern Irish recipes have been featured in *The New York Times*, *The Irish Times*, *The Sunday Times* (UK), *The Los Angeles Times*, *Saveur* magazine, and more.

When she is not cooking, writing, weeding, or photographing, you'll find her in the farmyard with her husband and son, milking cows, feeding calves and chickens, or loving up their two donkeys and amusing Airedale terrier, Teddy.

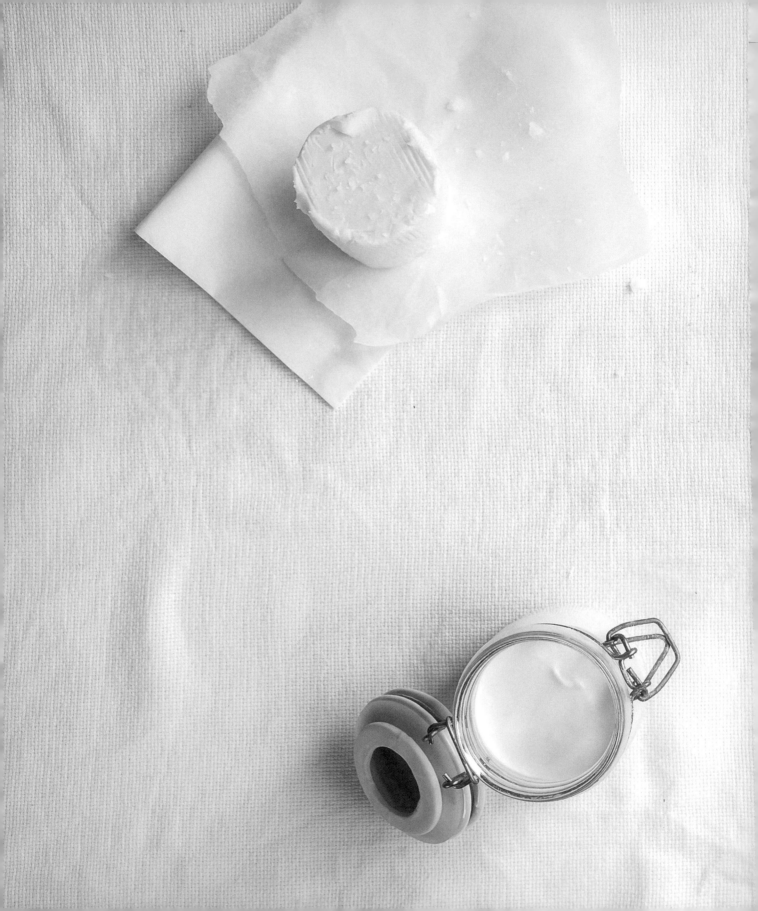